TOWARD

MEXICO'S

DEMOCRATIZATION

Parties, Campaigns, Elections, and Public Opinion

Edited by

Jorge I. Domínguez and Alejandro Poiré

Routledge New York and London

Published in 1999 by
Routledge
29 West 35th Street
New York, NY 10001

Published in Great Britain by
Routledge
11 New Fetter Lane
London EC4P 4EE

10 9 8 7 6 5 4 3 2 1

Library of Congress Cataloging-in-Publication Data

Toward Mexico's democratization : parties, campaigns, elections, and public opinion / edited by Jorge I. Domínguez and Alejandro Poiré.
    p.   cm.
    Papers of a conference held in Cambridge, Mass., Oct. 31, 1997.
    Includes bibliographical references and index.
    ISBN 0-415-92159-7. — ISBN 0-415-92158-9 (pbk.)
    1. Elections—Mexico—Congresses.   2. Mexico—Politics and government—
1988– —Congresses.   3. Political parties—Mexico—Congresses.   I. Domínguez,
Jorge I., 1945– .   II. Poiré, Alejandro, 1971– .
JL1292.T69   1999
324.972'0835—dc21   98-35528
                                                             CIP

CONTENTS

FIGURES

TABLES

PREFACE

Mexico's elections were among the last in Latin America in the twentieth century to be free and fair. But in the Latin American region, Mexican and Mexicanist scholars have been among the first to study Mexican elections employing the full array of analytical approaches ordinarily used to think about elections in long-established democracies.

This book has been made possible by the new-born eagerness and competence of Mexican citizens to fashion a democratic polity and by the emergence of a young and talented community of scholars, principally in Mexico and the United States, of Mexican elections. (Of the authors of this book, only Jorge Domínguez has gray hair.) As the twentieth century came to a close, no other country in Latin America had a comparable community of world-class scholars working on parties, elections, campaigns, and public opinion. This book brings together the writings of some of them.

The idea for the book began as a conversation between Domínguez and Alejandro Poiré; both had noticed that the best work in the study of these topics was being carried out by graduate students or newly appointed assistant professors. Certainly, few Mexicanist scholars above age forty employed the quantitative tools that were the daily bread of elections scholars elsewhere in North America and Europe.

With the enthusiastic support of Harvard University's David Rockefeller Center for Latin American Studies, a graduate student conference was organized and held in Cambridge, Mass., on October 31, 1997. With some additional research and revision, this book is the result of that gathering. We are grateful to the Center Director, Professor John Coatsworth, for his and the Center's support, and to Professors Merilee Grindle and Morris Fiorina for their insightful comments and suggestions during the conference. Debra-Lee Vasques took charge of the conference's organization with her usual skill and good cheer. The book's production was supported by

xi

Harvard University's Weatherhead Center for International Affairs. Theresa Spinale was the book's very able manager and producer. Melissa Rosati at Routledge has been the publisher every author wants.

We dedicate this book to the Mexican voter, long unappreciated but savvy, prudent, and committed.

Jorge I. Domínguez
and Alejandro Poiré

1

THE TRANSFORMATION OF MEXICO'S ELECTORAL AND PARTY SYSTEMS,[1] 1988–97

AN INTRODUCTION

Jorge I. Domínguez

In the dark nights of the 1970s, harsh dictatorships ruled over most Latin American countries. Mexico's willingness to grant asylum to Latin America's persecuted intellectual leftists, its loudly "progressive" social, economic, and foreign policies, and its government's subtle means to control political life and intimidate the opposition spared its "soft authoritarian" political system from the criticism it might have deserved. In the presidential elections of 1976, the candidate of the Institutional Revolutionary Party (PRI), José López Portillo, ran virtually unopposed and claimed 94 percent of the valid votes cast; the PRI also won every seat in the federal Senate and every seat in the federal Chamber of Deputies except for some specifically reserved for a nearly helpless, tolerated opposition. The PRI controlled every state governorship as well.[2]

The 1980s was the decade of democratization in Latin America; in country after country, more open politics, anchored in free and competitive elections, became the norm. By 1990 even in war-torn tyrant-rich Central America opposition victories had occurred in presidential elections in every country. Mexico's presidential election of 1988, however, was

1

marred by widespread and not unfounded accusations of electoral fraud. At last Mexico's political system came in for sustained criticism over its lack of democracy.

By *democracy* we understand a political regime where rulers are chosen in free and fair elections, held at regular intervals, in the context of guaranteed civil and political rights. Democracy requires a responsible government, that is, the accountability of the executive, administrative, and coercive arms of the state to the elected representatives, as well as universal suffrage and the nonproscription of parties. In a democracy, elections are competitive, and it is presumed that political change occurs only in accordance with rules and precedents.[3]

In the 1990s the Mexican political system moved considerably toward democratization. Its formal and informal institutions and practices were markedly different in the late 1990s from what they had been in the late 1980s. Its political parties—including the PRI—changed the way they operate and connect with voters. And Mexican voters themselves had discovered the values and instruments of democratic politics.

In this chapter I argue, first, that Mexico's political system has been democratizing slowly, and that the Mexican voter has been an important protagonist in this transformation. In the 1988 presidential election, voters shocked the political establishment with their demand for fundamental political change; they renewed those demands in the 1997 congressional and local elections. Second, voters could only succeed if the institutions of the national government made it possible. Thus electoral and other institutional reforms became an important aspect of the public agenda in the 1990s. Third, political parties provided the essential service of mobilizing the electorate and shaping both its views and their expression. Changes in parties, in campaigns, public opinion, and in the pattern of voter behavior are key parts of the story of Mexico's democratization as the millennium closes.

POLITICAL, INSTITUTIONAL, AND ECONOMIC LEGACIES

Mexico's political system has long been highly centralized. At its apex, the President of Mexico combined personal talent, impressive powers, and considerable technical resources, and he cultivated an aura of majesty to elicit deference and support. The machinery of politics at the president's service—the ruling party (PRI) and the government officials charged with managing political affairs—often governed effectively, but to maintain their political control, they also resorted regularly to electoral fraud and abuse of power.

The strongly presidentialist character of Mexican politics has been one of its most distinctive and enduring aspects; it explains the regime's most authoritarian features as well as the high stakes of presidential elections.[4] In practice, presidents chose their own successors as well as most state governors, members of Congress, judges, heads of state enterprises, and government officials down to midlevel bureaucrats. Presidents arbitrarily removed state governors,[5] PRI legislators, and labor union leaders who opposed them or performed poorly on the job. The constitutional prohibition of the reelection of members of Congress still prevents the development of a cadre of experienced and powerful legislators who might challenge the executive branch or at least monitor it effectively. This pronounced presidentialism—reproduced as executive dominance at the state and local levels—long enforced discipline and loyalty.

The ruling party dates its history to 1929, when the military chieftains and regional bosses who survived the Mexican revolution created the National Revolutionary Party[6] to put an end to two decades of violence and turmoil. Since then the PRI and its partisan predecessors have never acknowledged the loss of a presidential election and always controlled both houses of Congress. Until 1982 the official party always filled no fewer than 80 percent of the seats in the Chamber of Deputies; going into the 1988 national elections, the PRI still filled 72 percent of the seats in this chamber. Until 1988 the PRI controlled all the seats in the Senate. Until 1989 no opposition party member had ever been acknowledged as having won a gubernatorial election.[7]

The PRI's distinctness from the state was often difficult to discern. The PRI long blurred the boundaries between party and state. Not until the 1994 presidential election did Mexico begin to acquire legislation and means of enforcement to curb government financing of PRI election activities. The close connections between the government and the privately owned mass media had also given a marked advantage to the PRI especially in television coverage, even during the 1994 presidential election.[8]

Over the years the government and the PRI combined to commit electoral fraud with impunity. As Craig and Cornelius have noted, PRI-government agents stuffed ballot boxes, intimidated opposition candidates, disqualified opposition poll watchers, relocated voting places at the last minute, manipulated voter registration lists, issued multiple voting credentials to PRI supporters, manipulated voting tallies, and even nullified adverse electoral outcomes.[9]

The Salinas Presidency

The July 1988 presidential elections were a political earthquake. Carlos Salinas de Gortari, the PRI's candidate, claimed barely over one-half of the votes cast. The oldest established opposition party was the National Action Party (PAN). It is usually positioned on the center-right, favoring less government intervention in the economy than the PRI typically had over the years. For the 1988 elections the PAN nominated Manuel Clouthier, an entrepreneur. By the official count, Clouthier got 17% of the votes cast. In the months before the election a new political force emerged to the left of the PRI; its leaders objected to the measures adopted by President Miguel de la Madrid (1982–88), with PRI support, to reduce the government's role in the economy and to free up market forces. The left was led by Cuauhtémoc Cárdenas, a former PRI-backed governor of the state of Michoacán and son of one of Mexico's most revered presidents, Lázaro Cárdenas (1934–40).

The official count in the 1988 elections gave Cárdenas 32% of the votes cast, but he and his supporters claimed that Salinas and the PRI had stolen the election; Cárdenas and his supporters staged massive public protests in the weeks that followed. The PAN and Clouthier, too, sharply contested the results of the election as fraudulent. Although Salinas was installed as president (1988–94), the combined opposition parties commanded 48 percent of the seats in the Chamber of Deputies, the highest proportion ever.

The background to the momentous 1988 election included a prolonged economic recession during the preceding several years. Miguel de la Madrid became president in 1982 just as the international debt crisis broke out; although his presidency set the bases for Mexico's eventual recovery, there was no economic growth during his term. Mexico's gross domestic product (GDP) per capita fell each and every year of Miguel de la Madrid's six-year term—a cumulative drop of 12.4 percent. Real average manufacturing wages dropped by approximately one-third during those same six years. Consumer price inflation during de la Madrid's presidency was never below 60 percent per year and in some years exceeded 100 percent.[10]

Carlos Salinas further restructured Mexico's economy and reset it on a path of economic growth.[11] Consumer price inflation decelerated rapidly toward the low two-digit range. Gross domestic product per capita recovered at last, growing each year from 1988 to 1991, 1.4, 2.5, and 1.7 percent respectively. Voters rewarded Salinas and the PRI with election victory in the 1991 nationwide Congressional elections. Nonetheless, GDP per capita was still below the level achieved ten years earlier. Real average wages in manufacturing had also risen, but they were still lower than in 1980. During the second half of Salinas's presidency, the inflation rate dropped to the one-digit range. In 1994 real average manufacturing wages finally reached the 1980 level once again. But GDP per capita inched forward 0.9 percent in 1992, fell 1.2 percent in 1993, and rose 1.3 percent in 1994.[12] Mexico's economy had yet to benefit the ordinary citizen much.

Indeed, Mexico remained quite vulnerable to shocks, and shocks it did receive. On January 1, 1994, a revolt broke out in the southernmost state of Chiapas in protest against political, economic, and social conditions. Many of the rebels were indigenous people from the region. They called themselves Zapatistas, invoking the name of the Mexican revolutionary Emiliano Zapata, known for his commitment to land reform and to the peasants more generally. The revolt jolted the Mexican political establishment. In the days, months, and years that followed, the Mexican government combined repression and negotiation in its policies toward the Zapatistas. Although the rebellion was contained to one small region, it would remain for many years a symbol of both the injustices of the social system and the inability of the national government to address local problems effectively.

On March 23, 1994, Luis Donaldo Colosio, the PRI's presidential candidate, was assassinated. This was the first killing of a presidential figure since 1929. Along with the Zapatista insurgency, these two acts of violence gripped the country's consciousness as Mexico entered the 1994 presidential campaign. (The Colosio investigation proved inconclusive and the official version unpersuasive to the mass public.) Six days after Colosio's murder, with little pretense of internal party democracy, President Salinas and the PRI state governors chose former minister of education and Colosio's campaign manager, Ernesto Zedillo Ponce de León (1994–2000) as the PRI's new candidate for the presidency.

Zedillo faced two other main candidates for the August 1994 presidential election. The PAN nominated Diego Fernández de Cevallos, its leader in the Chamber of Deputies and an effective debater. The PAN generally endorsed Mexico's economic reorientation toward the market but challenged the lack of democracy. Cuauhtémoc Cárdenas ran for president again, this time as the candidate of the Party of the Democratic Revolution (PRD) which he founded from the smaller parties that first backed his candidacy in 1988. He, too, accepted the economic reforms but called attention to both the democratic and social deficits of the Mexican political system. To compete with them, Zedillo positioned himself as the candidate who could most be trusted to bring about change within the framework of order.

On August 21, 1994, Ernesto Zedillo was elected president of Mexico with 48.8% of the officially recorded votes. The PAN's Fernández de Cevallos came in second, with 25.9%, and Cárdenas third, with 16.6%; the small parties gathered the rest. The opposition parties had recovered from the 1991 national elections and done almost as well as had been officially recorded in the 1988 presidential elections. At least as important for Mexico was the much greater accuracy of the vote count.

Reforms of the Electoral Law |

In response to the allegations of widespread fraud in the 1988 presidential elections, and then, in 1994, in order to contain the political effects from the Zapatista rebellion and the Colosio assassination, the Salinas administration steered several electoral reform laws. Their combined result greatly ensured the integrity of the vote count on election day 1994.[13]

To guarantee representation of minority parties in the legislature, the number of senators per state was increased from two to four; three would be elected by simple pluralities, and one would be allocated to the party obtaining the second highest number of votes in the state. At the time of the reform, the opposition held only 5 percent of the Senate seats. In the Chamber of Deputies, no party would be permitted to hold more than 315 seats in the 500-member Chamber, thus making it impossible for a single party to change the Constitution by itself.

Since 1977 one-quarter of the seats in the Chamber of Deputies had been reserved for minority parties; these deputies were chosen through proportional representation. In 1986 the size of the Chamber was expanded to 500 members, with 200 seats to be chosen by proportional representation; all parties, including the PRI, could gain from these proportional allocations of seats.

The electoral registry, the lists of voters, and the voter identification cards would be subject to external audits. Every month each party would receive a copy of the electoral registry on magnetic tapes. Polling booth officials would henceforth be chosen through a double random lottery based on their month of birth and the first letter of their last name. That is, the local polling-booth officials would be ordinary citizens chosen independently of their known party affiliations, if any. Electoral ballots would have numbered slips to prevent the stuffing of ballots while preserving the secrecy of the vote. Upon casting their ballots, voters would have their fingers marked with indelible ink. Each voter would have a new voter card, with that person's name and address, voter identification number, photograph, signature, and fingerprint. To prevent the type of swift destruction of ballots that had occurred after the 1988 elections, no electoral lists or ballots could be destroyed during the six months following the election. Mexican citizens would be accredited as election observers, and formally designated "international visitors" would also be accredited to be present during the elections.

The General Council of the Federal Elections Institute (IFE) was overhauled. Six "citizen counselors" would be nominated by the political parties and elected by a two-thirds vote of the Chamber of Deputies (thus preventing any one party from imposing its will). Another five IFE members would be the minister of government (who chaired it), two senators, and two deputies; among the latter four, one from each chamber had to come, respectively, from the largest party and from the second largest party represented in that chamber. Each party would be allotted one hour on radio on the three Sundays prior to election day, but no partisan propaganda would be allowed on radio and television during the ten days before election day.

Nonetheless, serious problems remained because the PRI retained disproportionate strength, even drawing informally on government support. The campaign finance laws allowed the PRI to amass fortunes well beyond the fund-raising capacities of the opposition parties. The mass media remained extraordinarily biased in favor of the PRI. And some aspects of the electoral law remained unenforced. And yet, the cumulative effect of the reforms made the 1994 presidential election the first fair election ever held in Mexico.[14] As a result, the analyses of the 1994 election in the chapters that follow draw their evidence from a much more open political climate for a competitive election than had been the case in Mexico's past.

The Zedillo Presidency

Within days of his December 1, 1994, inauguration, Ernesto Zedillo faced a devastating financial panic that would soon plunge the Mexican economy into its steepest one-year decline in the time since Mexico has kept national economic accounts. In 1995, gross domestic product per capita fell 8.2 percent; real average wages in manufacturing dropped 13.6 percent. Also in 1995, the level of consumer price inflation was seven times that of 1994. Grim as 1995 no doubt was, President Zedillo courageously retained the market-oriented strategy. The president's perseverance, and the effectiveness of the economic reforms adopted during the two previous presidential administrations, paid off. The export sector led the economic recovery; the North American Free Trade Agreement (NAFTA), signed during the Salinas presidency (it went into effect on January 1, 1994), proved valuable to get the Mexican economy back on its feet. The recession was sharp but brief. Mexico's GDP per capita grew 3.4 percent in 1996 and then 5.2 percent in 1997—the best record since the beginning of the debt crisis in 1982. By 1997 consumer price inflation had dropped to the low two-digit range. Real average wages in manufacturing continued to slide every year, however; in 1997 they were 24 percent below the 1994 level.[15] This would cost the PRI in various state elections and in the 1997 nationwide elections.

The economic collapse greatly weakened the president and the PRI. There was widespread anger that the PRI had led the country once again toward the economic abyss. Opposition candidates, principally from the PAN, had been winning various municipal elections since the early 1980s, but in the mid-1990s the PAN's municipal victories greatly increased in number. The PAN also won several important state governorships. These PAN successes occurred first in the northern region, then throughout the country. The PRI began to face electoral competition in virtually every state of the nation.

The process of change also accelerated in 1995 because of a general perception that President Zedillo and his team were insufficiently skillful in politics. As Luis Rubio put it, "the government has been largely ineffective at explaining its objectives and convincing key constituencies about them." Moreover, Rubio also noted, the process of change had deinstitutionalized Mexico: "Almost every action undertaken over the past twenty years to liberalize politics came associated with the destruction—actual or de facto of a given ancestral (and usually no longer working) institution. None of the governments, however, was ever concerned with creating new institutions or shaping new structures for political interaction." As a result, factionalism, gridlock, and political violence increased. Much of the factionalism broke out within the PRI itself; especially noteworthy (and nearly unprecedented) was the successful defiance of presidential power by some PRI state governors.[16]

Reforms of the Electoral Law II

The Zedillo administration negotiated one more round of electoral reform, approved in the fall 1996.[17] The Federal Electoral Institute would have only nonpartisan members nominated by a consensual procedure in Congress, and the minister of government would no longer serve on it. The governor of the Federal District (Mexico City), hitherto appointed by the president, would be elected directly by the city's voters. One-quarter of the senators would be chosen through proportional representation in a national constituency. No party would be allowed more than 60 percent of the Chamber of Deputies, and the overrepresentation of the largest party in the Chamber (which results from the first-past-the-post method of choosing three hundred of its five hundred members) would be limited to 8 percent. A party would lose its registration if it failed to reach 2 percent of the votes cast; this clause would eliminate parties that at times had served as PRI vehicles to divide and fragment the opposition.

Public financing of the political parties was increased greatly, limiting private sources of financing to just 10 percent of total campaign expenditures. The amount of public financing allocated in 1997 was five times larger than the amount all parties claimed to have spent in 1994; 30 percent of these funds was distributed equally to all qualified parties while the remainder was allocated proportionate to the share of the vote each party had won in the previous election. The access of the parties to the mass media was also increased. The IFE bought 100 hours of television time and 125 hours of radio time and made it available to the political parties, relying on the same formula as for the allocation of public funds. These reforms in public financing and access to mass media made it much more likely that the opposition political parties could mount effective campaigns to challenge the PRI. And they did.

The 1997 National Elections

On July 7, 1997, nationwide congressional elections and some state and local elections were held.[18] The elections were generally free and fair; instances of voter intimidation and violence were the exceptions (the state of Chiapas was one of these exceptions).

For the first time ever, the PRI lost its majority in the Chamber of Deputies. The PRI won 39.1% of the vote for the Chamber of Deputies, the PAN won 26.6%, and the PRD 25.7%. Because the PRD vote was better distributed to win seats in districts where deputies were chosen by simple plurality, the distribution of seats in the Chamber was 238 for the PRI, 125 for the PRD, and 122 for the PAN. The Workers Party (PT) won 7 seats and the Green Environment Party (PVEM) won 8 seats. (Among the 32 senators elected in 1997, the PRI won 13, the PAN 9, the PRD 8, and the PT and PVEM one each.) In the election for the Chamber of Deputies, an opposition party won some simple-plurality seats in 22 of the 32 units of the federation; most of the states where the PRI retained its monopoly in plurality-district deputy elections were in the central or southern regions of Mexico.

The PAN won a majority of a state's delegation to the federal Chamber of Deputies in Baja California Norte, Guanajuato, Jalisco, Nuevo León, and Querétaro, and it won a plurality in Sonora. The PAN was highly competitive (that is, it garnered at least 35% of the votes cast) in Aguascalientes, Colima, Chihuahua, San Luis Potosí, and Yucatán. But for Yucatán in the South, the PAN was strong only in central and northern Mexico. The PRD won a majority of a state's delegation to the federal Chamber of Deputies only in Mexico City and in Michoacán. It was competitive (35% of the votes or more) in Campeche, Guerrero, Morelos, and Tabasco; it virtually tied the PRI in the state of Mexico—all states in central or southern Mexico.

Only the PRI drew significant support from all regions of the country, however. The PRI received at least 35% of the votes for the Chamber of Deputies in thirty of the thirty-two units of the federation; it received at least 40% of the votes in twenty-one states. Were the opposition parties to run separate presidential candidates in the presidential elections in 2000, the PRI retained a good chance of winning the presidency. Because of the regional distribution of the votes, however, by 1997 Mexico featured a two-party system in a majority of the states; this characteristic would enable the opposition parties to win many plurality-district deputy seats and many Senate seats. In that event, the PAN and the PRD could control both chambers of Congress after the elections in 2000 even if the PRI might control the presidency. If so, Mexico might have transited from single-party rule to divided government.

Coming out of the 1997 elections, the PAN had somewhat stronger depth and breadth than the PRD as a national party. The PAN controlled six governorships, including those of the important states of Jalisco, Nuevo León, and Guanajuato. The PRD elected Cuauhtémoc Cárdenas as governor of the Federal District in 1997 but it controlled no other governorship. The PAN held majorities in six state legislatures; the PRD did so only in the Federal District (Mexico City). PAN mayors governed nearly all of Mexico's largest cities; the PRD governed Mexico City. The PRI, alas, held many mayoralties but mostly in medium and small cities and towns.

The PRD owed much of its success in the 1997 elections to Cuauhtémoc Cárdenas's resurgence as a major national figure. Because Mexico's mass media are highly centralized in Mexico City, media coverage of Cárdenas's campaign in the city was broadcast nationwide, helping many PRD candidates ride his coattails. The PAN, in contrast, had no towering national figure. Its candidate for the government of Mexico City, Carlos Castillo Peraza, is an able intellectual who ran a terrible campaign that hurt the PAN nationwide. The PAN had expected to emerge from the 1997 elections as Mexico's second-largest party. Its good showing was disappointing, nonetheless, to its leaders and followers, whereas Cardenistas were elated that their leader had been catapulted as the opposition's front-runner for the presidential election in 2000. In this book, we pay considerable attention to the historic 1997 elections both because of the fairness of its procedures and the significance of its results.

THE MEXICAN VOTER: PART I

Professional social science surveys have been conducted in Mexico for decades. One of these, conducted for the five-country study that became *The Civic Culture,* had a great impact on thinking about Mexico and the views of Mexicans.[19] Until the 1980s, however, most surveys conducted in Mexico were proprietary, that is, they were for the exclusive use of the Mexican presidency, a political party (usually the PRI), or whichever organization commissioned it. Since the 1980s, and especially in the 1990s, many social science surveys conducted by particular organizations have become generally available, after some lag time. These include the large national surveys on which the chapters by Alejandro Poiré, Alejandro Moreno, Alberto Cinta, and Beatriz Magaloni rely; Chappell Lawson conducted his own survey in Mexico City with the assistance of one of the city's leading newspapers. Much is now known, therefore, about the Mexican voter.

Jorge Domínguez and James McCann were among the first to use such large national surveys as well as the contemporary tools of social science to develop a systematic analysis of the Mexican voter.[20] Because their work served as a baseline for studies that followed it, including several of the chapters in this book, the main points of their argument should be summarized.

By the late 1980s, Mexicans were much more likely to be interested in politics, to be attentive to political campaigns, and to discuss politics freely than they had been in the 1950s at the time of *The Civic Culture* survey. The Mexican electorate, moreover, was just as politicized as were the electorates of many democracies in western Europe and the United States. Mexicans opposed the participation of undemocratic institutions in political life, and they strongly favored the internal democratization of the ruling party's presidential nomination practices. There were some important, lingering authoritarian values, but Mexicans had clearly changed.

Mexico had also developed a national electorate. In their attitudes toward the values that serve as the cornerstone for the construction of democracy, Mexicans showed a narrowing over time in serious differences in terms of education and gender. Mexicans of all demographic types were ready for a more democratic polity than they were experiencing at the end of the 1980s. Differences in attachments to democratic values, consequently, did not divide Mexicans between a party of democrats and a party of authoritarians. There were democrats and authoritarians in all parties.

By the late 1980s, Mexicans were polarized in their assessment of various economic policies adopted by their government in response to the severe economic crisis that had afflicted them for most of that decade. Mexicans also showed consistency across issues. And yet while the level of issue polarization was high, the level of issue consistency was not. Attitudes toward some issues, such as the privatization of state enterprises, were not well related to other issues that are ordinarily considered to be part of the same economic worldview (e.g., freer trade, foreign investment). Even among economic issues that were related to each other in the public's view, the strength of association was modest. Nor did education, social class, and level of political interest serve as consistent explanations from one issue to the next. Mexicans were indeed divided over the issues but not cumulatively so: their views on one issue did not control their views toward other apparently closely related issues.

Domínguez and McCann also found that views on policy issues and on retrospective and prospective assessments of the nation's and one's own economic conditions were only marginally related to voter intentions, that is, attitudes toward economic matters were not the principal source of political contestation in the mass public. Supporters of freer trade, for example, backed different presidential candidates; many of those who held pessimistic expectations about Mexico's economic future nonetheless still intended to vote for the PRI. Domínguez and McCann were not surprised about their finding concerning the weak explanatory power of policy issues; that is not uncommon in democracies. They were surprised at the weak explanatory utility of retrospective and prospective economic assessments.[21] They found that expectations about the economy's future performance if a party other than the PRI were to win was one of the strongest explanations for voter attitudes, even if general expectations about the economy's future performance mattered little to explain voter intentions.

Sociodemographic cleavages were neither very important nor very consistent explanations for the party preferences of voters. Frequency of church attendance did not distinguish PRI from PAN voters, even though persistent absence from church did identify the Cardenista electorate. And regionalism, although unimportant in the 1988 election, became more so in the early 1990s.

Thus Domínguez and McCann concluded that partisan, institutional, and candidate assessments provided the stronger bases for the divisions in Mexican mass public opinion. PRI voters were likely to be loyal to the PRI in election after election, just as supporters of opposition parties were likely to be loyal to the opposition across elections. But partisan expectations were also important. In both 1988 and 1991 voters who believed that the PRI would get stronger, and voters who believed that the economy would suffer if a party other than the PRI were to gain power, were much more likely to support the PRI and much less likely to support the opposition. Moreover, the greater the approval for the incumbent president, the greater the likelihood of voting PRI.

These authors also found that opposition parties were organizationally ineffective. In 1988 the new Cardenista coalition reshuffled the voters among the existing parties but it did not mobilize the previously unmobilized, nor did it shift the underlying partisan allegiance of demographic or economic groups or sectors. Nor did the much older PAN develop a more capable organizational machinery. In the 1991 nationwide congressional elections, the 1988 Cardenista coalition fragmented. The divisions among the parties of the left were not substantive, however. Opinion alignments remained stable even if parties or coalitions splintered. As Domínguez and McCann put it, "a large pool of potential left-wing voters awaited the organizational reconstruction of Cardenismo."[22]

Finally, Domínguez and McCann argued that Mexican voters approached national elections by focusing on the fate of the party that had long governed them. They asked themselves, am I for or against "the party of the state" and its leader? Many voters asked themselves no other questions; they backed the PRI. Many other voters, ready to evict the PRI from office, asked themselves further questions. A much more ideologically competitive election faced them. The attitudes of Mexican voters, consequently, were understood in terms of a two-step model. Voters decided first on the PRI. For those open to the possibility of being governed by another party, but only for them, there was a second step. They supported an opposition party, and they chose among such parties motivated by policy preferences and social cleavage attachments.

Among these opposition voters, there was, however, a large minority of sophisticated strategic voters. These anti-PRI Mexicans wanted to defeat the government party so much that they suppressed their ideological preferences in order to back the party most likely to beat the PRI, even when such a party espoused views with which they disagreed. That is, in 1988 many voters with right-wing predispositions voted for Cárdenas; in 1991, many voters with left-wing predispositions voted for PAN candidates.

Expected Changes in Mexican Voting Behavior

Domínguez and McCann called their book *Democratizing Mexico* because they were conscious that Mexico was in the midst of a still-incomplete process of political change. By the very nature of their argument, some of their findings should hold only during a transitional period. In particular, three important conclusions were likely to change.

1. *In subsequent elections, retrospective and prospective performance should matter much more.*

The empirical work in *Democratizing Mexico* focused on the 1988 and 1991 national elections. In the 1988 election, Mexicans were overwhelmingly pessimistic about their country's and their own economic future and devastatingly critical of the recent past. There was little variation to distinguish PRI from opposition voters; a majority of voters who believed that current Mexican economic performance was bad, and a majority of voters who believed that their personal financial situation would worsen, still intended to vote PRI. In the 1991 election, Mexicans were overwhelmingly optimistic about the same issues and held a benign view of the recent past. Two-thirds of Mexicans believed that their personal finances were good and 70 percent believed that they would improve. Once again, there was too little variation to distinguish the PRI from the opposition.[23]

This was bound to change. There was a hint already in the 1991 elections when views of current personal finances had some impact in distinguishing between PRI and opposition voters.[24] Democratizing processes would have an impact on these perceptions in due course. Opposition party politicians would formulate and convey their criticism, helping to differentiate the voters. The greater transparency of political processes, evident already by the 1994 election and certainly by the 1997 election, would convey this information more effectively. The increased party funding and improved mass media access for the 1997 election would also facilitate a more nuanced and varied appreciation of the country's and their own economic circumstances. Retrospective and prospective assessments therefore should matter more than they did in the 1988 and 1991 elections.

2. *In subsequent elections, fear of political change should matter less.*

During the 1990s Mexicans came to be governed increasingly by PAN and PRD mayors and governors. By mid-decade, PAN governors and mayors governed over one-third of Mexico's population.[25] After the 1997 elections, a majority of Mexicans lived under either a mayor or governor from the PAN or the PRD. Some of these PAN and PRD public officials no doubt would turn out to be inept or venal, or, for whatever reason, not to the liking of many voters. Many of these PAN and PRD officials would govern effectively and well, however. Certainly the results of state and local elections in the 1990s, and eventually the outcome of the 1997 nationwide election, suggest that Mexicans were losing their fear of being governed by a party other than the PRI. The PRI might still draw disproportionate support from those who feared for the economy or for social peace if Mexico were governed by some other party, but the pool of fearful voters is likely to be much smaller.

3. *The two-step model should dissolve, in part as a consequence of these changes.*

But other considerations argue for the likely declining relevance of the two-step model. In their discussion of the 1994 election campaign, Domínguez and McCann noted that "for the most part the presidential candidates 'hugged' the political center."[26] This strategy blurred the differences among the three principal parties and certainly contributed to a declining fear of opposition victories. Moreover, this increasing moderation made it easier for a former PAN supporter to support Cárdenas and the PRD, and for a former PRI supporter to switch to either of the opposition parties. While strategic voting can be found in most democracies to some extent, much of the shift from one party to another in Mexico could be a process of "conversion," not just tactical thinking.

If these three large changes in the voting behavior of Mexicans were to occur, then Mexican voting behavior would resemble that of well-established democracies much more closely. If so, however, some of the factors that Domínguez and McCann had already discovered are likely to remain significant: the importance of partisanship in shaping voting behavior and the impact of presidential approval on the voter's choice, for example. These concerns are characteristically important in democratic elections in many countries.

Two other factors of possible significance might be volatility during a campaign and the impact of sociodemographic cleavages. Domínguez and McCann found that more than one-sixth of the voters in the 1991 national election decided for whom to vote in the twenty-four hours prior to voting. As standing commitments to the PRI weaken, such volatility may well increase. Secondly, sociodemographic cleavages matter in elections in various countries, certainly so in Canada and Europe, for example. It could be reasonable to expect that regional or other cleavages might deepen as Mexico's political parties seek to consolidate their hold over a pool of voters.

THE MEXICAN VOTER: PART II

This book focuses on the behavior of the Mexican voter and the role of political parties. The chapters that follow address principally the national elections of 1994 and 1997 bringing new evidence and providing fresh analytic perspectives. Their combined findings provide a subtle but clear picture of the Mexican voter and of the changes and continuities in voting behavior over time.

Social and demographic factors continued to have a minor role in shaping the partisan choice of voters in the 1994 presidential election, as both Alejandro Poiré and Beatriz Magaloni make clear. In this respect, there was strong continuity with the 1988 and 1991 elections. Mexico's social cleavages did not translate readily into political cleavages. Thus differences by levels of education, occupation, gender, and the like did not help much to explain the voting behavior of Mexicans; only region played some role.[27]

Retrospective economic judgments played a more important role in the 1994 election and an even more significant role in the 1997 election. Voters were more likely to vote for the PRI in 1994 and especially in 1997 if they judged that economic performance had been positive for the country and themselves; they were likely to support the opposition if they believed otherwise. This process helped the PRI in 1994 and hurt it considerably in 1997.

In this respect, the 1994 and 1997 elections differed from those of 1988 and 1991 but they should be understood as part of an historical process. A large minority of Mexican voters did not behave in 1994 as would be expected from a retrospective economic voting model. Poiré shows, for example, that voters who disapproved of the president's performance and who also believed that the national economy had not improved, that their own finances had not improved, and that the policies of the preceding six years should not be continued still had a 0.25 chance of voting for the PRI. These voters were highly consistent in their thinking, stunningly adverse to the ruling party, and yet their voting intention still featured some support for the PRI (although these voters were clearly the least likely to vote PRI). Similarly, Magaloni finds that 40 percent of voters who held strongly unfavorable views of the PRI still intended to vote PRI in the 1994 presidential election; in 1997, 20 percent of the voters who held strongly unfavorable views of the PRI still intended to vote PRI. As Magaloni shows, however, there was much stronger retrospective voting in the 1997 election. Thus the 1994 election may be thought of as transitional in this regard: it featured greater weight of retrospective voting, but it took the post-election financial collapse finally to persuade a large number of Mexicans to punish the PRI.

Approval of the president's performance continued to play a highly significant role in both the 1994 and 1997 elections. This is consistent with observed behavior in 1988 and 1991. Poiré also finds that party loyalty—the habits of voting for the same party—was significantly important in the 1994 election, as it had been in 1988 and 1991. Magaloni also discovers that voter expectations of how the PRI and the existing opposition would shape future economic performance had a strong impact on the voter's choice in both the 1994 and 1997 elections, also consistent with voter behavior in the two previous national elections.

This analysis indicates important elements of continuity across elections but also significant elements of change. As Poiré perceptively notes, performance mattered to the Mexican voter who behaved quite rationally. Magaloni provides an elegant approach to understand the process of change. She employs a statistical form of reasoning—Bayesian analysis—to think about political change. In dominant-party systems, voters must evaluate a party with a long history in government against opposition alternatives with no record in government, at least at the national level. Voters have very limited information about those alternatives and therefore are slow to render retrospective judgments against a ruling party that had seemed to govern effectively for a long time. This helps to explain both the low saliency of negative retrospective judgments until the mid-1990s and the quite gradual process of change; it also provides a good explanation for the two-step voting process to which Domínguez and McCann had alluded.

A Bayesian perspective indicates that voters update their information with the new evidence they observe. (Both Magaloni and Alejandro Moreno show that age makes a considerable difference in the process of learning: older voters are more reluctant to update information they have long deemed reliable.) As the PRI government's economic performance plummeted in late 1994 and early 1995, more voters broke with the ruling party. Moreover, many voters experienced state or local governments organized by a party other than the PRI especially in 1995 and 1996; this allowed them to update their information about these parties and learn that they could be trusted with greater political power—hence the opposition victories in 1997.

But how did this learning take place? A first, key concern is that Mexican politics in the 1990s occurred in a context of risk aversion and uncertainty generated by the limited and asymmetrical information about the ruling and the opposition parties. Poiré shows that the risk aversion of Mexican voters—the effect of the "fear" that had been part of every election since 1988—hurt the PRD disproportionately because, rightly or wrongly, it was the party perceived to be more closely associated with acts of violence, especially in the state of Chiapas in 1994.

Alberto Cinta makes the important, general observation that risk aversion pervaded the political system and strongly favored the PRI over all opposition parties (though his finding for the 1997 election also suggests that it hurt the PRD more). This is especially significant because the PRI is the party held in the most unfavorable light by Mexican voters, and yet, even in 1997, it received a plurality of the votes cast. Cinta also points out that relative uncertainty in information about the various parties is also a highly significant variable. (Attitudes toward risk are irrelevant for the voting decision if voters believe that they are fully certain in their judgment about the political parties.) The joint impact of risk aversion and uncertainty on the voter's choice is quite dramatic.

Under all circumstances, as Cinta's chapter shows, the general context of risk aversion gives an edge to the PRI. For example, voters who have positive views of both the PRI and the PAN and are certain about those judgments give 61% of their votes to the PRI. But the insertion of uncertainty as a factor can tilt the results sharply. Take the same example above and make just one change, namely, voters are positive but uncertain concerning their views of the PAN: these voters give 83% of their votes to the PRI, an increase of 22 percentage points.

For the PAN, the utility of affecting the degree of certainty is simply enormous. Consider another example. Voters who have negative views of both the PRI and the PAN and are certain about those views give 73% of their votes to the PRI. But under the same circumstances, if the PAN could make these voters less sure about their still negative views of their party, then the PRI receives only 31% of these votes. The PAN's capacity to create some doubt lowers the PRI share of the votes by 42 percentage points.

Although the PRD can also benefit from these swings, it gains much less than the PAN from the levels of uncertainty. The split of the votes between the PRI and the PRD is much sharper, and the cost to the PRD much more marked. There is less political maneuverability for the PRD to take votes from the PRI through modest campaign effects; to vote for the PRD, a voter must be clearly ready to break with the PRI. This finding by Cinta is quite consistent with another of Poiré's intriguing findings.

Poiré argues that both the PRI and the PRD benefited from standing partisan predispositions but the PAN did not. "In order to stay competitive," Poiré writes perceptively, "the PAN has to convince its voters over and over, while the PRI (and perhaps the PRD) shall enjoy chunks of loyal voters with a strong predisposition to virtually ignore the campaigns." That is why a good PAN campaign that could affect the image of the candidate and the party, and shift the effects of uncertainty to its favor, could make such enormous difference. For the PAN, therefore, a campaign must be addressed to voters it does not own and who may know little or nothing about the party.

For the PRD, in contrast, the campaign requires avoiding fragmentation and divisive issues, rebuilding the party organization, mobilizing the partisan predispositions of its voters, and tapping into the stable pool of voters that, since the 1991 election, had been bereft of effective leadership. The PAN must persuade the unconvinced, while the PRD must mobilize those already opposed to the ruling party.

The process of learning during the national campaign is the subject for Alejandro Moreno's chapter. He focuses on the role of the level of awareness and partisanship. Campaign awareness increases sharply with education, interest in political advertising, media exposure, and ideological commitments; residents of the Federal District are also more likely to be aware. Voters who are both aware and partisan are much less likely to change their views during the election campaign; these voters are likely to vote for the same party in election after election. Voters who are aware but weakly partisan are the most likely to be susceptible to changing their vote as a result of the campaign; in these circumstances, the opposition parties are likely to benefit disproportionately. The PRI performs best among voters who show little awareness of the campaign. Intense campaigning thus reinforces the partisan vote and makes the nonpartisan vote more volatile, producing a more competitive election.

There is an important and politically relevant exception. In general, strong and weak partisans are more likely to vote for the same party in election after election as campaign awareness increases; campaign awareness among these partisans becomes an obstacle to persuading them to switch their vote. (Thus media exposure and party identification are among the strongest predictors of voter consistency across elections.) PAN voters in 1997 were an exception, however. As campaign awareness increased, weak PANistas voted for a party other than the PAN. This behavior is consistent with the strategic voting among some opposition voters that Domínguez and McCann found in the 1988 and 1991 elections. As Moreno puts it, "many weak PAN identifiers probably weighed the chances of the PAN to win the 1997 elections, and if the chances weren't high, then weak Panistas preferred to vote for another party with higher chances to win." To cite Poiré once again writing about the 1994 election, the PAN has to convince its voters over and over—in 1997 the party failed at this task.

The Cárdenas mayoral election campaign in Mexico City in 1997 illustrates many of these propositions, as studied by Chappell Lawson. The key characteristics that explain the behavior of voters in Mexico more generally serve well to describe the Mexico City voter. Moreover, Lawson finds, as Moreno does, that the campaign reinforced the partisan commitments of the strongly partisan. Nonetheless, more than any other scholar, Lawson portrays a remarkably volatile electorate, much more willing to change its opinions and voter preferences than had hitherto been apparent. (To be sure, as Moreno's chapter also leads us to believe, the greater the level of education, the greater the consistency, and the lesser the volatility in these matters but voters at all levels of political awareness are susceptible to changing their views.) At issue is not just the existence of a substantial minority of very late-deciders (as Domínguez and McCann had found for the 1991 election) but the fact that "voting intention in March [1997] was an exceedingly poor indication of how people actually voted four months later."

As Lawson himself indicates, much of this volatility is similar to the campaign "noise" evident in other countries: "random fluctuations among voters with few fixed political views tend to cancel each other out." Thus this volatility may not be electorally significant, even though it marks the campaign experience. But a portion of the volatility reflects real changes in the attitudes of the electorate. Lawson's data show that there was considerable stability in voter preferences for the PRD, while the PAN vote in particular utterly collapsed during the campaign.

A significant proportion of Mexico City voters changed their voter preferences during the campaign, switching mainly from one opposition party to another (as Domínguez and McCann had also found). That is a major explanation for the Cárdenas victory in 1997. The PAN was defeated because it failed to articulate a clear antigovernment message; for truly convinced opposition voters, the PRD was the only credible option. This level of conviction, as Lawson points out, is different from the strategic voting identified by Domínguez and McCann for the 1988 and 1991 elections. In Mexico City in 1997, voters voted for the parties of their true preference. It remains to be assessed in subsequent elections whether these converts remain faithful to their newly discovered parties or whether, in retrospect, the final vote was just the resting spot of their volatility, or even whether these voters had simply rationalized what had remained strategic decisions all along.

Cardenismo resurrected in 1997 to recapture the pool of voters it first won in the 1988 elections and who were still available (albeit divided into several left-wing parties) in the 1991 elections. Mexican voters responded to the Party of the Democratic Revolution at long last as a *party*, voting not just for its leader as mayor of Mexico City, but also for hundreds of its candidates as members of Congress and of state assemblies and as mayors of other cities and towns.

Three of the reasons for the PRD's success, as Kathleen Bruhn notes, are found in the wider environment. Mexico's economic crisis begun in late 1994 gravely weakened the PRI; Cárdenas was the most readily identifiable opponent of President Salinas, and so supporting Cárdenas was the surest way to disapprove of Salinas. The electoral reforms approved in advance of the 1997 election campaign greatly strengthened the PRD by giving it significantly more funding and easier access to television. Finally, the party system had changed; several of the competing parties on the left that had taken about half of the left-wing vote in 1991 lost most of their voter support and even lost their formal registration as parties in 1997. With better funding in a fairer election, less competition for its voters, and winning plaudits for its history of anti-Salinismo, no wonder the PRD performed so much better.

Some of the reasons for the PRD's victory, however, are to its credit. Cárdenas and the PRD, Bruhn tells us, did not change their core ideology but they did reach out to voters more interested in its opposition message than in left-wing theology. They appealed to a wide array of voters, not just the core left-wing vote, and as we have seen, they succeeded. The PRD had become one more party hugging the political center.

Cárdenas and his party also accepted, at long last, some of the key ingredients of modern campaign strategy, tactics, and technology. In 1997 Cárdenas hired campaign consultants who persuaded him of the need to smile and who designed professional spots for radio and television. As Moreno and Bruhn report, the PRD's slogan—"now it's time for the sun to shine" (the sun is the PRD's symbol)—was by far the best-known slogan of the campaign. In 1997 Cárdenas prepared much better for a televised debate than he had done in 1994. He also kept his distance from the Zapatista insurgency in 1997 much more than he did in 1994, reducing thereby the fear that a PRD victory might be associated with violence. (Lawson found no evidence of fear as a campaign issue in 1997). More troubling is that many of the PRD's organizational weaknesses, including the risk of indiscipline and renewed fragmentation, had yet to be overcome fully. For the PRD to win the presidency in 2000, it must become a stronger and more disciplined organization able to plan for that victory and then capable of governing.

Electoral outcomes matter. Elections are not only the means for citizens to choose their rulers but also the instruments of democracy to empower the weak. This may happen over a wide array of social, economic, and political issues. In this book, we examine in detail only one of these matters, namely, the relationship between electoral outcomes and the condition of women in society. In Mexico, women for a long time have exemplified effective disenfranchisement even decades after women's suffrage. The proportion of women elected to Congress rose in 1988, dropped in 1991, rose again in 1994, and continued to rise in 1997. Linda Stevenson's chapter shows that there is a clear relationship between the proportion of members of Congress who are women, on the one hand, and the likelihood that Congress will attend to policies of special concern to women, on the other. The pattern of women's representation, just noted, created a natural experiment: when the percentage of women legislators dropped in 1991 so too did policy attention to women's issues. Increased women's representation in Congress, moreover, could be traced to the greater number and effectiveness of women's social movements, while the translation of newly found congressional strength into policy making owed much to freshly minted women policy entrepreneurs. Thus Mexico's democratic opening in the 1990s began to extend as well to meet the concerns of voters whose issues had been left unattended. Democracy was transforming the nation's institutions as well as the policies on which they focused.

CONCLUSION

Mexico heads for the twenty-first century with a much more competitive party system than it has ever experienced. Mexican voters can discern the likelihood that one party or another has a better chance of winning, and they act accordingly. Political parties have reinvented themselves. The PRI became an electoral institution, not just an arm of the government. The PRD became not just the home for the disgruntled still charmed by a "fatal attraction" for state intervention in the economy, but a real party capable of mounting impressive and successful electoral campaigns. The PAN has built a truly national party, governing various states and hundreds of municipalities.

And yet, important problems remain for the Mexican political system. Its parties and its politicians are barely learning how to cope with divided government where different parties control the presidency, the chambers of Congress, and many state and local governments. The voter's level of information about policy issues is low and the extent of volatility in public opinion is considerable. Although the role of fear and risk aversion in politics may be declining, it remains significant in various parts of the country. Elections have become much fairer, but pockets of intimidation and abuse persist, especially in rural areas.

The challenge for Mexico is to transit fully toward a democratic political system, with well-organized parties capable of fashioning effective policies. The nation's strongest asset may be its savvy voter, the long underestimated hero of the Mexican political transition.

NOTES

1. My past work on Mexican public opinion and elections could not have been possible without the insights, skill, and hard work of my friend and collaborator, Professor James A. McCann, Purdue University, to whom I remain most grateful.

2. For discussions of how the Mexican political system operated, see Wayne A. Cornelius and Ann L. Craig, *The Mexican Political System in Transition,* Monograph Series, no. 35 (La Jolla: Center for U.S.–Mexican Studies, University of California at San Diego, 1991); and Roderic Ai Camp, *Politics in Mexico* (Oxford: Oxford University Press, 1993).

3. For discussion, see Jorge I. Domínguez, *Democratic Politics in Latin America and the Caribbean* (Baltimore: Johns Hopkins University Press, 1998).

4. See, among others, George Philip, *The Presidency in Mexican Politics* (New York:

St. Martin's, 1992); Samuel Schmidt, *The Deterioration of the Mexican Presidency* (Tucson: University of Arizona Press, 1991); Rogelio Hernández Rodríguez, "Inestabilidad política y presidencialismo en México," *Mexican Studies* 10 (winter 1994): 187–216; Alicia Hernández Chávez, "Mexican Presidentialism: A Historical and Institutional Overview," *Mexican Studies* 10 (winter 1994): 217–25; and Miguel Angel Centeno, *Democracy Within Reason: Technocratic Revolution in Mexico* (University Park: Pennsylvania State University Press, 1994).

5. During Carlos Salinas's presidential term about half of the state governors were removed from office.

6. From 1938 to 1946 the official party was called the Party of the Mexican Revolution.

7. For further discussion, see Soledad Loaeza and Rafael Segovia, *La vida política mexicana en la crisis* (Mexico City: El Colegio de México, 1987); Soledad Loaeza, *El llamado de las urnas* (Mexico City: Cal y Arena, 1989); Juan Molinar Horcasitas, *El tiempo de la legitimidad: Elecciones, autoritarismo, y democracia en México* (Mexico City: Cal y Arena, 1991); and John J. Bailey, *Governing Mexico* (New York: St. Martin's, 1988).

8. The Mexican Academy of Human Rights and Civic Alliance/Observation 94 published the following: *The Media and the 1994 Federal Elections in Mexico: A Content Analysis of Television News Coverage of the Political Parties and Presidential Candidates* (Washington, D.C.: 1994); *Las elecciones federales en México según los noticieros "24 Horas" de TELEVISA y "Hechos" de Televisión Azteca, 30 de Mayo a 30 de Junio de 1994* (Mexico City: 1994).

9. Ann L. Craig and Wayne A. Cornelius, "Houses Divided: Parties and Political Reform in Mexico," in *Building Democratic Institutions: Parties and Party Systems in Latin America,* ed. Scott Mainwaring and Timothy R. Scully (Stanford: Stanford University Press, 1994).

10. Computed from Inter-American Development Bank, *Economic and Social Progress in Latin America: 1991 Report* (Washington, D.C.: 1991), 273; United Nations, Economic Commission for Latin America and the Caribbean, *Preliminary Overview of the Latin American Economy, 1988,* LC/G.1536 (New York: 1989), 17–18; ibid., *1992,* LC/G.1751 (New York: 1992), 43–45; ibid., *1994,* LC/G.1846 (New York: 1994), 41–42.

11. For further analysis, Carlos Bazdresch, Nisso Bucay, Soledad Loaeza, and Nora Lustig, eds., *México: auge, crisis, y ajuste,* 3 vols. (Mexico City: Fondo de Cultura Económica, 1992).

12. United Nations, *Preliminary Overview, 1992,* 41, 43–45; ibid., *1994,* 39, 41–42.

13. Council of Freely Elected Heads of Government, Carter Center, Emory University, *Electoral Reform in Mexico* (Atlanta: 1993); ibid., *Elections in Mexico: Third Report* (Atlanta: 1994); Instituto Federal Electoral, *Address of Dr. Jorge Carpizo, President of the General Council of the IFE, June 3, 1994* (Mexico City); Misión Técnica de la O.N.U, *Análisis del sistema electoral mexicano* (Mexico City: Instituto Federal Electoral, 1994).

14. Alianza Cívica/Observación 94, "La elección presidencial: Entre el escepticismo y la esperanza," *Perfil de La Jornada* (21 August 1994):1–3; Sergio Aguayo, *The Recent Presidential Elections in Mexico* (Washington, D.C.: National Endowment for Democracy, 1994).

15. United Nations, Economic Commission for Latin America and the Caribbean, *Preliminary Overview of the Economy of Latin America and the Caribbean, 1997,* LC/G.1984-P (New York: 1997), 50–52.

16. Luis Rubio, "The Politics of Economic Reform," in *Presiding over Change: Zedillo's First Year,* ed. M. Delal Baer and Roderic Ai Camp (Washington, D.C.: Center for Strategic and International Studies, 1997), 7–8.

17. Jeffrey A. Weldon, "Mexico's 'Definitive' Electoral Reform," *Enfoque* (fall 1996): 1–2, 12.

18. The statistics in this section are taken from Armand Peschard-Sverdrup, *The 1997 Mexican Midterm Elections: Post-Election Report* (Washington, DC: Center for Strategic and International Studies, 1997).

19. Gabriel Almond and Sidney Verba, *The Civic Culture: Political Attitudes and Democracy in Five Nations* (Princeton: Princeton University Press, 1963).

20. The next paragraphs draw closely from Jorge I. Domínguez and James A. McCann, *Democratizing Mexico: Public Opinion and Electoral Choices* (Baltimore: Johns Hopkins University Press, 1996).

21. See, for example, ibid., 9.

22. Ibid., 11.

23. Ibid., 95, 128, 130.

24. Ibid., 138.

25. Wayne A. Cornelius, *Mexican Politics in Transition: The Breakdown of a One-Party Dominant Regime,* Monograph Series, no. 41 (La Jolla: Center for U.S.-Mexican Studies, University of California at San Diego, 1996), 8.

26. Ibid., 176.

27. Poiré and Magaloni's findings differ on one important point. Poiré finds that the PRI did well in Mexico City, whereas Magaloni finds the opposite. This will require further research.

2

RETROSPECTIVE VOTING, PARTISANSHIP, AND LOYALTY IN PRESIDENTIAL ELECTIONS: 1994[1]

Alejandro Poiré

El domingo son las elecciones. ¡Qué emocionante! ¿Quién ganará?
—Jorge Ibargüengoitia, Mexico City, July 1976

INTRODUCTION

Sophisticated electoral analysis in Latin America is virtually in its infancy. To be sure, until only a few years ago, elections really did not matter much in the region. Still, now that the third wave of democratization seems to have settled in almost every one of its countries, elections are regaining analytical and political importance in the region. Although Mexico has certainly not yet staged such an impressive and pinpoint transition as the ones taking place in Chile, Argentina, and Brazil, for example, it has certainly accelerated its path out of the one-party hegemony it suffered until only some years ago.[2] Especially given the results of the federal contest of 1997, the fact is that elections have regained the analytical importance they always deserved but which was understandably negated under the Institutional Revolutionary Party (PRI) authoritarian rule.[3] The greater relevance of the subject is also methodologically oriented. Not only have the costs of better statistical analysis been exponentially reduced in the past few years but also the quality and availability of useful data to study these phenomena has been on the increase. Correspondingly, studies of Mexican

24

elections have started to show the enhanced statistical sophistication that is now easily available to test hypotheses regarding electoral behavior. However, a number of relevant theoretical questions are still lacking a more elaborate methodological assessment. Such is the task this chapter shall tackle.

In 1994 Ernesto Zedillo won what has been labeled the cleanest presidential election in Mexico's history—really not that surprising a title given our, to say the least, picturesque political past. As a candidate of the long-time ruling Partido Revolucionario Institucional, he obtained 50.2% of a total of more than thirty-four million valid votes.[4] The runner-up, Diego Fernández, from the right-oriented Partido Acción Nacional (PAN) garnered a historic high 26.7%; and in third place, from the left-leaning Partido de la Revolución Democrática (PRD) came the second-time presidential candidate and former member of the PRI, Cuauhtémoc Cárdenas; he gained 16.6% of the vote.[5]

Nineteen ninety-four will be remembered in Mexican political history as a highly dangerous year. The Chiapas uprising in the first day of the year and the assassinations of Luis Donaldo Colosio, the PRI's original candidate, in March and José Francisco Ruiz Massieu, the party's Secretary General, in September showed that political violence had erupted after decades of enforced social peace. Finally, the prospects for a quick economic boom were destroyed by the now infamous "mistake of December,"[6] which triggered an overwhelming capital flight and its corresponding recessive effects in 1995. In some sense, Mexico entered the twenty-first century of its history six years earlier than expected.

This chapter will address a small part of this history, by testing a model of the voters' decision in the Mexican presidential election of 1994 based on four sets of variables: performance evaluations, structural determinants, campaign influences, and political factors. We will show that:

1. Mexican voters were quite rational and retrospective in their votes.

2. Structural determinants were weak predictors.

3. Candidate images made a difference.

4. Political factors were also relevant.

In short, in 1994 Ernesto Zedillo won thanks to a combination of a still healthy reserve of loyal PRI voters, a great public image of then president Carlos Salinas and his policies, and mostly favorable television coverage. In addressing these issues, a number of relevant methodological and theoretical points will be made.

The study is organized as follows. The next section is a brief review of the major schools of electoral analysis, as an introduction to the current debate regarding the Mexican case. We then engage the Mexican debate by presenting a series of hypotheses for the 1994 presidential contest. These hypotheses are then tested against data stemming from a nationwide exit poll generously provided for this study by Warren Mitofsky. A final section discussing the results will be presented as a conclusion.

I. SCHOOLS OF ELECTORAL ANALYSIS

Electoral analysis can be divided in three major theoretical schools.[7] The sociological-demographic school, which is identified with the work of Seymour Martin Lipset and Stein Rokkan;[8] the psychological or party-identification one, which stems from the series of studies conducted by Campbell, Converse, Miller, and Stokes;[9] and the rationality school, following Anthony Downs's economic perspective. These different schools have followed different and, at times, divergent paths, partly deriving from the availability of useful data. A properly specified model of electoral behavior should recognize the contributions of each school and try to incorporate them in a coherent—and not eclectic—fashion.

The sociological school sees parties as the crystallization of underlying social cleavages in the electorate. Variables such as religion, ethnicity, or social class are the best predictors of an individual's electoral choice. Although this literature is perhaps most relevant for some "class-based" parties in Europe (e.g., the Socialist Workers' Party in Spain, the Social and Christian Democrats in Germany, and the Labour Party in Britain), some parties in the Latin American context also seem to represent clear-cut social cleavages.[10] The main theoretical problem with this school of thought is simple: sociological variables change very slowly over time and are therefore unable to predict quick shifts in electoral results. Instead of explaining a specific election, sociological variables may help determine the basic clienteles of political parties, but in competitive contexts elections are decided in the margins, where short-term factors appear to be most important.

The psychological school of electoral analysis has been dominated by the very U.S.-centered concept of party identification. This concept depicts an affective predisposition of the individual, learned in the early years, that is typically stable and asserted through time. This affective predisposition works as an interpretative tunnel through which the individual's evaluations of specific political objects—such as campaigns, candidates, and issues—are to be sorted out. It has been extensively used as the best predictor of U.S. elections but has also been subject to considerable theoretical review.[11] Political culture, more generally, shares some features with the party-identification concept: it is the result of early socialization and relevant experiences, it is relatively stable through time, and strongly influences the way in which we perceive the political world. Studies of Latin American elections have supported themselves in this school, although in a more tangential fashion. A partial reason for this is methodological: successful evaluation of the political effect of psychological or cultural traits is difficult to derive from aggregate data. Until fairly recently, reliable individual-level political data in the region was really very scarce. Theoretically, though, this school suffers from the same problem than the sociological one: long-term predispositions do not explain short-term swings in voting. What is even more important in Latin American terms, and is presented as an open question, is the effect of the relative instability of the party systems over the years, which might completely undermine any socialization-led perspective.

Also relying heavily on individual-level data, the rational approach to electoral analysis concentrates precisely on those short-term factors that might determine a voter's choice. Elaborating upon Downs's original perspective, voters are seen as maximizing a utility function which depends upon some expected package of benefits or policies to be provided by the winning contender; these choices in turn are weighted against the incumbent's performance.[12] Scholars of a number of countries in Latin America have also used rationality-based analysis,[13] but the fact is that very few of these analyses have used the methodological tools necessary to provide statistical validity to their conclusions.

From a methodological point of view, it must be said, electoral analysis in Latin America is in its earlier stages. Yet there is no longer a good reason for this since enough survey material is already available for analysis. To be sure, an increasing number of works shall quickly recover the lost time. However, the fact remains that there are still very few articles that allow us to test individual-level hypotheses.[14] The Mexican case—surprisingly enough—is perhaps the exception.

II. ELECTORAL ANALYSIS IN MEXICO: THE CURRENT DEBATE

Some of the most highly developed analysis of electoral behavior in Latin America corresponds to the Mexican case. Domínguez and McCann (DMC hereafter) have in many ways set the path to be followed: they have used comprehensive models, individual-level data, and reliable statistical techniques.[15] There is no doubt that Mexican electoral analysis has by now an important enough body of literature, covering the three schools of thought that we have depicted.[16] Still, it is DMC who have virtually set the current agenda of theoretical debate. What follows is a brief discussion of their model and two important responses to it.

DMC explain the voting behavior of Mexicans within a rational choice framework while relying heavily upon political variables. In accordance with other authors' depiction of the Mexican partisan spectrum as two-dimensional,[17] they argue that the 1988 and 1991 Mexican elections were a plebiscite over the institutional characteristics of the regime: "Voters ask themselves, above all, whether they continue to support the ruling party,"[18] and only later do they turn to an ideological dimension, composed of considerations of policy issues, government performance, and economic assessments.

They have also shown that the Mexican political culture is comparatively democratic,[19] and that partisan loyalty was an important predictor of the vote. But two findings of these authors were striking at the time, and one of them has been subject to considerable review. First, and contrary to a wealth of aggregate level data evidence stemming from the sociological approach, they found that social cleavages do not explain partisan attachments in Mexico. Second, they see no evidence of retrospective economic voting, *à la* Fiorina. The evidence they present comes from two nationwide Gallup polls—and is pretty convincing. But as we shall argue and others have noted, their conclusions need to be addressed in the light of new data and different techniques.[20]

Jorge Buendía[21] directly questions their model by stressing the importance of retrospective and prospective economic factors, presidential image, and risk aversion to explain the 1994 presidential vote. His evidence as well comes from a nationwide poll, but is obviously not directly comparable to DMC's; moreover, and as we shall see below, his model also has some specification problems. One of Buendía's claims about the DMC evidence is fairly straightforward. The indicator for retrospective evaluations on the latter's model is the voter's opinion about *current* economic conditions and not about their perceived change, which impedes the voter from entirely incorporating the impact of the incumbent on such conditions. As Buendía puts it, if the evidence for retrospective voting is not found, this may be due to the lack of a good indicator to capture it.[22] Buendía's work is also characterized by his refusal to include a measurement of party identification, due to its very high correlation with electoral choice. In his words, it "is practically equivalent to the vote and therefore the concept loses all of its explanatory power."[23] Finally, we should say that two of Buendía's specific results are directly comparable to ours: he finds that Mexican retrospective voting existed, but that it was mainly a sociotropic vote and not an individualist one. He also finds strong evidence about the effect of risk aversion hurting both opposition parties.

Alejandro Moreno and Keith Yanner[24] (MY hereafter) present a comprehensive model of the 1994 election based on a preelectoral nationwide poll and the same exit poll that is used in this study. Following the Michigan School, they find consistent evidence that partisan identification was a strong predictor of the vote. Contradicting DMC's and Buendía's claims, they see structural factors still closely related to the direction of the vote. Their evidence regarding retrospective and, in general, rational voting is not consistent across the two data sets. In the exit poll they find strong evidence of retrospective and issue voting, but in the preelectoral poll they only find some importance of specifically political issues.

Before we present our model, an overall assessment of these contributions is at hand. First of all, DMC's two-step model cannot be tested for the 1994 election, since some of the variables that they found to be central in explaining voting behavior in 1988 and 1991 were not measured then.[25]

Concentrating on the 1994 models, both MY and DMC present strong evidence that partisan loyalty or party identification has been a significant predictor of the vote. Even if it is too strong a predictor, its complete exclusion (as Buendía proposes) from a model of voting will probably bias the results of those variables highly correlated with partisanship; therefore, Buendía's move is a highly risky one. We here agree with MY in the sense that a standard, reliable measurement of party identification or loyalty must be developed for the Mexican case.[26] We shall address this issue below. Also, we will incorporate in our model a measure of risk aversion that only partially coincides with Buendía's findings.

On the other hand, MY's preelectoral model seems to be the perfect example of Buendía's claim. The only significant variable across all parties turns out to be party identification, although this could also stem from the inefficiency produced by a wrong model specification.[27] Still, if the trade-off is between inefficiency and probably wrong estimates, we prefer to back MY's approach and avoid supporting probably false hypotheses. Thus, we include a measure of long- and short-term party attachments in our model.

In sum, the central debate on the Mexican electorate concentrates on the relative weight that retrospective evaluations, party attachments, and specifically political factors (such as risk aversion) carry. This debate is clearly represented in the chapters that follow, concerning elections held after the one we study here. As we have stated, though, Mexican history has moved relatively fast during the last ten years, so these models are mostly single frames of a pretty speedy action tape. The point is that some factors could be very specific to transitional elections while others will continue being relevant for years to come.[28] We now proceed with a more specific methodological discussion.

III. MODEL, METHODS, AND DATA

To test our hypotheses we shall use individual-level data coming from Warren Mitofsky's national exit poll of Mexico's 1994 presidential election.[29] As we have seen, this same material has been used in other studies of the same election, but it is the contention of this chapter that a series of methodological issues have not been properly addressed, affecting the overall interpretation of the Mexican vote in 1994. The following section offers an assessment and proposes statistical solutions to these issues.

The proper way to test hypotheses about the effect of a set of independent variables on a nonordinal categorical variable is a multinomial logit procedure.[30] Apart from providing us with hypothesis tests for each variable included in the model, the procedure yields an estimated probability of occurrence for each of the categories of the dependent variable, given selected values of the explanatory variables. In other words, apart from letting us validate our hypotheses statistically, it will offer a neat depiction of the estimated effect of every factor in the probability of a voter choosing each party.

The multinomial logit procedure estimates, via maximum likelihood, a dependent variable with $m+1$ categories through m simultaneous equations. In our case, the dependent variable is the vote for the three major parties in 1994.[31]

Still, the procedure is not immune to the typical problems involved in more common estimation techniques. One of the central assumptions of the multinomial logit procedure is that the specification of the model is correct; if it is not a valid assumption, then all the results are put into question. As King, Keohane, and Verba suggest,[32] survey analysis is prone to problems of systematic measurement error, simultaneity, and endogeneity. Analyses of Mexican and Latin American elections have almost completely overlooked this issue, and it is here where they are found lacking. The methodological debate to which we want to contribute addresses exactly this kind of problem and concentrates on three types of variables: partisanship, loyalty, and political risk aversion.

A. Correcting for Partisanship and Loyalty

As we have seen, several authors argue about the importance of incorporating the individuals' electoral past as an explanatory factor of the present vote, whether it is from an identification perspective,[33] or from a straightforward partisan loyalty view.[34] Two variables included in the survey may help us address this question. One of them asks about the time when the decision to vote was made. The first category of response is, "I almost always vote for the same party." This variable measures a long-term predisposition of the voter to minimize his electoral analysis, and to vote regularly for the same party, almost regardless of the election. This long-term predisposition—*independent of party choice*—we will call *partisanship*.[35] The second variable asks the voters who they voted for back in 1988 and checks for its effect on the 1994 vote. This short-term feature we will simply call *loyalty*.

Unfortunately, these two variables face methodological problems. Should Mexican long-term partisans be similar—regardless of their preferred party? The answer does not seem to be yes, and there are at least two reasons for this. First, the PRD was only founded after the astounding outcome of 1988 election, which immediately puts it in a different category from the PAN and PRI, both having competed in elections for several decades now. Second, and due to the relatively recent break from the Mexican system's noncompetitive character, opposition partisans are simply very scarce relative to *Priísta* partisans. Thus, we should expect a high degree of endogeneity between preference for the PRI and a long-term predisposition to partisanship. To isolate the effect of being a "partisan voter"—of almost always voting for the same party—on a voter's electoral choice, we must recognize the fact that in the Mexican context being or not a Priísta will actually influence the probability of a voter being a partisan. Since we want to distinguish the effect of partisanship on an individual's chances of voting for one party, from the effect of party preference on long-term partisanship, we need to correct for endogeneity. In other words, if partisanship were to be included in our final model without any correction, then we would not be able to distinguish the real effect of long-term partisanship—the exogenous factor, from the Priísta preference that lurks beneath this answer—the endogenous factor.

In order to tackle this problem,[36] we shall derive a new variable from the voters' social characteristics, which estimates the cultural predisposition to stick to a party over time. In sum, by estimating partisanship (the probability of an individual answering "always" to our relevant question) as a function of the social characteristics of the subject, we are excluding whatever likelihood of being a partisan she could derive from her party preferences. Moreover, this procedure will produce unbiased and consistent estimates when we incorporate the new variable in the final model.[37]

A similar problem appears when we try to incorporate the voter's answer to the question about the 1988 presidential election, to check for the effect of short-term loyalty. The official—and highly contested—results were PRI 49.9%, PAN 16.9%, and the Frente Democrático Nacional, the coalition supporting Cárdenas, 31.7%.[38] However, the aggregate answers to such question in the Mitofsky poll are: Salinas (PRI) 64.1%; Clouthier (PAN) 15.3%; Cárdenas (FDN) 16.0%.[39] This difference stems from two factors: one of them is random error in the voter's memory; another is a straightforward lie on their behalf. It is fairly evident that good opinions about Salinas and his tenure systematically affected the people's recollection of what they did six years before. In this case, using the variable without any correction could once again bias our estimates in the rest of the model. To solve this problem,[40] we could have used the respondent's social characteristics as an instrumental variable to avoid the measurement error—just as we did for the partisanship variable, but in this case we do have authentically exogenous information to correct for the voters' peculiar memory patterns. As is shown in Appendix B, we will use the official results from the 1988 election for each of the thirty-two states of Mexico, in order to perform a linear transformation of the variable "vote in 1988." This transformation yields a weighted value for each response to this question and will produce in the survey an aggregate result (both by state and nationwide) identical to the one obtained from the real election, thereby reducing the measurement error in the 1994 survey.

The following caveats should be kept in mind: although there is good reason to suspect the official electoral results for the 1988 election, all of the available surveys from that time resemble the official figures relatively closely;[41] moreover, none of the surveys has enough information about the state by state results to be used as a more reliable source. This would suggest the appropriateness of using the official results to implement the correction. Finally, the incorporation of the corrected 1988 vote will result in the exclusion of the younger voters, which represents around 20 percent of the sample. Although this figure is not negligible, the theoretical thrust of this chapter is to evaluate a series of competing hypotheses about the Mexican electorate in 1994—where the impact of partisan loyalty seems to be crucial. We therefore prefer to include the loyalty variable and leave the analysis of first-time voters for further work. In sum, the transformed variable for the 1988 vote corrects for the measurement error via trustworthy exogenous information and will avoid biased and inconsistent results in our final model.

To summarize, party attachments are relevant in explaining electoral behavior in Mexico in two senses, each providing specific methodological challenges. First, it is a long-term predisposition to vote for the same party (partisanship), which can only be used in a model if it is effectively separated from the effect of partisan preference. This is done here by using instead the probability of a voter being a partisan as estimated from his social characteristics. Second, it is a behavioral characteristic of the individual, which can have a strong short-term effect (loyalty); the indicator we use is the voter's recollection of her last presidential vote. This variable presents a systematic measurement error, which is corrected by weighting it with the state by state results of the 1988 election.

By providing a detailed account of the statistical techniques used to address these problems, we hope to evoke a deeper methodological and theoretical discussion.

B. The Fear Debate

Ask any observer of the recent years of Mexican politics for a one-word explanation of the 1994 triumph of the PRI; most often the answer will be "fear." In various ways, electoral studies have tried to address the fact that after decades of one-party rule, risk-averse voters might continue to vote for the PRI even if they have strong reason to believe that it will do poorly. Simply because, for the Mexican case, as Fiorina would put it, Magaloni has argued, and Cinta's work in this volume discusses in detail,[42] they attach a very large variance to the expected benefits from an opposition government because they lack any concrete evidence of it. Moreover, the very rocky year of 1994 was the perfect scenario for a vote dominated by conservative concerns. The Chiapas uprising in the first days of the year and the assassination of the original PRI presidential candidate, Luis Donaldo Colosio, sent a clear signal to the electorate that peace and order were at stake.

The Mitofsky survey tried to address this issue directly, by asking the voter what was the main reason for her vote, and giving her as an option the popular Mexican saying, "más vale malo por conocido que bueno por conocer" (something like "better the devil you know").[43]

The risk aversion variable, although highly appealing a priori, has methodological problems similar to the ones presented by the partisanship variable. Once again—and this is a problem that needs to be addressed directly—the use as an explanatory variable of the uncorrected answer of the voter will impede us to distinguish *which part of his risk aversion predates the electoral decision* (and is therefore a relevant explanatory factor) *from the part of his risk aversion that stems from his partisan preference* (and is then a factor determined by our dependent variable).[44] The correction for endogeneity is similar to the one used for the partisan loyalty variable: an estimate of the probability of being risk averse is derived via logit from the social characteristics of the respondent and this variable is used instead of the voter's direct response to the question.[45]

As we have seen, other authors analyzing the 1994 elections have used the risk aversion hypothesis but without correcting for endogeneity, which could lead to erroneous conclusions. Still, and just as it is the case with the partisan loyalty variables, it is imperative to recognize the fact that political risk aversion is dependent upon partisan preference.

In short, this study strives to provide a statistically dependable assessment of the effect of risk aversion, partisanship, and loyalty in the Mexican voter's electoral decision. It also contends that proper incorporation of them in future models of Mexican voting is compulsory.

C. The Explanatory Variables

By this time, and thanks to the methodological discussion, we have already disclosed some of the central parts of our model, the explicitly political factors:

1. a measurement of *risk aversion* corrected for endogeneity;

2. a measurement of long-term *partisanship* also corrected for endogeneity; and

3. weighted estimates of the past presidential vote as a measure of *loyalty*. Still, it is time to depict the rest of the components of the model. The

political factors contained in it are only one among four batteries of indicators: social and regional determinants; performance variables; campaign factors; and political variables. What follows is a brief assessment of the logic underlying the expected effect of each variable.[46]

First we should consider the social clienteles of the Mexican parties in 1994. As we have seen, a lot of the literature has centered upon these as relevant explanatory variables. Although we follow DMC to contend that they will very improbably determine the vote—especially when considering short-term changes of opinion—we first have to test their significance in order to reject such a hypothesis. Especially, and given the huge amount of theoretical and empirical evidence of sociological determinants of the vote, it seems safe to start by including all the social information available. The voter's gender and age do not have any theoretical importance a priori,[47] but it has been argued that voters with elementary education or less and those in the minimum levels of income form the typical PRI social base.[48] Also, some occupations are expected to favor some parties,[49] especially public servants and peasants might consistently favor the PRI due to relatively strong corporatist ties between these sectors and the official party; likewise, workers in the private sector might be expected to favor the opposition disproportionately. Finally, some regional differences in the parties' competitiveness should be incorporated. First and foremost, it may be argued that the presence of state governors from the PAN will favor Panista candidates. Although Diego Fernández lost the presidential race in each of these states, we still lack statistical evidence concerning the specifically political effect of this variable in the individual voter's choice. Given our previous argument, we should expect rational voters from Baja California, Chihuahua, and Guanajuato to have lowered the variance they associated to an opposition triumph, since they already had experienced electoral turnover in the executive branch of their own states. We therefore included a dummy variable for voters belonging to those states in the equations estimating risk aversion.[50] Also, although electoral contestation was already growing in most of the country by the early 1990s, the two main opposition parties had a highly regionalized basis of support, with the PAN concentrating its constituents in the central and northwestern states, and the PRD being stronger in the South and Mexico City. A number of dummy variables for these regional indicators will be included in the first, saturated model, in order to test for their significance, and will be discarded if irrelevant to avoid inefficient estimates.[51]

However, this chapter basically contends that performance factors count, and do so heavily. These will mostly be determined by a voter's retrospective evaluations of the role of the incumbent. Also, partisan choice should depend upon an analysis of the prospects offered by each party if winning the election—as signaled by their policy offers. Our database contains three indicators of retrospective evaluations: the voters' assessment of Salinas's performance as a president, as well as their perception about the changes in both the national and personal or family economy during Salinas's tenure. Regarding policy positions, the survey asks the citizen whether he or she thinks that the economic policies followed by Salinas should be continued or significantly changed by the next president. This question also implies a retrospective judgment but clearly tries to link the voters' view of economic policy with the proposals coming from the different parties for the next term.

These four indicators constitute our central "performance" battery. Specifically, and given the fact that 1994 was such a turbulent political year, it seems fair to assume that voters felt that there was a lot at stake in the presidential election. Under these conditions, we believe that expected utility concerns should be most important.[52] We therefore expect voters to reward Salinas and his policies by voting for the PRI, or to punish him and his party by voting for the opposition.[53] Moreover, the policy question provides us with the opportunity to differentiate voters along economic lines. Since the PAN offered its legislative support to most of Salinas's initiatives in economic policy, we should expect voters disagreeing with his policy to favor the more leftist-leaning PRD stronger than they would favor the PAN.

In any presidential election, and in spite of a strong party-oriented vote, candidates themselves are usually the axes of a voter's decision. Apart from a certain assessment of the incumbent's performance, of the policy proposals of alternative parties, and of other long- and short-term political factors, the rational voter will incorporate the candidates' appeal and their personal attributes in her electoral decision. Even from a party-based perspective, it could be argued that candidates are the most powerful signaling devices of a party's political offer. The database contains two questions that allow us to test for the significance of such factors. First, respondents were asked whether the candidate or the party mostly guided their vote. Later, they were asked for the rationale behind their candidate choice and were given four major attributes to assess: honesty, experience, closeness to the people, and personality. We constructed a series of interaction terms which indicate those respondents which "voted their candidate" and the attribute they selected for such purpose. To this respect, the only relevant hypothesis a priori refers to the benefits that Ernesto Zedillo should have garnered from his experience as a top-level public administrator, which was underscored by his first campaign lemma: "He knows how to do it."[54]

Campaigns should matter, especially if the notion of a first-time-ever competitive election is prevalent—and this was probably the case in Mexico 1994.[55] The role of the media and most importantly of television during the campaign will undoubtedly be remembered. In spite of the occurrence of the first nationally broadcast presidential debate in Mexican history, one of the central complaints of the opposition, coming more poignantly from the PRD, referred to the unfair treatment received by their candidates on television.[56] The survey used allowed us to assess the effect of television through two elements. First, there is the general coverage of the campaigns, which could have had a direct effect in the electoral decision. The hypothesis in this chapter is that it did have an effect, which was biased in favor of the candidate of the PRI.[57] Second, the presidential debate staged around three months before Election Day gave the three major candidates ninety free minutes of a leveled playing field on which an immense share of the electorate could compare them. Journalistic reports would agree that Diego Fernández, the normally vociferous polemicist from the PAN clearly won the debate, and that both Ernesto Zedillo from the PRI and Cuauhtémoc Cárdenas from the PRD had disappointing performances.

In order to test these hypotheses we used information from two questions in the survey. To test for the overall effect of the campaign, we will use a dummy variable, which will indicate whether the voter obtained from the TV (or other source) the information that was most relevant for her electoral choice. If the "unfair treatment" hypothesis is correct, we expect those getting most of their information from TV to be prone to vote for the PRI. To test for the effect of the debate in itself, we construct an interaction term between the TV as most relevant source of information variable and a variable indicating that the electoral decision was taken "after the debate." This term (TV*debate) will allow us to distinguish between the overall effect of TV coverage and the effect of the debate, *but only for the TV faithful*—therefore isolating its impact. In short, if the voter did not get his most relevant information from TV, then it follows that the debate was not that influential—even if his decision was taken on the days following such event. Also, if the voter did get the most important information from TV, we will have separate estimates of the effect of the overall campaign *and* the effect of the debate. Our hypothesis is that this interaction term should strongly influence the vote in favor of the PAN's "Jefe Diego."

More generally, campaign influences shape the way in which voters evaluate the political offers put forth by the parties. To the extent that a wealth of information is easily available, a voter's evaluations about the past, expectations about the future, and opinions about incumbents' performance might change during campaigns.[58] The effect of these variables is therefore not inconsistent at all with what we call a rational voter but simply highlights the fact that the transmission of some crucial political information needs to be addressed in a systematic way.[59]

Finally, the political variables we have already discussed will be included. The initial model is therefore composed of the following elements:[60]

1. Social and regional determinants (nine variables): male; postelemen-

tary education; minimum-income earners; housewives; public servants; workers in the private sector; peasants; Mexico City; and the South.[61]

2. Performance elements (four variables): approval of Salinas's presidential performance; improvement in the national economy during his tenure; improvement in personal and family economy during the *sexenio*; and desire to see Salinas's economic policies continued.

3. Campaign issues (six variables): vote was candidate-oriented *and* candidate was preferred for his personality, his experience, his honesty, or his closeness to the people; TV was the most important source of information; and decision was taken after the debate *times* TV was the most important source.

4. Political factors (six variables): estimated exogenous value of risk aversion; estimated exogenous value of partisanship; party loyalty (estimation via weighted vote in 1988 for PAN, PRI, and FDN); and belonging to a state governed by the PAN.

The initial saturated run, containing twenty-five variables was purged from variables that were statistically insignificant; or without major theoretical importance.[62] The final model included eighteen variables and yielded the results shown on Table 2.1.

IV. MODEL RESULTS
A. Predictive Power of the Model

The results in the final model are remarkable. Our analysis will be subdivided in two sections. The following one is an overall assessment of the validity of the model and of its predictive power, which opens a prelude to the specific interpretation of the generated estimates. Each and every variable included in the model is statistically significant for at least one of the equations run, which gives us reason to believe that the specification is correct. Moreover, its predictive efficacy is relatively high. The model greatly enhances the accuracy of our electoral predictions based on the information given by the relevant variables.[63]

In the case of the people who voted for the PRI, the model's estimates will accurately predict an overall 83.7% of the sample (86% of the 1,279 who voted for it and 80% of the 909 who didn't). The proportionate reduction of error (PRE) statistic, which calculates the proportion of improvement in prediction relative to the modal category, in this case is 0.61. For both opposition parties, the predicted probabilities do equally well. When estimating the probability of voting for the PAN, the total number of cases

Table 2.1
Final Model of Electoral Choice, Presidential Election 1994

Iteration 0: Initial Log Likelihood = −2082.3631   Number of observations = 2188
Iteration 6: Final Log Likelihood = −1238.6715   Pseudo R^2 = .405

Explanatory Variable	PAN / PRI		PRD/PRI	
	ß	s.e.(ß)	ß	s.e.(ß)
Social and regional determinants				
Minimum family income	−0.214	0.20	0.575**	0.27
Mexico City	−0.898***	0.21	−0.687***	0.26
South	−0.707***	0.27	0.014	0.30
Performance elements				
Approved Salinas's performance	−0.798***	0.15	−1.410***	0.20
National economy improved in the *sexenio*	−0.634***	0.15	−0.804***	0.21
Personal economy improved in the *sexenio*	−0.519***	0.14	−0.476**	0.21
Continuity in economic policy	−0.783***	0.14	−0.976***	0.22
Campaign issues				
Voted candidate's: Personality	1.117***	0.22	0.093	0.33
Honesty	0.535***	0.20	−0.134	0.30
Closeness to the people	0.365	0.25	0.562*	0.29
TV most important source of information	0.109	0.14	−0.455**	0.18
TV * debate	1.093***	0.22	0.804**	0.32
Political factors				
State governor is from the PAN	0.032	0.23	−1.645***	0.43
Estimated risk aversion	−1.205	3.12	−7.787*	4.28
Estimated long-term partisanship	−0.962*	0.53	0.405	0.72
Corrected vote in 1988: PAN	1.741***	0.26	−0.712*	0.37
PRI	−0.953***	0.34	−2.791***	0.42
FDN	0.550***	0.15	0.839***	0.15
Constant term	1.378***	0.47	2.491***	0.61

*** statistically significant with $p < .01$
** statistically significant with $p < .05$
* statistically significant with $p < .1$

correctly predicted is 82.6% (88% of the 1,612 who didn't vote for it, 67% of the 576 who did), and the PRE statistic is 0.34. Finally, for the PRD, the total number of cases correctly predicted is 90.5% (94% of the 1,855 who voted against it, 69% of the 333 who voted for it) and the PRE statistic is 0.38. In short, the model improves our a priori prediction of electoral choice by 44.3%

Given the assumptions and corrections implemented, we have provided evidence supporting the hypothesis that the model's specification is correct and its estimates valid. We now turn to the analysis of the specific estimates.[64]

Structural Determinants of the Vote

The social-demographic battery is, as expected, the least solid one in terms of its explanatory power. After eliminating all of the other variables in this battery due to their insignificant coefficients, we are left with only three relevant indicators. Regional differences are still important. It is clear that the South still does not offer a warm welcome to Panistas, underscoring its profile as a central-northern party (−0.7). The South, more clearly, was up for grabs between the PRD and the PRI during the 1994 election (0.01). One of the surprises of this contest, which is clearly reflected in our model, was the PRI's strong showing in the Federal District. The net effect of a voter being in Mexico City favored the PRI against Panistas (−0.89) and Perredistas (−0.68).[65] Finally, and as the only sociological variable still relevant in analyzing electoral choices, a low-income level helped distinguish the Perredista and Priísta clienteles. The PRD was relatively more successful than the PRI in capturing the vote of the least favored (0.57), but this variable failed to affect the odds of voting for the PAN.

C. Performance Elements

Income and region may still relatively segment Mexican voters, but this may also be an effect of the parties' strategies during the campaign. The implication may be that Mexico City in 1994, with its forty congressional seats and very large proportion of the electorate (more than 12 percent of the valid votes) was considered a strategic goal of the PRI, and its spending there may have been very effective.[66] What is certain by now is that voters were very rational and calculating when they attended the polls. As any other voter in any country of the world, Mexicans based their decision mainly on a retrospective and prospective evaluation of the incumbent and his party. Each and every one of the coefficients in the rationality battery has the expected sign. Good opinions of Salinas (−0.79 for PAN, −1.41 for PRD) and his policies (−0.78 for PAN, −0.97 for PRD) helped Zedillo and the PRI. Moreover, Mexicans were as much sociotropic (−0.63 for PAN, −0.8 for PRD) as individually interested voters (−0.51 for PAN, −0.47 for PRD), and perhaps even more the former.[67] Also as expected, the better the opinion about Salinas's policies, the worse the PRD would do. In sum, there is not much chance for rebuttal: Mexican voters were pretty rational in their choices. Table 2.2 illustrates such findings. In it, the predicted probability of voting for each of the parties is computed from the model, for a number of different possible combinations of performance evaluations.[68]

Table 2.2
Impact of Retrospective and Prospective Assessments on Party Choice

Presidential Approval?	National Economy?	Improvement of Personal Economy?	Policy Continuity?	Predicted Probabilities		
				PRI	PAN	PRD
Yes	Yes	Yes	Yes	0.87	0.11	0.02
Yes	Yes	No	Yes	0.80	0.17	0.03
Yes	Yes	Yes	No	0.74	0.21	0.05
No	Yes	No	Yes	0.61	0.28	0.11
No	Yes	Yes	No	0.53	0.32	0.15
No	No	No	Yes	0.44	0.39	0.17
No	No	Yes	No	0.36	0.41	0.23
No	No	No	No	0.25	0.49	0.26

Table 2.2 should be self-explanatory, but we must underline that the sway of these evaluations is impressive. When the average Mexican voter approved Salinas's performance, thought both the country and her family's economy had improved through the *sexenio*, and agreed with the continuation of his policies, the probability of her voting for Zedillo was 0.87, for Fernández 0.11, and for Cárdenas 0.02. On the contrary, when all these evaluations were not favorable, the probability of voting PRI came down to 0.25, as opposed to PAN's 0.49 and PRD's 0.26! To put it bluntly, Salinas won the Mexican election of 1994 throughout his tenure as much as it was won by the PRI and its candidate during the campaign.

D. Campaigns: TV and Candidates

But campaigns mattered as well. Television made a difference, although not as big as it could have been expected. Fulfilling our expectations, Diego Fernández was king of the debate (1.09), and the nondebate effect of TV on his prospects was not significant. For the PRD, though, the impact of the electronic media was noteworthy. Its net effect on those who said their most important source of electorally relevant information was the TV and did not make a decision in the days right after the debate, was to hurt Cuauhtémoc Cárdenas (−0.45). The model shows that although his performance in the debate disappointed many, it actually helped his electoral prospects. This effect is seen thanks to the construction of the interaction term TV*debate, which has a significant coefficient of 0.8. In other words, while the overall coverage of TV decreased Cárdenas's probabilities of being chosen by a voter, his performance in the debate significantly countered this negative effect.

The overall conclusion seems to be that TV did play a big role, although most importantly through the debate. Given the open and leveled stage of the presidential debate and due to the large audience attending it, ninety

minutes of competition between the three candidates resulted in important losses for a then troubled Ernesto Zedillo.

Candidate attributes also played a role, in general terms. Three variables
were left in the final model (experience not being a significant predictor).
Zedillo suffered against Cuauhtémoc, who was rewarded for his apparent
closeness to the people (0.56), and against Fernández , who benefited from
those who appreciated his honesty (0.53) and personality to govern (1.11).
Candidate traits mattered, and Zedillo was unable to capitalize personally
on his larger experience. The two opposition candidates were significant
components in the electoral equations of their parties. On the other hand,
these results also imply that straightforward party concerns were relatively
more important in explaining both the PRI and PRD votes.[69]

E. Political Variables

Political factors deserve a close, careful look. We will start with the effect of
a PAN state governorship. First, its effect is negligible in explaining the PAN
vote, which implies that the presidential race in those states cannot be seen
as a referendum (positive or negative) on the local authorities. In other
words, the rationale behind the probability of voting for the PAN against
the PRI was the same regardless of whether or not a voter lived in a Panista
state. But this was not the same for the PRD: the effect of a local PAN governorship on the PRD vote was clearly negative (−1.64). What PAN state
chief executives accomplished in the presidential race was to reinforce local
bipartisan competition between the PRI and the PAN.

Loyalty was a big factor determining the 1994 vote, all coefficients in our
model being statistically significant. The PRD tended to be favored by its
1988 supporters (0.83), and it had a hard time drawing support from former
Panistas (−0.71) and especially Priístas (−2.79). The PAN, in contrast, was
also favored by 1988 Panistas (1.74) and punished by Priístas (−0.95), but it
fared better than the PRI from the pool of former Cardenistas (0.55). What
this implies is that 1988 FDN voters quite improbably became PRI voters in
1994, but that some actually switched to the PAN. Six years after the apparent realignment that the 1988 election produced, with groups of Priístas
switching allegiance in favor of Cárdenas, the fracture was partially closed in
1994.[70] Relations between the government and PRD were harsh all through
the *sexenio.* On several occasions, then PRD president, Cuauhtémoc
Cárdenas, denounced Carlos Salinas's illegitimacy, neoliberal policies, and
his government's repression against Perredistas across the country. Salinas
himself was careful to contrast his policies and personality against what he
labeled "the new reactionaries."[71] Therefore, it is reasonable to find—as we
saw in the retrospective indicators—less distance between the government
and the PAN and a larger distance between the former and the PRD.

Actually, this may be the evidence that gets us as close as possible to an assessment of DMC's two-step model. They contend, once again, that "a core political division existed across elections between the PRI and all opposition parties."[72] After such judgment, both ideological orientations and strategic factors come into play. Although we are ready to argue that the evidence they present also speaks of a strong retrospective vote in spite of their own claims, we are also ready to state that some FDN supporters might have consistently turned to the PAN out of strategic considerations, just as they report for the 1991 election.[73] However, PAN and PRD clienteles seem to be further differentiated by other factors, to which we turn our attention below.

Our evidence shows that the PAN and the PRI were relatively successful in retaining their old clienteles in the short run, and the former even gained from old FDN voters, which had some trouble in rebuilding the large 1988 coalition. Was this due to a long-term partisanship? Apparently not, emphasizing the crucial differences between PAN and PRD electorates.

After all, long-term partisanship—the tendency of voters to repeat their electoral choice in every election—was not a consistent predictor across the model. It did hurt the PAN (−0.96), but the effect on the PRD, however positive, was not statistically significant. This implies that although the PAN was highly successful in retaining the support of its voters from the 1988 election, this was mostly due to a rationalization of the voter along the *sexenio* and the favorable impact caused by its candidate, as we have seen. The effect of this variable is seen most clearly in Figure 2.1. In it we show the probability of voting for each party for increasing levels of partisanship.[74]

As can be seen, both the PRD and especially the PRI benefit from a partisan predisposition, while this predisposition hurts the PAN. Above we discussed the methodological problems involved with this variable and argued that the exogenous effect of partisanship was the relevant explanatory variable that needed to be isolated. We here offer statistically significant evidence of this long-term predisposition on the Mexican voter. It should be kept in mind what *partisanship* measures here. It is distinct from *party identification*—the feeling of closeness or sympathy with a party. It simply tells us to what extent we can expect a voter to disregard recent information when deciding for whom to vote. Our results do not deny that PAN identification exists, they simply show that in order to stay competitive, the PAN has to convince its voters (even those who might like it) over and over, while the PRI (and perhaps the PRD) shall enjoy chunks of loyal voters with a strong predisposition virtually to ignore the campaigns.

The explanation for this phenomenon can be two-fold. On the psychological-cultural side, Priístas are bound to be loyal voters, and therefore a discussion of performance elements, candidate and campaign influences, and the like is destined to be useless in their case. On the rational choice

Figure 2.1
Effect of Long-Term Partisanship on Party Choice

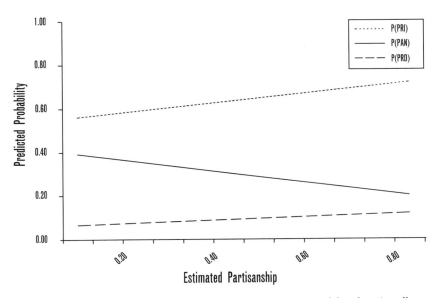

*Probabilities are calculated using the final specification of the model and setting all other variables at their means. Values for estimated partisanship are rounded to the second decimal.

side, partisanship is explained as follows: there are certain groups of voters for which the trajectories of their expected utility from voting change less over time and are especially robust to campaign influences. These voters expect some benefits from voting for a party that are not perceived to change as much due to the election's results. These are voters for whom the expected utility of voting includes an *almost constant* benefit derived from one of the parties, and therefore any investing in decision-making processes is a waste. These could be individuals directly linked to the political party or with a good opinion of the benefits derived from a party through history.[75] In contrast, voters lacking this "external" link or good historical record might face greater marginal variance in their expected electoral utilities over time, which will make them more prone to reestimate it more frequently.

The strong impact of short-term loyalty suggests yet another refinement of this argument: in general, voters are not going to spend much time evaluating the expected utility of their vote; they will make a "rationally careless investment decision."[76] To the extent that the past immediate vote seems to be a strong predictor of the present vote, this would imply that over short periods of time the trajectories of the expected electoral utilities do not vary greatly—and therefore voters are prone to repeat their choice. In other words, for a voter to take the care of changing a standing decision,[77] a significant jump in the expected benefits derived from a party would be needed.[78] In short, realignment hypotheses about the Mexican electorate should underscore these important findings: PAN voters seem to be more concerned with short-term elements than those of the PRD and PRI. This is shown both by the negative impact of partisanship in Panistas *and* the stronger effect of candidate traits on PAN votes.[79]

The analysis of the risk aversion feature was also discussed in the methodological debate. As we did with the long-term loyalty variable, we isolated the effect of nonpartisan determined risk aversion. It turned out, as expected, to benefit the longtime ruling PRI. But the story does not end there. Its effect was only statistically significant against the PRD (−7.78), and not against the PAN. In other words, the simple argument that the PRI benefited from the electorate's fear does not find support in the available evidence. Impressionistic perceptions abound in this regard, but what political science tells us is that it only hurt the PRD, not the PAN. The reason for this? As it has been argued elsewhere,[80] whether it is as a victim or as a felon, the PRD was associated with violence throughout Salinas's *sexenio*. Moreover, the experience of states with PAN governors effectively diminished the expected variance associated to this party, therefore consolidating bipartisan competition. Our findings are supported by those reported by Moreno and Yanner, and Buendía. The former show, in their first model, that a voter who feared violence after the election might favor the PAN's candidate,[81] while Buendía offers evidence that risk aversion hurt the opposition and favored the PRI. Our correction for endogeneity helps us construct a finer argument: when people were driven by some kind of rational fear, they were only driven away from the PRD, since they had far worse expectations about this party's possible incumbency than the Panista one. This effect is clearly seen in Figure 2.2, where the probability of voting for each party is plotted against the whole range of values of the estimated probability of being risk averse.

Figure 2.2 shows that for the average voter the shift from minimum to maximum levels of risk aversion changed the probability of voting for the PRI from 0.55 to 0.68. This increase of about 13 percentage points was mostly won from the PRD, whose chances of being selected dropped from 0.17 to 0.05, while the probability of voting for the PAN remained virtually constant at 0.28.[82]

Although the effect of risk aversion is clearly to increase the PRI's prospects and diminish the PRD's, the evidence suggests that there is a great deal of exaggeration in accounts of the 1994 election as one dominated by fear or risk aversion. Not only does the variable come out as only tenuously significant, but most importantly in practical terms, risk aversion

Figure 2.2
Effect of Risk Aversion on Party Choice

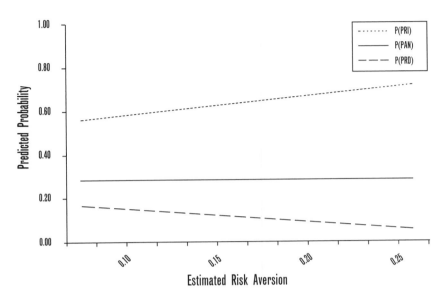

*Probabilities are calculated using the final specification of the model and setting all other variables at their means. Values for estimated risk aversion are rounded to the second decimal.

simply did not affect the runner-up's prospects, which implies that the PAN's inability to challenge effectively the PRI was due to different factors already discussed.

V. CONCLUSIONS

This chapter has offered significant evidence about the variables determining the Mexican electorate's choice in the August 1994 presidential election. In brief:

1. People voted their pockets and their evaluation of Salinas's performance and his economic policy.

2. Mexicans were influenced by their last presidential vote: loyalty played a big part. Partisanship was significant only in explaining PRI advantages over the PAN.

3. Voters were also drawn by the candidates' personality traits, especially so in the PAN's case.

4. Television coverage played a significant role, particularly when it was opened for the first-ever nationally transmitted presidential debate between the three major candidates.

5. Some regional differences in the parties' strength still mattered.

6. Last, but certainly not least, fear or risk aversion played a secondary role, only hurting the PRD in favor of the PRI.

This chapter has also proposed statistical refinements that aim to enrich Mexican electoral analysis. It has provided a satisfactory model of voting behavior that arguably improves upon others using the same available data. It tests hypotheses about the effects of a series of variables in the Mexican voting behavior in 1994. Still, it must recognize its limitations. As MY put it, in spite of the excellent quality of the data in the Mitofsky exit poll, it is not enough to test a series of hypotheses that seem to be relevant.[83] The now famous two-step model is a case in point. Other issues that might have been relevant in the 1994 campaign were not included in the questionnaire, as were the handling of the Chiapas uprising, the overall prospects for democratization, and the like. In sum, although we contend to present the best possible specification given the variables available, this simply does not imply that we have found "the model" of presidential electoral behavior. Nevertheless, if the task was to spur a richer methodological debate, we think we have accomplished it.

In theoretical terms, we have tried to address head-on some of the major debates regarding Mexican elections. We have shown that in 1994 risk aversion was not the defining element and that retrospective evaluations and loyalty were. Also, we have assessed carefully the role of partisanship, candidates, and television. These findings have an increased significance for the study of Mexican presidential elections and electoral behavior more generally. One step ahead should be the modeling of such findings within a general rational choice framework. In working toward such task, we have offered a number of suggestions regarding the form of the utility function of the voter confronting a presidential vote in Mexico.

APPENDIX A

1994 Election Exit Survey

From Cámara de la Industria de la Radio y la Televisión, conducted by Mitofsky International, Inc., and BIMSA.

C) Sex.

D) How old are you?

E) What is the highest level of education that you have achieved? None, primary, secondary, high school, and university or more.

F) In general, do you approve or disapprove of the way President Salinas has governed the country? Approve, approve to some extent, disapprove.

G) Do you think that the economic situation of the country has improved or deteriorated since President Salinas took office? Improved, remained the same, deteriorated.

H) Compared with the situation before President Salinas's term, how would you describe your current economic situation? Better, the same, worse.

I) What is your main occupation? Unemployed, public sector employee, private sector employee, professional, informal economy, part-time job, student, housewife, other (which corresponds mostly to peasants).

J) When did you decide to vote for the candidate or party you chose today? Always vote for the same party, from the time I knew who the candidates were, after the televised debate, in the last few days.

K) From which of the following sources did you receive the information that most helped you decide your vote? Street propaganda, newspapers, radio, TV, direct contact with the candidate, other.

L) Would you like the next president to continue with President Salinas's economic policies, or would you rather see some important changes? Continue, change.

M) In regards to whom you voted for, why did you vote for this candidate or party? Like the candidate, like the party, don't like the others.

N) Which of the following is closer to the reason for which you chose your candidate? Has personality to govern, has experience to govern, is honest, is close to the people.

O) What is your family's total monthly income? 0 to 3 minimum wages (mw), 3 to 10 mw, 10 to 30 mw, 30 mw or more.

P) For which candidate or party did you vote for president of the nation today? (A sheet resembling the electoral ballot plus the following questions was given to the voter in order to be answered and deposited in a separate box).

Q) You voted for such party or candidate because you think . . . ? Family and personal situation will improve, country situation will improve, other reason.

R) In the 1988 elections, which presidential candidate did you vote for? Manuel Clouthier (PAN candidate), Carlos Salinas (PRI candidate), Cuauhtémoc Cárdenas (FDN candidate), Rosario Ibarra (PRT candidate), other, couldn't vote.

S) The presidents that have governed Mexico for the past sixty-five years have come from the PRI. Which of the following reasons motivated you to vote for the party you chose today? The PRI is still the best choice, in politics it's "better bad but known than good but unknown," voted opposition to protest, want the opposition to win.

T) Did anyone try to force you in any way to vote for a specific party? Yes, no.

APPENDIX B
Corrections for Explanatory Variables[84]

1. Partisanship and Risk Aversion
    Two variables presented endogeneity problems: partisanship and risk aversion. Both were substituted for the predicted values resulting from estimating the observed value as a function of a series of social determinants. What this procedure implies is that we effectively identify the part of the explanatory variable, which cannot be influenced by the voter's previous opinions, and use it as a confident source for explanation of the voter's opinions regarding electoral choice. This will allow us to test hypotheses of the effect of risk aversion and long-term partisanship *independent of party preference* in our model.
    The model used was identical in both cases; it was a logistic regression of the dichotomous dependent variable on the following structural variables: sex, age, education, occupation, income, and region. This last variable was decomposed in the three most politically relevant categories, namely Mexico City, the South, and those states with PAN governors, leaving the rest of the states as a reference category. In the case of partisanship the dependent variable was coded 1 for those who said "I almost always vote for the same party," and 0 for the rest of the categories concerning the time of the decision. In the case of risk aversion, the dependent variable was coded 1 for those answering "más vale malo por conocido," and 0 for the rest. The resulting estimated variables yielded the following descriptive statistics:

Variable	Mean	Std. Dev.	Min.	Max.
Estimated Risk Aversion	.1647	.0434	.0617	.2431
Estimated Partisanship	.5305	.1810	.1094	.8809

2. The 1988 Vote
    The procedure used for correcting the systematic measurement error in the reporting of the 1988 vote can be construed in a similar fashion to the endogeneity one. We are looking for an instrumental variable which will help us capture more clearly the effect of one of the relevant explanatory variables. In this case, by comparing the results of the survey to those of the actual election, we know that there was a consistent inflation of the PRI vote and an underreporting of the opposition vote, especially the FDN (now PRD). The linear transformation to obtain such value is straightforward and follows the 1988 presidential election results by state. Instead of using values of 1 for the reported response, we used a weighted value ($kpty88_i$), which reflects the ratio between the official result by state

(%off$_i$), and the aggregate result by state in the national survey (%sur$_i$), according to the following formula:

$$kpty88_i = \{\%off_i / \%sur_i\}$$

which repeated for each party across the thirty-two states yields ninety-six different values to be substituted for the original responses accordingly.

Granted, this process does not completely eliminate the measurement error, since the survey is not representative at the state level, but it does diminish its systematic component and potentially biasing effect. It's the best possible compromise between the exogenous information from the official results and the response by each individual to the survey question.

NOTES

1. I wish to thank Jorge Domínguez and Jim Alt for thorough revisions of earlier versions of this chapter. Federico Estévez also provided insightful and useful suggestions. The final outcome is, of course, only the author's responsibility. I also want to thank CONACYT and the Fundación México-Harvard for financial support. I dedicate my work in this volume to Leslie.

2. For an excellent overall discussion see Jorge I. Domínguez and James A. McCann, *Democratizing Mexico: Public Opinion and Electoral Choices* (Baltimore: Johns Hopkins University Press, 1996).

3. Juan Molinar Horcasitas, *El tiempo de la legitimidad: Elecciones, autoritarismo, y democracia en México* (Mexico City: Cal y Arena, 1991).

4. BANAMEX, *México Social* (Mexico City: 1996), 625.

5. The rest was captured by the smaller Partido del Trabajo (2.8%), and five other minor parties: Partido Verde Ecologista de México, Partido del Frente Cardenista de Reconstrucción Nacional, Partido Auténtico de la Revolución Mexicana, Partido Popular Socialista and Partido Demócrata Mexicano (Banamex, 1996).

6. As Salinas popularized what he thought was a terrible policy mistake on behalf of the newly elected President Zedillo and his economic team.

7. We here follow Jack Dennis, "The Study of Electoral Behavior," *Political Science Looking to the Future, Vol. III: Political Behavior*, ed. William Cratty (Evanston: Northwestern University Press, 1991): 51–89; Beatriz Magaloni, "Elección Racional y Voto Estratégico: Algunas Aplicaciones para el Caso Mexicano," *Política y Gobierno* I, no. 2 (1994): 309–44; and Juan Molinar Horcasitas and Rafael Vergara, "Los Estudios Sobre el Elector Mexicano. Cuatro Enfoques de Análisis Electoral en México"(El Colegio de México, Mexico City: 1996, mimeographed).

8. Seymour M. Lipset and Stein Rokkan, "Cleavage Structures, Party Systems and Voter Alignments: An Introduction," in *Party Systems and Voter Alignments: Cross-National Perspectives*, (New York: The Free Press, 1967): 1–64.

9. Angus Campbell, Philip E. Converse, Warren Miller, and David Stokes, "The Impact and Development of Party Identification," *Classics in Voting Behavior*, eds. Richard G. Niemi and Herbert F. Weisberg (Washington, DC: CQ Press, 1993): 224–34.

10. For a complete review, see Scott Mainwaring and Timothy R. Scully, eds., *Building Democratic Institutions. Party Systems in Latin America* (Stanford: Stanford

University Press, 1993). Probably the Chilean case is the one most amenable to such interpretation.

11. See Morris P. Fiorina, *Retrospective Voting in American National Elections* (New Haven: Yale University Press, 1981).

12. One of the most complete models of this type is still Fiorina's (1981); Anthony Downs, *An Economic Theory of Democracy* (New York: Harper and Row, 1957).

13. For the case of Chile from 1952 to 1973 see James W. Prothro and P. E. Chaparro, "Public Opinion and the Movement of the Chilean Government to the Left," *Chile: Politics and Society,* eds. Valenzuela and Valenzuela (New Brunswick, NJ: Transaction, 1976), 67–109. For the Argentine case in 1983, see Eduardo Catterberg, *Argentina Confronts Politics: Political Culture and Public Opinion in the Argentine Transition to Democracy* (Boulder, Col.: Lynne Rienner, 1991).

14. Even Mainwaring and Scully's edited volume (1993) presents mostly descriptive evidence. On their behalf, however, it must be said that the task of their volume is less to analyze the Latin American voter than it is the Latin American party systems.

15. Apart from their 1996 book, see their two published studies: Jorge I. Domínguez and James A. McCann, "Shaping Mexico's Electoral Arena: The Construction of Partisan Cleavages in the 1988 and 1991 National Elections," *American Political Science Review* 89, no. 1 (March 1995): 34–48; ibid., "Whither the PRI? Explaining Voter Defection in the 1988 Mexican Presidential Elections," *Electoral Studies* 11, no. 3 (1992): 207–22.

16. See Molinar and Vergara, "Los Estudios Sobre el Elector," for a complete review.

17. See Molinar, *El Tiempo*; and Magaloni, "Elección Racional," for example.

18. Domínguez and McCann, "Shaping Mexico's Electoral Arena," 34.

19. Domínguez and McCann, *Democratizing Mexico,* 23–50.

20. The specific model they present cannot be tested for the 1994 presidential election, and that is why their book only shows descriptive evidence for this case. The point of this chapter is not, however, to offer the "only" model of electoral choice in Mexico and rebut all others, but to try to contribute to a theoretical and methodological debate by carefully reviewing the most relevant models in light of the available evidence.

21. See Jorge Buendía, "Economic Reform, Public Opinion and Presidential Approval in Mexico, 1988–1993," *Comparative Political Studies* 29, no. 5 (October 1996): 566–92.

22. Ibid., 3.

23. Ibid., 7.

24. Alejandro Moreno and Keith Yanner, "Predictors of Voter Preferences in Mexico's 1994 Presidential Election," (1995, mimeographed).

25. Using the same data they used, an explicit two-step modeling strategy should allow to test directly the main claim of their work. This chapter, however, will only deal with the 1994 presidential contest.

26. Moreno and Yanner, "Predictors," 12.

27. They include five variables which are shown to be completely irrelevant in the final specification; ibid., 17.

28. This is a central consideration to keep in mind when analyzing Domínguez and McCann's models. These elections (1988 and 1991) were held in specifically transitional settings, and their results could be judged from that standpoint. However, if this point is to be taken at face value, the question remains: Is the 1994 election still transitional? We argue that if we are going to assume that some elections are transitional and

others are posttransitional, 1994 belongs to the second category. This would be the case because it was played under an electoral code which—for the first time—was approved and mostly followed by the three major parties, and the possibility of a PRI loss was not out of the question.

29. The total number of cases was 5,635.

30. See Alfred Demaris, *Logit Modeling: Practical Applications* (Newbury Park, Cal.: Sage, 1992); S. Hosmer and Stanley Lemeshow, *Applied Logistic Regression* (New York: John Wiley, 1989); and John H. Aldrich and F. Nelson, *Linear Probability, Logit and Probit Models* (Newbury Park, Cal.: Sage, 1984).

31. Therefore, the model will take the following general form:

$$\log \{P(\text{vote for PAN}) / P(\text{vote for PRI})\} = Z_a$$
$$\log \{P(\text{vote for PRD}) / P(\text{vote for PRI})\} = Z_c$$
$$\text{where} \quad Z_a = ß_{0,a} + ß_{1,a}X_1 + ß_{2,a}X_2 + ß_{3,a}X_3 + \ldots + ß_{j,a}X_j + \varepsilon_a$$
$$\text{and} \quad Z_c = ß_{0,c} + ß_{1,c}X_1 + ß_{2,c}X_2 + ß_{3,c}X_3 + \ldots + ß_{j,c}X_j + \varepsilon_c$$

The ß coefficients report the net effect of the presence of a variable—controlling for the rest—on the logarithm of the odds between voting for each of the opposition parties and the PRI. Therefore, the estimated conditional probability of voting for each of the parties can be calculated as follows:

$$P(\text{vote for PAN}) = e^{Z_a} / \{1 + e^{Z_a} + e^{Z_c}\}$$
$$P(\text{vote for PRD}) = e^{Z_c} / \{1 + e^{Z_a} + e^{Z_c}\}$$
$$P(\text{vote for PRI}) = 1 / \{1 + e^{Z_a} + e^{Z_c}\}$$

which will obviously yield a sum of 1. Finally—and before further exploring the methodological issues at stake—it should be kept in mind that a lot of the assumptions underlying the use of this model depend upon the asymptotical properties of maximum likelihood estimation. In other words, the coefficients yielded by the model will be consistent only if the number of cases is large enough. On this see Demaris, *Logit*, 78. Fortunately, the data set allowed us to run the final model with 2,188 cases.

32. See Gary King, Robert Keohane, and Sidney Verba, *Designing Social Inquiry* (Princeton, NJ: Princeton University Press, 1994), 185–86.

33. See Fiorina, *Retrospective Voting*; Moreno and Yanner, "Predictors"; and Campbell et al., *Classics in Voting*.

34. See Domínguez and McCann, *Democratizing Mexico*, also Alejandro Poiré, *Lealtad Partidista y Desalineación Electoral en la Elección Presidencial de 1994* (B.A. thesis, ITAM, Mexico City, 1995).

35. What I call *partisanship* is to be distinguished from the concept of *party identification*. Whereas the latter refers to a psychological attachment to a specific party, the former simply describes a characteristic of a voter to avoid updating her beliefs every time she casts a vote. In other words, for a voter with a strong party identification, partisanship implies that his vote will *always* be identical to his party identification.

36. We here follow King et al., *Designing*, 185–96; and Robert Pindyck and David Rubinfeld, *Econometric Models and Economic Forecasts* (New York: McGraw-Hill, 1991), 157–68.

37. The specific procedure is detailed in Appendix B. It is a logit estimate of the probability of being a partisan as explained by a voter's social characteristics.

38. DIANA, *Elecciones a Debate, 1988* (Mexico City: DIANA, 1994), 21.

39. The fact that the PRD did not compete in the 1988 election is a minor problem in terms of the loyalty hypothesis, since Cuauhtémoc Cárdenas ran as presidential candidate both in 1988 and 1994. Moreover, as will be seen below, candidate appeals were not as strong in explaining the vote for the PRD, which speaks about the incipient—yet probably increasing—partisanship of the Perredista electorate.

40. We now follow King et al., *Designing*, 150–58; and Pindyck and Rubinfeld, *Econometric*, 159–62.

41. DIANA, *Elecciones*, 41.

42. Fiorina, *Retrospective Voting*, ch. 4; Magaloni, "Elección Racional," 323.

43. Alberto Cinta's work in this volume actually clarifies this point. This question measures the concavity of a voter's utility function, but still fails to address entirely the variance attached to the expected incomes—which are ultimately determined by the policy bundles offered by parties. In order to take a cut at this issue in our estimation of the risk aversion variable, and given the data available for 1994, we will ask the following question: Should the presence of governors coming from the PAN have any effect on voters' risk aversion? We discuss this below.

44. The endogeneity of this question was probably increased by the wording it used, since the voter was asked about his choice of the two sayings when applied to political matters (see Appendix A). I'm indebted to Federico Estévez for this insight.

45. A second element should be addressed when using this variable from the Mitofsky database. There is strong reason to believe that it will overestimate the opinion of the literate electorate, since it was not asked by the pollster but included in a separate sheet where the voter would reproduce her ballot and answer a few confidential questions. In order to check for possible selection bias, a Heckman procedure is at hand. This procedure will also render an estimated probability of answering in the affirmative to the risk aversion question using the social variables as instruments, but it will run a simultaneous equation controlling for the fact that some observations are more likely to be observed than others—typically due to the research design (in our case, the probability of having an answer to the rationale question was highly correlated with education, age, and preference for one of the large parties). The Heckman procedure was run but selection bias was not significant, so the standard logit correction procedure was used. See William H. Greene, *Econometric Analysis* (New York: MacMillan, 1993), 711–13; and Stata Corporation, *STATA Reference Manual* (College Station, Texas: Stata Press, 1995), 438–45.

46. See Appendix A for the questionnaire used.

47. Except for the supposedly *machista* overtones of the PAN candidate, which will also be tested via the inclusion of the housewives variable. See Adolfo Aguilar Zínzer, *¡Vamos a Ganar! La Pugna de Cuauhtémoc Cárdenas por el Poder* (Mexico City: Océano, 1995) for an almost immediately classic account of the campaigns. Also, Magaloni and Moreno argue in this volume about the importance of an age gap in the Mexican electorate, particularly when considering evaluations of the PRI's historical performance. This variable will have less relevance in our study, precisely because we are eliminating from our sample those in the group age between eighteen and twenty-four to allow for the analysis of party loyalty.

48. And which also favored the FDN in 1988, Juan Molinar Horcasitas and Jeffrey A. Weldon, "Elecciones de 1988 en México: Crisis del Autoritarismo," *Revista Mexicana de Sociología* 52, no. 4, (October–December 1990).

49. Ibid.

50. In the model, this variable will be included as a "political factor," to the extent that the logic behind grouping these voters is strictly political and not a geographical one. See Appendix B.

51. At this point, the need to make a choice is clear. Sociological factors are the only exogenous information we have to estimate the correct values of the risk aversion and partisanship variables. On the other hand, if we include both the estimates and the social variables in the final model, we suffer the risk of multicollinearity and therefore of inefficiency. Although the correlation matrix shows this to be a negligible problem in this model, the a priori choice was to include the corrected values along with the social variables that helped estimate them. We would rather suffer some inefficiency, and therefore be unable to provide significant conclusions, than use the wrong specification and yield wrong significant conclusions.

52. Specifically, presidential elections in Mexico are the ones in which the expected magnitude of returns is the largest—by far—from the voter's point of view. This has strong normative and positive implications and suggests a way toward a theory of "structure-induced" electoral behavior. As a hint toward this discussion, I have elsewhere considered voting as a "rationally careless investment decision." See Alejandro Poiré, "Turnout as a Rationally Careless Investment Decision: An Application to the Mexican Case in 1994" (Harvard University, Department of Government, 1997, mimeographed). From this point of view, the patterns of expected returns for voters—and therefore their electoral behavior—are structured by institutional features such as reelection, centralism, and so on. Theoretical questions stemming from this analysis include the following: Can parties and politicians do anything about it to shape the electoral equilibrium? How does this shape local versus national party elites' strategies toward issues as federalism and electoral reform? The PAN's relentless insistence on strengthening municipal governments' fiscal capacities illustrates this point.

53. An alternative approach to the analysis of this variable is to collapse the three retrospective variables into one single measure. However, this will result in a loss of information, both from a statistical and theoretical point of view. Especially, our results demonstrate that the three variables were separately statistically significant.

54. Before being appointed as the PRI's presidential candidate, Zedillo had been secretary of the Ministry of Budgeting (1988–92) and of Education (1992–93) under Salinas.

55. The best way to study the effect of a political campaign in a voter's electoral decision is through a panel survey. Chappell Lawson's chapter in this volume is the first-ever published analysis of its kind for any Mexican election.

56. The very fact that fair access to the media was one of the central points on Zedillo's proposal for electoral reform in 1995 speaks for itself. Also, see Aguilar Zínzer, ¡Vamos a Ganar!

57. It should be kept in mind that 60.1% of the respondents to the poll said that they obtained the most relevant information for their choice from watching television.

58. In a first-ever competitive election, the relative changes in the expected utility of voting are big enough to offset the relative costs of gathering more information during the campaign for a voter. Also, the media will make more information available, further increasing the probability of campaigns being relevant.

59. American electoral studies have searched through this path consistently, following the seminal work of Philip E. Converse, "The Nature of Belief Systems in Mass

Publics," in *Ideology and Discontent,* ed. David Apter (New York: The Free Press, 1964), 201–61. Also, Moreno's contribution to this volume is the most thorough analysis yet of such sort for the Mexican national electorate.

60. Given the precedent discussion, it is clear that the model's specification was carefully prepared. However, another clarification is at hand: a common—yet in my view not recommended—way to code the dependent variable (electoral choice) is not the vote for the three major parties, which implies running a multinomial model, but rather to run three dichotomous separate logits, each estimating the probability of voting for each party. This procedure loses relevant information yielded by the simultaneous equation estimation used in the multinomial logit: it cannot differentiate which of the nonincluded relevant categories of the dependent variable is hurt or benefits from the effect of the explanatory variable. More importantly, perhaps, it assumes a peculiar decision process by the voter, that is, a series of dichotomous comparisons between pairs of parties.

61. The political South is composed of the allegedly Perredista-prone states of Chiapas, Guerrero, Michoacán, Oaxaca, and Tabasco.

62. For the process of model selection see Hosmer and Lemeshow, *Applied Logistic,* and Aldrich and Nelson, *Linear.* The log likelihood of the initial saturated model was −1231.6251, yielding a reduction from the constant-calculated log likelihood, or pseudo R^2 of 40.85%.

63. Two categorizations of the estimated probabilities of the model are at hand. The first one simply predicts a value of 1 for those cases with an estimated probability higher than 0.5 and 0 for the rest; the alternative choice is to set a cutoff point which will equal the number of affirmative predictions of the model to the number of observed positive cases. The proportionate reduction of error (PRE) statistics yielded by these methods are very similar. In cases as the one we are handling it seems better to use the second one, since we know that the real probabilities of voting for opposition parties were well below 0.5; in this case, the cutoff points used were as follows: PAN $\cong$ 0.33; PRI $\cong$ 0.60; PRD $\cong$ 0.33.

64. In the following paragraphs, the numbers between parentheses are the estimated coefficients of the multinomial logit, for easy reference. Their significance is reported in Table 2.1.

65. While this finding contrasts with Magaloni's for the same election in this volume, it's probably adequate to underscore here two differences between her analysis of this election and the one presented in this chapter: first, her study is explaining PRI defection, and therefore the choice of a dichotomous dependent variable is preferred; second, our sample excludes the younger in order to account for the impact of party loyalty. This in itself could account for the difference, implying that younger voters were much less lenient with the PRI, especially in Mexico City, as Magaloni argues.

66. An aspect of the campaign that must not be forgotten is the immense advantage held by the PRI in terms of funding and spending. Whether by legal or illegal paths, bundles of money were spent by the official party in the campaigns, certainly much more than the opposition could afford. Although we lack accurate estimates of the true monies spent, there is evidence that only in the small state of Tabasco, which cast only 1.8% of the national valid votes and staged a gubernatorial race in nearby dates, the PRI spent almost eighty million dollars. See the newspaper *Reforma,* Mexico City, February–April 1995.

67. This finding speaks to the differences in specification between our model and

Buendía's, who does not find any significant effect of retrospective individualist vote, and whose model's predictive efficacy is lower than it is for the one presented here (not higher than 73% for any of the parties and less than 60% for both the PAN and PRD).

68. The values are calculated according to the formula laid out in note 31, with the rest of the variables in the model held at their means for this exercise. Another possibility is to use the modal categories in each variable, but we prefer to illustrate the average voter, not the typical one.

69. To a certain extent, this is also reflected by the partisanship variable; see below.

70. See Molinar and Weldon, "Elecciones de 1988." What the results of the 1997 elections would suggest, however, is that to some extent Salinas's tenure was only a safety patch on top of a major—yet not lethal—wound. Bruhn and Domínguez's chapters in this volume speak to the importance of PRD's organizational revival to explain its resurgence and probably reopening the now more than ten-year-old stab.

71. Anecdotal evidence illustrates this point. Right after his sixth and last presidential address to Congress, Salinas was asked about the interruptions and protests staged by PRD representatives during his speech. He simply grinned and said, "I don't see them, I don't hear them." ("Ni los veo, ni los oigo.")

72. Domínguez and McCann, "Shaping Mexico's Electoral Arena," 41.

73. We believe that what Domínguez and McCann call political factors are a combination of political preferences in an institutional dimension, risk aversion, typical retrospective judgments about the incumbent's performance and party identification, but this discussion is spurious without the proper data.

74. The levels of partisanship are within the range produced by the endogeneity correction procedure. The rest of the variables in the model are held at their means to yield the estimated probabilities of vote.

75. This argument draws heavily on John Aldrich, "Rational Choice and Turnout," *American Journal of Political Science* 37 (1993): 246–78; Poiré, "Turnout as a Rationally Careless Investment Decision." A more developed view is presented in Magaloni's contribution to this volume.

76. Poiré, "Turnout as a Rationally Careless Investment Decision."

77. This interpretation basically follows Fiorina's representation of party identification as a "standing decision" as determined by cumulative retrospective evaluations. However, it differs to the extent that it relies heavily on changes in the marginal variations of the expected utilities of the voters as being the crucial explanatory variable, as opposed to the total value of the calculus of voting for any of the parties. Needless to say, more careful theoretical elaboration is required.

78. Just how significant is "significant" is yet to be addressed. A related question should be more carefully studied from a theoretical perspective: Can these elements be the building blocks of an individually based theory of electoral realignment?

79. These two interpretations need not be mutually exclusive. Should the PAN's negative score on partisanship be explained by the strong appeal of Diego's candidacy, the model would not show significant coefficients for *both* types of variables.

80. Moreno and Yanner, "Predictors," 8.

81. Ibid., 17.

82. Once again, we use the final specification of the model, the average values of every other variable, and the range of estimated values of the risk aversion variable.

83. Moreno and Yanner, "Predictors," 14.

84. Corrections performed following King et al., *Designing,* 150–96; and especially Pindyck and Rubinfeld, *Econometric,* 152–68.

3

GENDER POLITICS IN THE MEXICAN DEMOCRATIZATION PROCESS

ELECTING WOMEN AND LEGISLATING SEX CRIMES AND AFFIRMATIVE ACTION, 1988–97

Linda S. Stevenson

> We cannot speak of democracy while a society exists that maintains half of its human potential in a handicapped, undervalued situation, in subordination to the other half of society; we cannot speak of democracy while the dignity and human rights of women suffer; we cannot speak of democracy until we women occupy the place in society that we deserve.
>
> —Gloria Brassdefer, Congressional Deputy for the
> *Partido Revolucionario Institucional*
> (PRI), Mexico[1]

As is eloquently expressed in the words of this female political leader, the struggle for women's rights is intricately linked with the fight for democracy. While women make up approximately half of the citizenship of any given political system, rarely have they been able to express their demands or shape their societies through high-level positions of political leadership, or via significant levels of representation in the governing bodies of their societies. Although Brassdefer refers to the situation in Mexico, over the last fifteen years proponents of gender equality have battled for women's rights within the struggles of civil society groups and movements demanding democracy[2] in countries moving toward democratic consolidation.[3]

However, as the euphoria fades and the nitty-gritty work of democracy begins, for many people, especially those with less political power such as women, serious questions again arise. Who is benefiting from this form of "democracy"? How and when will the demands of specific groups with less direct representation in institutional politics be heard and heeded? What new forms of politics need to be employed to get women's issues onto the nation's political agenda?

Within the literature on democratization, general consensus was reached years ago with regard to the importance of procedural definitions of democracy, such as universal suffrage and respect for civil liberties.[4] More recent studies of democratic transition in Latin America added that the military must be controlled by a civilian government and that opposition parties must have a realistic chance of winning office and affecting policy.[5] But what about politically underrepresented groups, such as women, having a realistic chance of winning office and affecting policy? Moving beyond these conventional measures of democracy, I propose that new measures for the *depth* of democracy are now necessary.

More recent and worrisome observations of the social side of democratization show that the roots of democratic development are not very deep. Without strong roots, the sustainability and substantiveness of democracy may be in jeopardy. This has led to a requestioning of just how deep the roots in any democratic system—emerging or advanced—are for those who have not historically or culturally held political power. O'Donnell observed this problem in labor-industry relations.[6] Diamond has also raised important questions by comparing the traditional measures of democracy in the so-called "emerging democracies" with their poor or worsening human rights records.[7] In advanced democracies, Guinier pointedly shows the lack of progress for minority ethnic populations in the United States in her work,[8] while Mazur problematizes the depth of democracy in France by systematically showing the weak implementation of women's equal employment opportunity policies.[9]

In relation to these questions in the Mexican case, the locus of the fight for women's rights shifted when new political spaces opened up after opposition parties gained strength through the watershed in Mexico's democratization process of the hotly contested presidential elections of 1988.[10] In 1988 there were significant gains for a more proportionally representative democracy in terms of the percentage of women elected to the Congress—12.2 percent won positions in the Chamber of Deputies and 18.8 percent in the Senate. However, in the ensuing decade the electoral results for women and legislation of issues especially pertinent to women were mixed. Thus, the purpose of this study is to determine more clearly which factors best explain variation in the election of higher percentages of women into the Congress and party leadership, and in the potential for successful passage and implementation of public policies related to women's issues.

A unique aspect of my approach to this topic is that the theoretical framework and hypothesis come from three generally distinct bodies of social science research. Focusing on women's political participation in each area, I draw from literature about social movements, political institutions, and policy-making processes. The hypothesis has two related parts: (1) if women's political participation increases in or across the political spheres of social movements, the Congress and political party leadership, and in policy-making arenas, then legislation specifically addressing women's issues will be passed; and (2) if the laws passed are adequately implemented for women, then the given society in which this occurs becomes more genuinely democratic. Findings to the contrary may show where the roots of democracy still need to be strengthened. Ultimately I argue that observations and findings using the methods common in the three different literatures need to be related more rigorously to theories of democratic transitions and consolidation.

In order to examine women's participation in recent electoral and policy processes, I utilize Kingdon's concepts from *Agendas, Alternatives, and Public Policies*.[11] In general terms Kingdon discusses how the "streams" of issue problems, apt politics, and ready proposals must run together in a given moment in order for an issue to successfully be able to obtain agenda status and be moved successfully through the policy-making process. Beginning with Kingdon's framework, I evaluate the "streams" of problems, politics, and proposals in the cases of the women's issues of sex crimes and affirmative action favoring women. In these two policy cases I find truth in Kingdon's idea that the three streams must run together. But then I move beyond Kingdon's concepts to consider the issue of *implementation* of the policies, as well as to uncover the contextual factors that were pertinent to making the streams flow.

In this chapter my research compares women's electoral success with the degree of legislative success of feminist demands in the corresponding congressional period, beginning with the election of 1988. I examine women's representation in the Chamber of Deputies and the Senate as the numerical proportions changed over the course of the elections in 1988, 1991, 1994, and 1997. In relation to these variations, I document the corresponding legislative efforts of female deputies and senators on the issues of sex crimes and affirmative action quotas in the four legislative periods of 1988–91, 1991–94, 1994–97, and the beginning of the 1997–2000 period. The data used is primarily from secondary sources, with some references to interviews I conducted in Mexico in 1995. Parts of the implementation processes are assessed here, but presentation of more conclusive results will be included in future work, as data collection is still in process.

In a society commonly known for its *machismo*,[12] these advances by and for women in institutional politics appear to be extraordinary. However, by examining women's participation in the Congress and in party leadership during the last ten years, and determining the key variables and necessary conditions for the policy success of women's issues, it will be easier to see whether they were extraordinary, or whether such forms of politics are gradually becoming more ordinary.

The next section of this chapter presents a theoretical framework of democratic transitions and consolidation in relation to gender politics in Latin America, relative to the questions about democratization on microlevels of politics and for underrepresented groups in institutional politics. Of particular importance is the explanation of the concept of "critical mass," or a threshold for a minority group in a given political entity, and how it applies to women's representation. Next, Kingdon's framework is set forth and applied to the cases of sex crimes policies and affirmative action quotas for electoral lists. The conclusion highlights the key factors evident from the case studies that relate to the hypothesis that increased women's political participation can be a democratizing force, and makes recommendations for continuing and related future research.

GENDER POLITICS AND DEMOCRATIZATION IN LATIN AMERICA: A BRIEF OVERVIEW

The number of women gaining access to legislative bodies has gradually increased throughout Latin America in the last fifteen years.[13] These women politicians have designed and promoted the passage of a number of woman-specific public policies, at a rate unprecedented in the policy-making history of the region.[14] Two key issues achieving significant levels of attention and legislation in the policy processes cross-nationally include violence against women and affirmative action quotas favoring women on electoral lists. Laws designed to counter violence against women have been proposed and passed in Brazil, Costa Rica, Nicaragua, and Bolivia in the last decade.[15] Mandates for affirmative action quotas favoring women on electoral lists were passed on a national level in Argentina in 1991,[16] and more recently on lower levels of governance in Brazil and in some political parties in El Salvador.

Both of these issues were among those listed on the *Platform for Action* of the Fourth International Conference on Women, sponsored by the United Nations, which took place in Beijing, China in September 1995.[17] Based upon the observations of twenty-seven women political leaders I interviewed in 1995[18] and the great number of Beijing follow-up meetings

Figure 3.1
Percentages of Female Deputies and Senators in the Mexican Congress: 1952–97

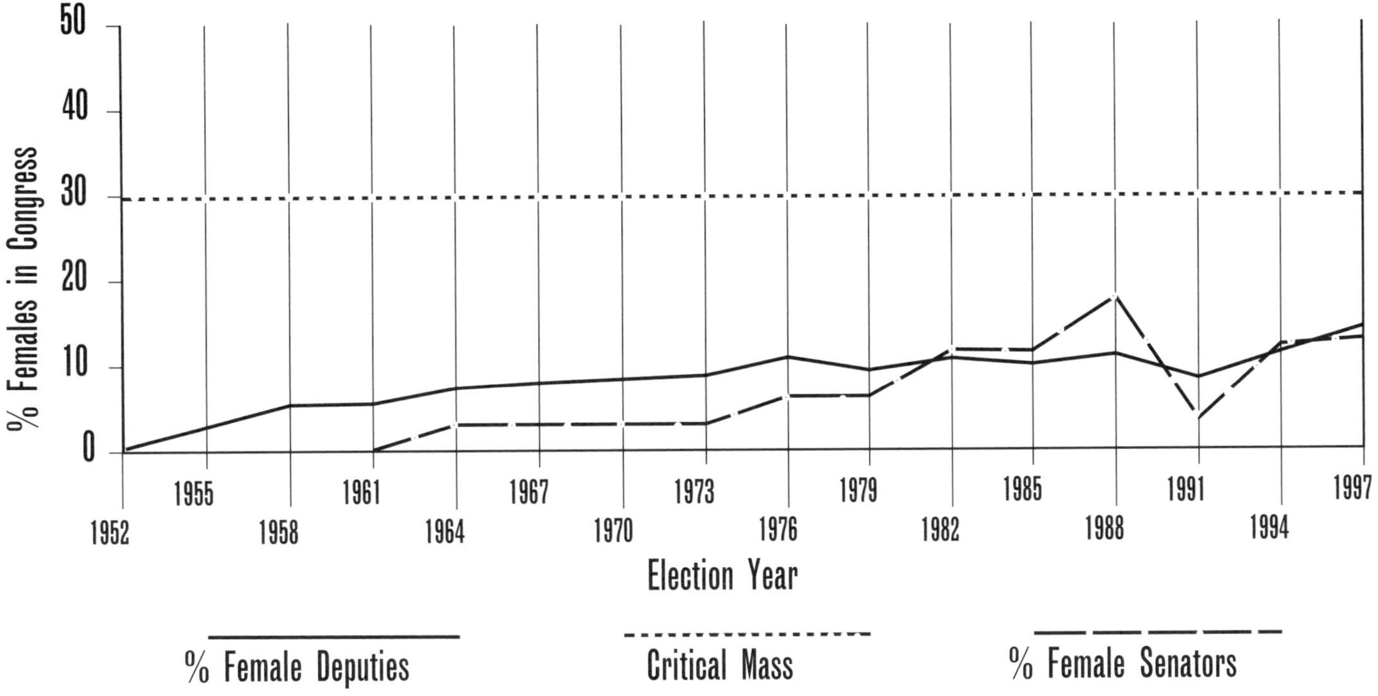

Sources: Fernández 1995a, 1995b; Martínez 1993; Federal Electoral Institute 1997 (See Table 3.1)

in Mexico that have occurred during the last two years, it appears that the existence of international pressure or a demonstration effect of legislative efforts by and for women in other countries is an important factor in strengthening the political work of women in movements, political parties, and the Congress in Mexico. Whether or not international consciousness or a demonstration effect is significant in the general picture of women political leaders getting policies passed, in the period from approximately 1994 to 1997, the "Beijing effect," as I call it, must be taken into account. The numerous preparatory and follow-up meetings provided the opportunity for a diverse range of women's groups, regionally and nationally, of all different ideological backgrounds to work together. Having to reach consensus on a wide variety of issues relevant to women's lives—notably a nonpatriarchal form of doing politics— enabled many in these circles to form new alliances which have become the basis for political work since the conference. My continuing research on these issues will enable me to determine more precisely the degree of impact of the "Beijing effect" on the gendered policy processes from 1988 through 1997.

Since the first woman was elected to the Chamber of Deputies in Mexico in 1952, the number of women in the Congress has risen gradually and steadily until 1988 (see Figure 3.1).

For the purposes of this chapter, specific focus is placed on the four most recent elections (see Table 3.1).

In 1988 the numbers of women elected reached new heights, with sixty-one elected to the Chamber of Deputies, (12.2 percent), and twelve elected to the Senate (18.8 percent). In 1991 however, the number of women elected decreased significantly. But then the numbers again ascended in the 1994 and 1997 elections, although not beyond those reached in 1988. This fluctuation of the degree of women's congressional electoral success is analyzed further in the section on affirmative action.

Several key factors came into play at the same time in 1988. First, there was broad-based awareness and agreement that the dominant form of politics was failing. After years of the lack of implementation of political reforms passed in the 1970s and the severe economic crises that plagued Mexico in the 1980s, participation in social and political movements increased, many of which expressed their discontent toward the PRI.[19] Second, opposition parties on the left and right provided viable alternatives to the PRI project. A new highly competitive left-leaning coalition, the Frente Democrático Nacional (FDN), which was later transformed into the Partido de la Revolución Democratica (PRD), was formed to challenge the political status quo with the leadership of Cuauhtémoc Cárdenas. On the right, the Partido Acción Nacional (PAN) also made strides in consolidating several of its regional bases—to the point of being the first opposition party to win a gubernatorial election in sixty years.[20]

Table 3.1
Percentages of Female Deputies and Senators Elected: 1988–97

Election Year	% Female Deputies	% Female Senators
1988	12.2%	18.8%
1991	8.0%	3.1%
1994	13.8%	13.3%
1997	17.2%	21.9%*

*This percentage is the proportion of women elected as a part of the 32 Senate positions which were up for election 1997. Of the total 128 Senate seats, the total percentage of women for the 1997-2000 legislative period is 15.7 percent.
Sources: Fernández 1995a, 1995b; Martínez 1993; Federal Electoral Institute 1997.
Anna Poncela Fernández, *Participación política: Las mujeres en México al final del milenio* (Mexico DF: Colegio de México, 1995a); Anna Poncela Fernández, "Las Mexicanas en el Congreso de a Unión y en el ejecutivo hoy," FEM, año 19, n. 147, June, 1995; Alicia Martínez, *Mujeres Latinoamericanas en cifras: México* (Santiago, Chile: Instituto de la Mujer, Ministerio de Asuntos Sociales de España, y Facultad Latinoamericana de Ciencias Sociales, 1993); Federal Electoral Institute (IFE), "Votación por Distritos (300)," (Mimeograph, IFE, Mexico, DF: 1997); Federal Electoral Institute (IFE), "Candidatos por circumscripción: Diputados de representación proporcional," (Mimeograph, IFE, Mexico DF: 1997); Federal Electoral Institute (IFE), "Senadores que permanecen de la LVI Legislatura a la LVII," (Mimeograph, IFE, Mexico DF: 1997); Federal Electoral Institute (IFE), "Conformación de la Cámara de Senadores: LVI–LVII Legislaturas," (Mimeograph, IFE, Mexico, DF: 1997).

But how are these changes in women's political representation and Mexico's democratization process related, if at all? Most of the literature on political transitions ignores or excludes the role of women's mobilization and their ways of doing politics in the explanations of transition and consolidation.[21] However, there are several scholars who argue that women's greater political participation and the democratization processes are mutually beneficial to one another.

Jaquette and the contributors to her volume on the women's movement in Latin America describe the importance of a number of different kinds of women's movements in the transitional processes in seven countries.[22] In Basu's collection of works on women's movements in seventeen countries and regions, Lamas, et al. describe how the women's movements in Mexico worked across class, race, and ideological lines in order to get their demands heard and attended to by those with power.[23] In *Waves of Democracy*, Markoff uses the varying rates of achievement of women's suffrage in different countries as an indicator of democratization.[24]

In addition, the concept of "critical mass" has arisen as one of the most important concepts being employed by researchers who take into account the role of women in institutional processes and by multilateral agencies promoting women's political participation. As was first described as a soci-ological phenomenon in corporations by Kanter,[25] and then first docu-mented in the Scandinavian legislatures,[26] when a minority group reaches a 30 percent proportion in the given group or a political body such as a leg-islature, sociocultural and political obstacles such as patriarchy or rigid party ideology can be overcome more easily. The minority then is less like-ly to be impeded or intimidated by the larger group and may feel more free to deviate from the dominant norm in favor of other demands specific to the minority group with which they identify.

A strong proponent of the idea that "critical mass" matters in politics, Staudt argues that until women are fairly represented—by women—in leg-islative bodies, with at least a chance for them to reach a critical mass in order to overcome the cultural barriers of male dominance in institutional politics, the robustness of a nation's democracy remains in question. Her work compares women's representation measured by proportional repre-sentation in legislatures worldwide.[27] Thomas provides further support for the notion of "critical mass" by demonstrating a correlation between a near or more than 30 percent critical mass of women in U.S. state legisla-tures, and higher levels of policy output addressing women's needs and demands.[28] Based in part on studies such as these, proponents of women's political participation are promoting and initiating gender-equalizing quotas—working at least toward the 30 percent threshold—in many legis-latures around the world.[29]

Nevertheless, many people continue to be skeptical of the substantive-ness of women's initiatives, including their visible yet incremental progress in the legislatures, given the strong legacies of masculine and patriarchal politics, especially in Latin America.[30] Moreover, studies of the relationship between women's presence and women's political benefits in political insti-tutions in advanced democracies have not produced clear evidence to sup-port the idea that improvement in women's lives is directly related to the efforts of female legislators. Mazur's examination of equal opportunity employment policy in France during a forty-year period shows that the passage of these gendered policies was merely "symbolic reform."[31] This may also be the case of the implementation of gendered policies in Mexico. And to complicate the issue further one must take into account the high degree of the influence of "co-optation" or coercion, and corporatism in Mexican politics.[32]

Thus the questions remain: Is Mexico's democratization process bene-fiting women and their rights? Are the gendered policies passed promoting change for women that was impeded by the one-party system, or are the policies merely symbolic? Although definitive answers may not be easy to attain on these issues, the examination of changes in female representation since 1988 and progress and evaluation of pro-woman policies do provide important insights into the understanding of the relationship between minority group politics and democratization in the Mexican context.

PROBLEMS, POLITICS, AND POLICY PROPOSALS

In relation to the actors in any given policy scenario, Kingdon discusses the importance of having "policy entrepreneurs" inside and outside of government who can apply their respective forms of pressure at the appropriate moment, in promotion of a certain policy.[33] In the United States this includes interest groups, academics, researchers and consultants, media, elections-related participants, and pollsters. In the case of the issues under examination in this study, a similar list of actors existed, with an important variation on "interest groups." Instead of interest groups as they are known in the United States, key actors in Mexico were women's and feminist movements, pro-woman nongovernmental organizations, and other sympathetic civil society groups, such as human rights groups and citizens' movements.

Kingdon describes the need for three "streams" of policy-related processes or conditions to flow into each other or coexist, in order for a policy to have a chance of moving forward in the policy process. These three streams are: (1) the problem; (2) the politics; and (3) the policy proposals. First, the problem or issue needs to be or to project the image of being urgent. An attention-drawing crisis might occur to trigger news coverage, so that it gets into the press, onto the airwaves, and into the minds of a large number of people. Second, the politics of the moment need to be receptive to working on the issue. Thus, not only do the politics of the parties in power matter (e.g., in the United States, Democrats or Republicans in the Congress or in the White House), but also the "public mood" or public opinion,[34] pressure from voters, and interest group actions.

Third, the concerned policy communities need to gain consensus on clear policy proposals or alternatives to the status quo policy, so that they are ready to lobby for their proposals at the moment the other two streams begin to run together. Then, as the strength of combined streams grows, a "policy window" is necessary for the actors to be able to push the streams into the legislative arena and out again, with success. A policy window is a political moment that may be caused by such political shifts as elections or a change in power, which open "windows" for issues that are not usually on the agenda (the concept of *coyuntura* is also appropriate for the description of the timing of the existence of a policy window).

A prime example of the documentation of this policy process is found in Nelson's *Making an Issue of Child Abuse.*[35] Nelson analyzes how concern for child abuse shifted from being a private issue to a public issue, gaining coverage in the U.S. media, attaining agenda status in Congress, and achieving important reforms to antiquated legislation on the issue. The issue got onto the agenda in the early 1970s. This was a political moment when the wave of the U.S. feminist movement was at its peak, and when the Republican party, which might not be as inclined to legislate the issue as the Democrats, was frantically looking for issues to keep people's faith in their party in the wake of President Nixon's resignation.

Although her overall assessment of the reforms is positive, Nelson points out some of the difficulties of opening up the complexities of this issue to legislation and institutionalized state responses. For example, psychological medication of the abuser in isolation from other contextual factors will only partially solve the problem. The social aspects of integrating an abuser back into a family or a community are of concern and are not adequately addressed by the legislation.

Parallels can be drawn between difficulties related to child abuse legislation in the United States and the sex crimes initiatives and penal code reforms, as well as affirmative action quotas in Mexico. The sex crimes legislation takes what was considered a private issue and makes it public— in both contexts. The U.S. feminist and women's movements were at a peak moment in their existence and ability to build coalitions when the child abuse legislation obtained agenda status, as were the feminist and women's movements in Mexico when the two issues arose. Both parties that were in power in the United States and Mexico at these different moments were in troubled times: the Republicans after Watergate and the PRI after the economic crises of the 1980s and the controversial presidential victory in 1988. Finally, as with the limited response by the state in the United States, Mexican advocates of the broader, feminist form of the penal code reform proposals on sex crimes, which called for a reconceptualization of the treatment of the victims within the state's criminal justice system, were disappointed with the early governmental responses. The next sections present sketches of the recent history of the sex crimes and affirmative action policy processes in Mexico, in relation to Kingdon's three streams of problems, politics, and policy proposals.

LUCHAS LEGISLATIVAS: SEX CRIMES

Policy initiatives on reforms to the penal code were presented in the Chamber of Deputies in the late 1960s without significant success.[36] They did not arise again until the early 1980s. At this time, a Mexican feminist organization was formed in 1981 called "The Network Against Violence Toward Women," in the wake of the first and second U.N.-sponsored international conferences of women, held in Mexico City in 1975 and in Copenhagen in 1980. This national organization spearheaded data collection and case documentation to begin to quantify everyday acts of violence against women. The data that were gathered provided the first statistical breakdown on the pervasiveness of sex crimes and proved invaluable in calling attention to the urgency of the problem.

One of the state-level organizations in Sonora, the Center for Support Against Violence (CECOV), which was a part of the national network, pioneered the gathering of data on the subject. Their early data provide an idea of "the problem" of sex crimes and are fairly representative of general trends found in later studies. Of the 279 reported cases of rape perpetrated between 1987–89 in the state of Sonora, the following data summarize the situation. According to sex and age, the victims were: (1) adults—95% women, 5% men; (2) adolescents—80% women, 20% men; and (3) children—60% girls and 40% boys. In relation to age, 70% were adults, 20% were eleven to eighteen years of age, and 10% were between the ages of three and ten years. The most common places for rape to occur were in the home, accounting for 70% of cases, and in schools, 16%. Incidents in public places accounted for 6% of the cases, while 4% occurred in isolated places and 4% in hospitals. Of the aggressors, 50% were relatives of the victim and 35% were acquaintances, while only 14% were strangers and 1% was conjugal rape. Formal denouncements were made in only 3% of the reported cases.[37]

These statistics and those from other studies played an important role in delineating the problem of sex crimes.[38] But it was not until 1988 that a proposal of reform to the penal code on sex crimes was presented in the Chamber of Deputies by Deputy Hilda Anderson of the PRI.[39] This was at the moment when there were more female representatives in the Chamber of Deputies than there had ever been before. However, the following day, just after Carlos Salinas de Gortari of the PRI was inaugurated as president in December of 1988, one of the first proposals handed down from the Executive branch was a reform to the penal code on sex crimes. This may have been part of the work of the PRI to regain its image after the elections. But at the same time perhaps it was a move to reinforce that although the PRI was a "modern" party in some ways (e.g., proposing gendered policies), with regard to presidential-congressional relations, it was still business as usual. The Executive version of the proposal on sex crimes passed, while the congressional proposal based on consensus of many policy entrepreneurs was swept aside. This may be viewed as an indicator of the continuing strength of presidentialist politics at this time.

The Executive reform changed the penalty for perpetration of rape from eight years to fourteen. But the Executive reform represented only a small part of a much deeper reform proposed by the feminist movement and legislators aligned with them, concerning the rights of the victims, not just the penalty for the crimes. Although from the Executive's perspective it appeared that the three streams of problem definition, politics, and proposals were running together on the issue, the streams of the feminists who initially proposed the legislation had not yet connected. The female legislators had their work cut out for them on the issue for the next three years of their legislative term.

With regard to getting the problem of sex crimes onto the political agenda, neither the statistics nor the weak reform made headline news. Although they contributed to the growing public concern around the issue, they did not provide sufficient weight to build support for further promotion of the reforms. In the Congress, the women legislators and civil society groups organized a forum on sex crimes, which brought together experts from multiple perspectives. The thrust of the presentations was that it was not only time for reforms on the issue, but for a reconceptualization of the victims and how they should be treated and cared for by the state. Finally in 1989 a plan for the creation of state agencies to treat the victims was proposed and passed— by those working through Congressional channels, not the Executive. The first agencies specialized in sex crimes were opened in the state of Tabasco and then in two of the sixteen *delegaciones* (similar to "districts" in U.S. political geography) in the Federal District.[40] But this was only the beginning of what was needed for real change.

In March 1989, while meetings and proposals occupied those working on sex crimes legislation in the Congress, nineteen young women from middle-class families in the south of Mexico City transformed the issue with a collective scream for help. These women were raped and decided to come forward and press charges against their aggressors.[41] The fact that these women came from middle-class families and neighborhoods broke the stereotype that these kinds of crimes generally took place in poor neighborhoods, thus providing more fuel for the fire of public outrage and demands for a political response since a new and economically stronger sector of society was affected. But more significant yet was the common denominator of the profile of their aggressors—they were all judicial police.

Not only did the collective charges against an arm of the state despised by many Mexicans for their corrupt and violent ways draw more attention to the women's call for help and for justice, it was like a torrential downpour causing the three streams of problems, politics, and policies to flood one into another. The cases brought the issue into the mainstream press. They created new links between human rights groups and feminists, as together they documented and fought the impunity of the judicial police.[42] Without the mutual support across the different civil society nongovernmental organizations and movements, it is unlikely that the feminists would have been able to make the impact needed to push the issue forward. They were confronted by a number of forces within the bureaucracy and the state that vigorously resisted the unmasking of these crimes, as it was perceived as a risk to the fragile legitimacy and public tolerance of the state apparatus. The cases were almost closed due to "inconclusive evidence."[43]

Nevertheless, the victims and their sympathizers pressed on, increasing public consciousness of the issues of violence against women and the indiscriminate violence by the judicial police (the state) toward its citizens, not just these particular nineteen young women victims. Although the process was dragged out by the obstacles in the judicial process and signified great costs for the victims and their families, four of the aggressors were finally charged and put in prison. Other aspects of the cases are still being tried up to the present. The extended duration of the process allowed a number of groups to organize effectively around the issue and expand the base of mass and elite support necessary to get the issue of sex crimes onto the congressional agenda.

In February 1990 meetings were held with the attorney general of the Procuraduría General de Justicia del Distrito Federal (PGJDF), to organize working commissions on how to form and execute a broader plan of specialized state agencies that would respond to victims of sex crimes and work to ameliorate the problem. In May 1990 the next set of reforms were presented in the Chamber of Deputies by the female legislators, with widespread support from a diverse range of feminist, women's, and human rights organizations.

To give a more concrete and personal sense of this important achievement, I have included a translation of Dr. María de la Luz Lima de Rodríguez's "Note for your Archive" written to the Attorney General's Office describing the presentation of the first version of the Reform to the Penal Code on Sex Crimes and Sexual Harassment on May 17, 1990 in the National Congress. Dr. Lima is one of the primary authors and advocates of the legislation in the Congress.

> *A Note for Your Archive:*
> On May 17, 1990, we arrived at the Auditorium of the National Congress in Centro Médico, more than 5000 women of all tendencies and sectors.
>
> Excited, it seemed as it if was the birthday of each one of us. Without concern for our different affiliations or tendencies, we formed a great coalition that was felt when Hilda Anderson, deputy for the Institutional Revolutionary Party and current Secretary of the Chamber of Deputies, began to read the document [the new proposal for reform to the penal code on sex crimes]. For us, every line was a social revindication that we felt gave meaning to our existence and gave value to the importance of our work and our ideas, now on a national level.
>
> When some paragraph was read containing transcendental material, cries of joy could be heard. With a thirst for justice, we stood up and cried out our common slogans.
>
> . . . it had been many years of struggle. One could see faces with similar thoughts: "Finally!", "We've been waiting a long time for this day!"

The male deputies just watched, perplexed. A few laughed, but the laughter was of the nervous, disconcerted type, without knowing where these ideas came from, who was setting the norms, what was going on?

Some of the male deputies . . . looked at us with great respect and seriousness. Afterwards, one asked the question: "Doctora, why these reforms? Why?"

I told him that thousands of victims in the Attorney General's office had been received, so severely battered or affected by the crimes that we had to participate in the drafting of this initiative.

In the corridors one could see women of diverse tendencies—happy, amazed, wanting to convince themselves that what they were living was real.

It was a great day, a moment of emotion and change in our country.

Local deputies from all over the country were invited to the meeting. It was with euphoria that they said they would take this initiative back to their states to make it a reality there too.

Someone asked: "Why didn't this initiative come from the President?"

Because in Mexico, democracy can be exercised, the channels exist. At times citizens do not use them, or when they don't work, they only passively wait. Women, who it seems always have to wait, now have put themselves to work and to legislate for women, for the respect of their children, and for the grandeur of their nation. For Mexico![44]

In July 1990 the proposal on sex crimes, with some modifications, passed in the Chamber of Deputies—377 votes in favor and 0 votes against.[45] In October the Attorney General's office created two new specialized agencies: the Center for Support of Missing Persons (CAPEA) and the Center for Attention to Intrafamiliar Violence (CAVI). In November a second forum took place in the Chamber of Deputies, of similar magnitude to the first held in 1989. In December 1990 the Senate passed the reform to the penal code into law. In March 1991 the Attorney General's office created a fourth kind of specialized agency, the Center for Therapy in Support of Victims of Sex Crimes (CTA).[46] Finally the original feminist policy entrepreneurs managed to bring the streams of problems, politics, and proposals together and to find a policy window through which to let it flow.

Thus, during the LV legislative period, from 1988 to 1991, support for the first part of the hypothesis is garnered since when the greatest number of female legislators ever were present in the Congress, significant advances occurred on the gendered issue of sex crimes. The formation of a nonpartisan plural group, let alone that it was of female legislators, to push the issue was also a noteworthy deviation from the norm of agenda setting in relation to each deputies' party identification. Although a PRI deputy presented the proposal, it was the work of a diverse group for many years, inside and outside of institutional politics, that finally led to the presentation of the initiative.[47]

However, the momentum behind these efforts slowed in the next legislative period when the percentages of women in the Congress abruptly declined after the 1991 election (note dip on Figure 3.1, and percentages in Table 3.1). Apparently having only single digit percentages of women in the Chamber of the Deputies and the Senate was not sufficient for keeping women's issues on the agenda.[48] This was a great disappointment for women who had been working hard to develop a new feminist institutional strategy using the Congress, after working from the outside for so many years.

But pressuring from a variety of positions in nongovernmental organizations and movements was what the women working on these issues knew best, so after they got over the failure of their strategy, activity increased among the civil society organizations and networks, organizing forums and using the media to try to keep "the problem" on the congressional agenda. In 1994 another initiative on sex crimes again passed successfully. In February 1994 the Specialized Unit for Legal Attention to Victims of Sex Crimes (ADEVI) was created by the Attorney General's office to serve the victims of sex crimes.[49]

In 1995 new initiatives began at different levels of politics. In the Federal District an initiative was proposed to improve the protection of the rights of victims, supported with signatures from 13 female senators, 41 female deputies, 148 male deputies, and 9 female Federal District Assembly representatives.[50] National meetings on sex crimes were held in 1995 and 1996 with support from the Attorney General's office. The strategy shifted to building common knowledge and support for future initiatives by broadening the sphere of state support in other administrative circles, such as the Attorney General's office, the Secretariat of the Interior, and the Secretariat of Health.

The coalition of women's and feminist groups were primed for the political moment of the 1997 elections. The heads of these organizations in Mexico City, now experienced "policy entrepreneurs" after nearly a decade of concerted work inside and outside of the Congress, were prepared with a larger repertoire of strategies to get their issues onto the political agenda. At the same time, the network and consensus building across the country not just among the elites in the capital, owed in part to the "Beijing effect," provided a broad base of support for a new set of initiatives. Moreover, it appears that the feminist methods of horizontal, nonpatriarchal politics made an impact, even in the context of the Congress, where masculine, patriarchal forms of politics dominate.

On June 23, 1997, two weeks before the July 6 elections, the feminist political group Diversa held a forum to announce five demands (and proposals for legislation) for the new Congress—regardless of which parties won—to work on in the coming legislative period, from 1997 until 2000. All eight political parties sent representatives to hear and sign onto the accords. Thus this public act marked a definitive moment for feminists in what had been a gradual shift from a nonpartisan to a multipartisan posture in rallying support for their demands on the institutional political agenda. The five demands included: (1) the right to freedom from discrimination based on gender; (2) clearer regulation of the rights and responsibilities within the family (especially paternal responsibility to provide economic child support whether or not he is present in the household); (3) legislation prohibiting firing of women workers when they become pregnant and forced pregnancy tests when applying for employment; (4) installations of day care in the workplace; and (5) more progressive legislation for treatment of intrafamiliar violence.[51]

As can be seen with the evolution of the issue of sex crimes, the focus shifted from a feminist outcry to an appeal to a multipartisan, broader base of support. The issue was transformed into a family issue, which concerns all of Mexican society, women *and* men, and ideologically left- and right-leaning activists and politicians. Naturally there are pros and cons to the change in strategy, but those will become evident as the new legislative period unfolds.

In the next section I present a similar sketch of the problems, politics, and policy proposals on the issue of affirmative action. Following that section I discuss the overlap of the two issues and the sequencing in relation to legislative periods and corresponding numbers of women in the Congress.

LUCHAS LEGISLATIVAS Y ELECTORALES: AFFIRMATIVE ACTION

As previously observed in Figure 3.1, during the course of the four elections since 1988, female political representation gradually increased in the Congress and party leadership, with the exception of 1991. The 1991 decline provided proponents of women's representation in the Congress with one more reason to promote a quota of 30 percent.

Furthermore, the successful policy outcomes of the female deputies and senators in the 1988–91 legislative period, which finally responded to the demands of feminists and women's groups, made it evident that their presence in these positions was essential for the advocating for gender equality and women's issues through the politics of congressional legislation. At the same time and perhaps more importantly, female deputies and senators contributed to the shift in the balance of power between the Executive and Legislative branches by utilizing different forms of consensus-building politics related to the Congress (countering its rubber-stamp image), which contributed to making the Congress a more credible political institution. But in 1991 the problem of the lack of female representation in the Congress crystallized when all could see the difference in women's legislative success between the periods before 1988 and then during the 1988–91 legislative period, relative to the corresponding numbers of women in the chambers.[52]

Thus, the women of the PRD set to work to try to insure their presence in the leadership of their party, based on the belief that the left-leaning ideology of the party should support equal rights for women.[53] In 1993, the issue of quotas favoring women achieved agenda status at the PRD's second national congress. After much debate, a 20 percent quota passed, mandating that 20 percent of the individuals on the uninominal and plurinominal candidate lists be women. In the 1996 party congress, the PRD women continued to push the issue and a 30 percent quota passed. This time the mandate applied not only to the electoral lists but also to the National Executive Council (CEN) of the party, the highest level of leadership in the party.[54]

For the women of the PRD, inside their party at least, the streams of problems, politics, and proposals came together. But not for long. Despite these efforts within the PRD, the results of the 1991 election were a disaster for female party members—in the PRD, as well as the PRI and the PAN. As noted in Table 3.1, the numbers of women elected declined sharply: only forty women won in the Chamber of Deputies (8.0 percent), and two in the Senate (3.1 percent).

The main reason for this decline is that after the near loss of power in 1988, the PRI pulled out all the stops to regain power in the 1991 elections. One of those measures may have been to run the most certain candidates possible and, apparently from the perspective of the PRI leadership, very few female candidates qualified. At the same time, Accetolla shows that a decline in the number of women elected in midterm elections is part of a larger pattern, known as the *"flor del sexenio."*[55] Over time more women (the metaphor is of women as *"flores"* [flowers]) won in the six-year term elections— the presidential elections—than in the midterm elections. The reasons for this pattern are unclear as a comprehensive study of all the factors that may be at play is yet to be done.

More critical perspectives point out that accusations of fraud again arose after the 1991 elections, as the PRI won overwhelmingly in many areas. From the feminist perspective, some believe that the exclusion of women from winning positions was a form of punishment for exposing the role of the state[56] (the judicial police) in the rapes of the nineteen women in Mexico City.[57]

At the same time, the feminist demands on politicians at this moment may have been too radical. Most politicians—male or female—were not ready to accept issues like the decriminalization of abortion, the right to free exercise and respect of one's sexual preference, and the legalization of prostitution.[58] Lastly, the coalition between diverse groups of women during this period, the Convención Nacional de Mujeres por la Democracia (CNMD), formed only a few months before the election. Members of the group needed more time to resolve internal differences in order to clarify strategies and determine how to implement them. Regardless of the electoral loss in 1991, the formation of the CNMD did set a precedent for the creation of feminist and politically active women's groups thereafter, serving as a part of their collective political learning.

During the three-year period from 1991 to 1994, the focal point of the struggle for affirmative action for women moved back from the PRD and the Congress to civil society. As mentioned in the section on sex crimes, the idea of partisan affiliation lost strength, and in fact the PRD coalition nearly fell apart.[59] The concept of *ciudadanía* (citizenship) took its place. Groups such as Alianza Cívica and the Movimiento Ciudadano por la Democracia (MCD) arose with great numbers of adherents from working and middle classes and support from an ideologically broad range of political elites. They organized around issues which would eliminate electoral fraud—such as the renewal of the electoral registry and other electoral reforms in 1993. At the same time, the common work between feminist and female activists and those working for democratic reform reinforced alliances between activists across movements concerned about similar issues. This was another key factor in building support for women's issues in the parties and in the Congress after 1994.

In 1994, the year of the presidential elections, the greatest task was to try to convince the Mexican citizenry that their votes mattered and, more importantly, would be respected.[60] The uprising of the Zapatista Army for National Liberation (EZLN) in January 1994, followed in March by the assassination of the PRI's presidential candidate, Luis Donaldo Colosio, made the demand for respect of citizens' rights even more urgent. As a result, for the first time in Mexico's history, national and international observers (officially known as "international visitors") were permitted to watch the electoral proceedings, in support of efforts to ensure fair and free elections.[61]

The results of the 1994 elections exhibit a recovery in the number of female deputies and senators elected from 1991, although the percentages did not reach those of 1988. Sixty-nine women were victorious in the Chamber of Deputies (13.8 percent), and seventeen in the Senate (13.3 percent). Key factors that affected this recovery from the 1991 decline include: influence of the PRD's quota law (although the 30 percent mandate was not fulfilled as seen below in Table 3.2); a significant degree of mobilization of women in the citizens' movements; the positive effects of the *flor del sexenio* factor; and growing public discussion and notice of female candidates such as Cecilia Soto of the Partido de Trabajo (PT), and their impressive political skills. The symbolic importance of female candidates for female voters has been found to be significant in the United

States, and it may be in Mexico also, because it gives female voters candidates with whom they can identify as women and therefore more reason to "talk politics" and perhaps to vote or participate politically.[62]

Although those in the opposition were disappointed by the PRI victory of the presidency in 1994, few could argue that the elections had been stolen, as in the previous two elections. In relation to the 1994 election being the first national election when the PRD had a quota law of 30 percent favoring women, the election of 11.9 percent females as deputies looked like a very poor showing. However, since the fulfillment of the quota is related to the placement of women candidates on the electoral lists, fewer women were elected in part due to the party's losses as the PRD had significant electoral losses all over the country in 1994.

At the same time, the 1994 elections manifested that the mass mobilization of "citizens" could have an important impact on making progress toward democracy, in the classic terms of achieving free and fair elections. But for many in these movements the achievement of a free and fair "electocracy" was not sufficient. Demands continued for electoral reforms, and among those was the call for increased attention to the political participation of women —some sought this in the form of national quotas favoring women, while others continued to oppose the idea.

In 1995 there was a flurry of governmental and nongovernmental activity around women's issues in preparation for Mexico's representation in the United Nations Fourth International Conference of Women in Beijing, China, held in September of that year. In preparation for the conference, a National Council of Legislative Advisors was formed in the Congress. By a mandate from the Executive level, a new agency called the National Program for Women (PRONAM) was established to collect data and serve as a governmental support for information on women's issues from 1995–2000. As women political leaders now had more experience working inside institutional channels, the initiative taken by the Executive was more readily accepted as one more way to work on women's issues (albeit a rather weak one), rather than as a way to try to quell feminist demands.

Although there were multiple consultations amidst the nongovernmental organizations and movements leading up to the conference, the "Legislative Consultation" in the Congress did not take place until late August. With regard to the promotion of quotas, this grouping of women's organizations did not support the concept.[63] Nevertheless, the debate raged on when the *Platform for Action* from the international conference came back from Beijing—with a strong recommendation to promote quotas for women's representation in their respective legislative bodies.[64]

With the weight of the international recommendation and increasing numbers of women pressuring for quotas, the PRI began to reconsider its position.[65] The stream of politics shifted, and PRI women were ready with

Table 3.2
Percentages of Female Deputies and Senators Elected by Party:
1994 and 1997 Elections

Election Year	% PRD Female Deputies	% PRD Female Senators	% PRI Female Deputies	% PRI Female Senators	% PAN Female Deputies	% PAN Female Senators
1994	11.9%	0%	8.0%	5.0%	7.8%	0%
1997	24.0%	25%	15.1%	23.1%	12.4%	22.2%

Sources: Fernández 1995a, 1995b; Federal Electoral Institute 1997.
Anna Poncela Fernández, *Participación política: Las mujeres en México al final del milenio* (Mexico DF: Colegio de México, 1995a); Anna Poncela Fernández, "Las mexicanas en el Congreso de la Unión y en el ejectivo hoy," FEM, año 19, n. 147, June 1995; Federal Electoral Institute (IFE), "Votación por Distritos (300)," (Mimeograph, IFE, Mexico DF: 1997); Federal Electoral Institute (IFE), "Candidatos por circumscripción: Diputados de representación proporcional," (Mimeograph, IFE, Mexico DF: 1997); Federal Electoral Institute (IFE), "Senadores que permanecen de la LVI Legislatura a la LVII," (Mimeograph, IFE, Mexico DF: 1997); Federal Electoral Institute (IFE), "Conformación de la Cámara de Senadores: LVI–LVII Legislaturas," (Mimeograph, IFE, Mexico DF: 1997).

a proposal.[66] At the party's 1996 convention, the proposal was made and finally accepted as a recommendation—not a mandate—to include no more than 70 percent of the candidates of the same sex on electoral lists.[67] Shortly thereafter, the same issue was accepted as a recommendation in the October 1996 electoral reforms to the Código Federal de Instituciones y Procedimientos Electorales (COFIPE).[68] While the PRI and PRD, as well as some of the smaller parties, passed internal party mandates and recommendations of the like, the PAN continued to refuse to consider quotas in their party.[69] Table 3.2 shows the party breakdown for the 1994 and 1997 elections concerning the effect of the 30 percent gender quota mandate in the PRD statutes, implemented after 1991, and the impact of the same recommendation in the PRI, related to the reforms to the Federal Electoral Code, approved in 1996. Thus far, despite the legislation and recommendations, it is evident that the 30 percent level has not yet been reached within any of the three major parties.

Nonetheless, after attaining at least a minimum degree of approval of quotas in two of the three major parties on the national level, action on similar proposals has since moved out to the state governments. In the state of Sonora, a 20 percent quota was passed in the state legislature in June 1996. In Chihuahua, a 30 percent quota was approved in July 1997, and most recently, a 30 percent quota was passed by a slim margin in the state of Oaxaca.[70]

Table 3.3
Percentages of Female Deputies and Senators Elected by Party: 1997

1997 Election	% Female Deputies	% Female Senators	% Substitute for Senator
TOTAL	17.2%	21.9%	37.5%
PRD	24.0%	25.0%	37.5%
PRI	15.1%	23.1%	46.1%
PAN	12.4%	22.2%	22.2%
PT	14.3%	0%	0%
PVEM	50%	0%	50%
Indept.	50%	0%	0%

Source: Federal Electoral Institute 1997.
Federal Electoral Institute (IFE), "Senadores que permanecen da LVI Legislatura a la LVII," (Mimeograph, IFE, Mexico DF: 1997); Federal Electoral Institute (IFE), "Conformación de la Cámara de Senadores: LVI–LVII Legislaturas," (Mimeograph, IFE, Mexico DF: 1997).

In the elections that took place July 6, 1997, the number of women elected reached beyond the 1994 numbers in the Chamber of Deputies, but still did not match the 1988 peak in the Senate. As was shown in Table 3.1, 17.2 percent were elected to the Chamber of Deputies (eighty-six of five hundred), and 21.9 percent in the Senate (seven of thirty-two).[71] Related to the issue at hand Table 3.3 shows the difference by party and includes data on the "substitute for senator" (*suplente*) position. Neither the PRI nor the PRD reached the 30 percent level of female representation. Both the Partido Verde Ecologista Mexicana (PVEM) and the Independents attained 50 percent levels of female representation, although having only one of two is not a fair sample from which to generalize. But it is important to note that the internal mandate of the PVEM with regard to gender equality is to have 50 percent female/male leadership and candidates. In the fourth column of Table 3.3, the "Substitute for Senator" (*suplente*) statistics show the high percentages of women who take secondary positions in the electoral contests. A critical perspective of the percentages in the secondary positions is that it is an obvious relegation of women to second-class status, and demands that more women should have access to primary positions. At the same time, a more reformist perspective views these high numbers with optimism, arguing that women are gaining fundamental political learning by being a part of the process, which may then lead to their ascension into primary positions in the future.

From the viewpoint of the feminist political group Diversa, and other women's groups and networks, such as the Asamblea Nacional de Mujeres,[72] the results of the 1997 elections were quite positive. Having 17.2 percent female deputies and 15.7 percent female senators for this legislative period from 1997 to 2000 is a deviation from the midterm election decreases that have occurred historically and a great boon for the women's groups. In addition, the hopes and expectations of those promoting equity for women have increased with the election of PRD leader Cuaúhtemoc Cárdenas to the mayoral position of Mexico City. Many believe that when the PRD's leftist ideology becomes incarnate in the numerous positions appointed by Cárdenas in December 1997, feminist and women's issues will have possibilities of legislation and implementation previously unattainable (or unthinkable) in Mexico.

FUTURE ISSUES FOR SEX CRIMES AND AFFIRMATIVE ACTION QUOTAS LEGISLATION

The three "streams" of problems, politics, and proposals ran together at several moments after 1988, permitting gendered policies on sex crimes to become law.[73] The Attorney General's office and Secretariat of the Interior also are producing some impressive statistics on how many victims have been served by the agencies. These reports show that the new agencies are being effective.[74] However, the bureaucratization of a political issue, especially in Mexico, can be more problematic than positive, as is discussed by Sloan in his early work on policy analysis in Latin America.[75] With historical precedents of corruption, patronage, and frequent rotation of personnel inhibiting acquired wisdom and serious evaluations of previous policies in the bureaucracies, little real progress is made when the issue is bureaucratized.[76]

Sloan's summary of the Mexican bureaucracy provides useful criteria for assessing how the legislative response to the sex crimes policies will fare in the newly formed agencies. He states that without (1) a strong public service tradition; (2) a free press, and (3) a strong independent judiciary, the strategy of bureaucratic development may be corrupted easily, and hence its political purpose defeated.[77] Translated into Kingdon's terms, the bureaucratization of the politics and policy outcome may very well block the flow of the streams—but in the implementation process. Until I gather more data on this part of the policy process—implementation—the following assessment of the application of these three criteria to the sex crimes policies is preliminary.

In relation to Sloan's criteria of a strong public service tradition, although Mexico is not known for such a tradition, the new proposed plans, complete with specific training guides may aid in developing bureaucracies that are less corrupt and personalistic, and more humane. However, more varied methods of evaluation will need to be employed to observe how well the agencies are really working.[78] With regard to Sloan's second criteria of a free press, although the printed press in Mexico is relatively free, radio and television communication have been and are more controlled by the government. As most people get their news from radio and television,[79] reform of party coverage by the radio and TV media was a major issue in the 1997 elections and is under consideration for further reforms. Equity of campaign coverage in the television media for the different political parties was a specific focus of citizens' movements and human rights groups in 1997.[80]

Also in addition to Sloan's criteria of importance of the watchful eye of the press on governmental processes, the increasingly important role of nongovernmental organizations (NGO) must also be noted. Their work has become essential in serving as watchdogs over their respective issues and pressing for reforms in their governmental counterparts if the agencies are not being effective.[81] For example, the data gathered and support provided by NGOs was fundamental to the efforts of the penal code reforms.

Nonetheless, aside from some advances made with regard to the first two necessary conditions for a bureaucracy to carry out its functions effectively, Sloan's third condition, that of a strong independent judiciary, continues to be absent from Mexican politics. Not only for the victims of sex crimes but also for the general population, the lack of a strong judiciary greatly limits Mexico's democratic consolidation process. As long as perpetrators of sex crimes, be they relatives of the victim or judicial police, continue to go free because either the charges are dismissed due to bribes or impunity, or the victims calculate that their chances of winning the case are so slim they do not bother pressing charges, the roots of Mexico's democratization process will not have a firm foundation.

In addition to Sloan's criteria, another factor impeding implementation is the deep influence of patriarchal and clientelistic politics in Mexican political culture. In spite of the progress made in the legislation of sex crimes and affirmative action policies, and the hopes pinned on the women in the Congress and on Cárdenas's administration in the Federal District during the next three years, these factors are still present. Prominent Mexican feminist Marta Lamas captured this concern clearly with her classic phrase: "Cuerpo de mujer no guarantiza conciencia de género," "a female body does not guarantee gender consciousness." Relative to this work, Lamas's phrase means that not all female legislators necessarily want to support women's issues, even those determined via consensus, such as those outlined by Diversa and the Asamblea Nacional de Mujeres.

A few recent examples reveal the complexities of the congressional and legislative challenges to come. Since the beginning of the new legislative term in late August 1997 the results for women have been mixed. In the formation of the commissions and definition of who will have the leadership positions thereof, female legislators were able to achieve the formation of a special commission, established for the duration of this legislative period (with hopes that it may become permanent—say the feminists), called the Commission on Equity and Gender. Promotion of gendered issues will be greatly facilitated with the congressional budget and legal capacity of this commission. However, at the same time, the number of women appointed to the presidencies of the other sixty-one commissions was very low, with only three appointed. Once again the the 30 percent quota of women in leadership positions was not fulfilled.[82]

CONCLUSIONS

The purpose of this chapter is to contribute to the understanding of the intersection of gender politics and democratization. I present data in support of the argument that there is a positive association between women's advances in institutional politics and the democratization process, as observed in the case of Mexico from 1988 to 1997. Moreover, I examine a new angle of this intersection by utilizing concepts and methods from the literatures of social movements, political institutions, and public policy analysis, to document and analyze the significance of the correlation between the varying percentages of women in the Mexican Congress and gendered policy initiatives and successes during this period.

The thesis of the study has two parts: first, if there are more women in a given legislative body, and especially if the percentage of women reaches a critical mass (or 30 percent of the given body), then the female representatives will better represent the demands and interests of the feminine half of the nation's population; and therefore, secondly, if this sector of the population's interests and demands are better represented in the Congress, then the polity is more genuinely democratic.

Borrowing a form of analysis more common in studies of advanced democracies, I utilize Kingdon's framework of the streams of problems, politics, and policy proposals to examine the significance of the gender breakdown of the results of the last four elections in relation to the policy initiatives and successes of the penal code reform on sex crimes and affirmative action quotas. Although the collection of data is yet incomplete, the ebbs and flows of gendered policy proposals and passage does appear to be correlated with the presence of higher percentages of women in the Congress. Proponents of policies on sex crimes made the most progress during the legislative period from 1988 to 1991, when the percentages of women in the Congress were the highest ever.

Then when the percentages of female legislators dropped between 1991 and 1994, there was a severe decline in the number of initiatives proposed. The locus of women's organizing efforts moved back to civil society. After the 1994 elections, when the percentages rose up to the 13 percent mark (in both chambers), some initiatives were presented early in the legislative period. But it was not until after female legislators gained strength from the recommendations of the Beijing International Women's Conference in 1995 for quotas favoring women that they were able to make concerted efforts to promote and obtain approval for quotas in 1996 and 1997.

Relative to the results from the current legislative period, it is evident that at this point with the percentages of female legislators still being far from 30 percent, other external factors are important to make up for the lack of a female legislative critical mass. My continuing research will determine more precisely what these factors are, but several key factors emerged from the policy analysis of these two cases of sex crimes and affirmative action quotas. First, at the macrolevel the Mexican political context was in a key moment of change that allowed for new actors with different forms of "doing politics" to gain space. Thus the conditions of (1) a troubled status quo, such as has been the case with the PRI, and (2) viable political alternatives, as were the PRD and the PAN, were important in opening up the policy windows for new initiatives.

Next, as Kingdon discusses, there must be a group of policy entrepreneurs able to recognize opportunities and ready to make policy proposals on their issues. In the Mexican case from 1988 to 1997 the presence of the following actors as policy entrepreneurs was significant: a strong feminist movement and other civil society movements, such as the urban popular, human rights, and citizens' movements—with which the feminists built alliances, and of course, the female legislators. With regard to the idea of a "critical mass" of women legislators, the data from these case studies suggest that a critical mass of 13 percent in both chambers, *when these other conditions and actors were present,* is sufficient to allow the effective legislation of gendered policies for women.

In addition to these contextual factors and actors necessary to create the conditions for successful legislation by a formerly underrepresented group, I believe that international pressure or a demonstration effect from other countries on the same or similar policy issues had a significant impact on the process in Mexico. However as the data collection on this factor is still incomplete, this must be taken as a speculative conclusion. At the same time, the question of the degree of adequate implementation of these policies has only been partially answered in this chapter. Without implementation, policy successes become merely symbolic, and thus, democracy for the given underrepresented sector of the population remains superficial. In my ongoing research on these policies I plan to gather data to enable a more complete evaluation of these policies' implementation.

Finally, it is my hope that this study can serve as a model of how to apply different forms of analysis, in this case electoral and public policy analysis, to the research agenda of those concerned with the rights of women and other groups underrepresented in institutional politics in other places or on other policies. Analysis of the potential for success of less powerful sectors of the population via legislative forms of politics are of particular importance, especially in the cases of countries moving into the stage of consolidating their democratic processes.

As can be observed with the case of women in the Mexican Congress, despite the rhetoric of Mexico being in a democratic transition, advances for women while important, have not been constant. In order for democracy's roots to deepen and to then be able to nourish the society and all of its citizens, not only a powerful few, advances for less powerful groups in the legislative arena need to be consistent and deep enough so that the majority of citizens perceive themselves as being fairly represented. With adequate representation, the legitimacy and credibility of political institutions such as the Congress in Mexico, can be established and maintained and the roots of democracy strengthened.

NOTES

Acknowledgments: Research for this chapter was made possible with support from the Fulbright García-Robles United States–Mexico Commission, the Provost's Development Fund of the University of Pittsburgh, and the Heinz Social and Policy Program of the Center for Latin American Studies of the University of Pittsburgh. I owe special thanks for support of my work on this chapter to fellow collaborators Jorge Domínguez and Kate Bruhn, María Luisa Tarrés of the Colegio de México, Gloria Careaga of the Gender Studies Program at the National Autonomous University of Mexico (UNAM), Ophelia Ceja of Comunicación e Información de la Mujer, A.C. (CIMAC), Dag MacLeod, Sam Smucker, Melissa Jameson, and my mother, Sarah Stevenson.

1. Lucía Lagunes Huerta, "Día Internacional de la Lucha contra la Violencia: Sólo habrá democracia cuando la mujer ocupe su lugar en la sociedad: Brassdefer," trans. Linda S. Stevenson, *Doble Jornada* (2 December 1991): 11.

2. Jane S. Jaquette, ed., *The Women's Movement in Latin America: Participation and Democracy* (Boulder, Col.: Westview Press, 1994); Barbara J. Nelson and Najma Chowdhury, eds., *Women and Politics Worldwide* (New Haven: Yale University Press, 1994); Elizabeth Adell Cook, Sue Thomas, and Clyde Wilsox, eds., *The Year of the Woman: Myths and Realities* (Boulder, Col.: Westview Press, 1994).

3. Guillermo O'Donnell, Philippe C. Schmitter, and Laurence Whitehead, eds., *Transitions from Authoritarian Rule: Latin America* (Baltimore: The Woodrow Wilson International Center for Scholars, 1986); James M. Malloy and Mitchell A. Seligson, eds., *Authoritarians and Democrats: Regime Transition in Latin America* (Pittsburgh, Penn.: University of Pittsburgh Press, 1987); Scott Mainwaring, Guillermo O'Donnell, and J. Samuel Valenzuela, eds., *Issues in Democratic Consolidation: The New South American Democracies in Comparative Perspective* (Notre Dame, Ind.: University of Notre Dame Press, 1992).

4. Robert A. Dahl, *Polyarchy: Participation and Opposition* (New Haven: Yale University Press, 1971).

5. Terry Lynn Karl, "Dilemmas of Democratization in Latin America," *Comparative Politics* 23, no.1 (1990): 1–21; Adam Przeworski, "Toward Self-Sustaining Democracy," in *Issues in Democratic Consolidation: The New South American Democracies in Comparative Perspective,* eds. Scott Mainwaring, Guillermo O'Donnell, and J. Samuel Valenzuela (Notre Dame, Ind.: University of Notre Dame Press, 1992).

6. Guillermo O'Donnell, "Democracy and Social Life?" in *Issues in Democratic Consolidation: The New South American Democracies in Comparative Perspective,* eds. Scott Mainwaring, Guillermo O'Donnell, and J. Samuel Valenzuela (Notre Dame, Ind.: University of Notre Dame Press, 1992).

7. Larry Diamond, "Is the Third Wave Over?" *Journal of Democracy* 7, no. 3 (July 1996): 20–37.

8. Lani Guinier, *The Tyranny of the Majority: Fundamental Fairness in Representative Democracy* (New York: The Free Press, 1994).

9. Amy Mazur, *Gender Bias and the State: Symbolic Reform at Work in Fifth Republic France* (Pittsburgh, Penn.: University of Pittsburgh Press, 1995).

10. In the middle of the vote count, when it appeared as though the PRI might lose, the entire computerized system suddenly broke down. Not until nearly two weeks later was a final count announced, the PRI winning the presidency with 50.2%.

11. John W. Kingdon, *Agendas, Alternatives, and Public Policies,* 2d ed., (Boston: Little, Brown, 1995).

12. Marta Lamas et al., "Building Bridges: The Growth of Popular Feminism in Mexico," in *The Challenge of Local Feminisms: Women's Movements in Global Perspective,* ed. Amrita Basu (Boulder, Col.: Westview Press, 1995).

13. Teresa Valdés Enchenique and Enrique Gomáriz Moraga, eds., *Mujeres Latinoamericanas en cifras: Tomocomparativo* (Santiago, Chile: Instituto de la Mujer, Ministerio de Asuntos Sociales de España y Facultad Latinoamericana de Ciencias Sociales, 1995).

14. Alida Brill, ed., *A Rising Public Voice: Women in Politics Worldwide* (New York: The Feminist Press at The City University of New York, 1995).

15. María de la Luz Lima Malvido, *Modelo de Atención a Víctimas en México* (Mexico City: Imagen Impresa, S.A., 1995).

16. Gloria Bonder and Marcela Nari, "The 30 Percent Quota Law: A Turning Point for Women's Political Participation in Argentina," in *A Rising Public Voice: Women in Politics Worldwide,* ed. Alida Brill (New York: The Feminist Press at The City University of New York, 1995); Mark P. Jones, "Increasing Women's Representation Via Gender Quotas: The Argentine Ley de Cupos," *Women in Politics* 16, no. 4 (1996): 75–98.

17. United Nations, *Beijing Declaration and Platform for Action: Fourth World Conference on Women: Action for Equality, Development and Peace* (presented at the Fourth International Conference on Women, Beijing, China, September 15, 1995).

18. Linda S. Stevenson, "Las mujeres políticas y la izquierda en México: Reclamo de un nuevo espacio en la política institucional," in *Género y Cultura en América Latina,* ed. María Luisa Tarrés (Mexico City: El Colegio de México, forthcoming).

19. Joe Foweraker and Ann L. Craig, eds., *Popular Movements and Political Change in Mexico* (Boulder, Col.: Lynne Reiner Publishers, 1990).

20. Victoria E. Rodríguez and Peter M. Ward, "Introduction: Governments of the Opposition in Mexico," in *Opposition Government in Mexico,* eds. Victoria E. Rodríguez and Peter M. Ward (Albuquerque: University of New Mexico Press, 1995), 8.

21. For example, in his review article "On the Third Wave of Democratization" in *World Politics* 47 (October 1994): 135–70, Doh Chull Shin makes no reference

whatever to the works done on women's roles and gender analysis in relation to political transitions.

22. Jaquette, *The Women's Movement.*

23. Lamas, "Building Bridges."

24. John Markoff, *Waves of Democracy: Social Movements and Political Change* (Thousand Oaks, Cal: Pine Forge Press, 1996).

25. Rosabeth Moss Kanter, *Men and Women of the Corporation* (New York: Basic Books, 1977).

26. Drude Dahlerup and Elina Haavio-Mannila, "Summary," in *Unfinished Democracy: Women in Nordic Politics,* ed. Elina Haavio-Mannila (Oxford: Pergamon Press, 1985).

27. Kathleen Staudt, "Women in Politics: Global Perspectives" (paper presented at the Women in Contemporary Mexican Politics conference at The Mexican Center of Institute for Latin American Studies, University of Texas at Austin, 7–8 April, 1995).

28. Sue Thomas, *How Women Legislate* (New York: Oxford University Press, 1994).

29. In relation to the Mexican case, note the dashed line on Figure 3.1 at the 30 percent mark.

30. For a thorough explanation of the concepts of "gender" relations and specifically "masculine" forms of conducting politics, see Georgia Duerst-Lahti and Rita Mae Kelly, "On Governance, Leadership, and Gender," in *Gender Power, Leadership, and Governance,* eds. Georgia Duerst-Lahti and Rita Mae Kelly (Ann Arbor: University of Michigan, 1995); and on patriarchy in Mexico, Judith Adler Hellman, *Mexican Lives* (New York: The New Press, 1994).

31. Mazur, *Gender Bias.*

32. James Malloy, ed., *Authoritarianism and Corporatism in Latin America* (Pittsburgh, Penn.: University of Pittsburgh Press, 1977).

33. Kingdon, *Agendas,* 179–84.

34. James A. Stimson, *Public Opinion in America: Moods, Cycles and Swings* (Boulder, Col.: Westview Press, 1991).

35. Barbara Nelson, *Making an Issue of Child Abuse: Political Agenda Setting for Social Problems* (Chicago: University of Chicago Press, 1984).

36. Lima, *Modelo de Atención,* 13.

37. Amalia Rivera, "Las reformas a la ley sobre delitos sexuales: Significado y perspectivas," *Doble Jornada* (6 August 1990): 12.

38. The Mexican Association Against Violence Toward Women, (COVAC) carried out an important opinion survey on these issues in 1995. One of their key findings was that the most frequent incidence of intrafamiliar violence was against children, with 61.2% suffering from either physical or emotional abuse. Abuse of mothers followed, with 20.9 percent of mothers suffering from such violence.

39. Cámara de Diputados del "LIV" Congreso de la Unión, "1 Para El Distrito Federal en Materia de Fuero Común y Para Toda La República en Materia de Fuero Federal. Iniciativa para Reformar el Título Décimoquinto 'Delitos Sexuales,' Capítulo I, Artículo 260 Bis, presentada por la C. Dip. Hilda Anderson Nevares de Rojas, a nombre de las Diputadas integrantes de la "LIV" Legislatura. Primer año, Sección Primera, Número 315, Comisión de Justicia. 28 de diciembre, 1988.

40. Lima, *Modelo de Atención,* 29.

41. Sara Lovera, "El movimiento feminista debe replantear estrategias: El coraje organizado, invaluable lección de jóvenes violadas," *Doble Jornada* (6 February 1990): 8–9.

42. Americas Watch, *Human Rights in Mexico: A Policy of Impunity* (New York: Human Rights Watch, 1990); *Americas Watch, Unceasing Abuses: Human Rights in Mexico One Year After the Introduction of Reform* (New York: Human Rights Watch, 1991).

43. Lovera, "El movimiento," 1990.

44. María de la Luz Lima Malvido, "Nota para tu archivo," letter to Asesora Jurídica del Procurador General de Justicia del Distrito Federal, 17 May 1990.

45. Lima, *Modelo de Atención*, 77.

46. Procuduría General de Justicia en el Distrito Federal, "Acciones." (Subprocuraduría de Atención a Víctimas y Servicios a la Comunidad. Dirección General de Atención a Víctimas de Delito: Mayo 1997); Barbara Yllan and Marta Torres, former directors of the Center for Therapy and Support (CTA), interview with Linda Stevenson at the Procuraduría General de la Republica, Mexico City, 21 January 1998.

47. Yllan and Torres, interview with Linda Stevenson, Republica, Mexico City, 21 January 1998.

48. An alternative thesis to the straight percentages is that the variable that better explains the change is the particular elite configuration of the women (and men sympathetic to women's issues) in and near to the deputies and senators elected, and their degree of feminist consciousness. Such analysis is beyond the scope of this work, but is included in the broader investigation of the topic.

49. Procuduría General de Justicia en el Distrito Federal.

50. Lima, Modelo de Atención, 257–62.

51. Araceli Yáñez Santamaría, *Avancemos un trecho: Por un compromiso de los partidos políticos a favor de las mujeres. Memorias del Foro* (Mexico City: Fundación Friedrich Ebert, 1997).

52. Patricia Mercado and Elena Tapia, "Primeras reflexiones de dos candidatas de la Coordinadora Feminista: La participación en las elecciones de agosto de 1991," *Doble Jornada* (2 September 1990): 3.

53. Amalia García Medina, interview with Linda Stevenson at the PRD office, Mexico City, July 1995.

54. Rosario Robles, interview with Linda Stevenson at the Cámara de Diputados, San Lazaro, Mexico City, July 1995.

55. Jennifer R. Accettola, "La Flor de un Sexenio: Women in Contemporary Politics" (Master's thesis, Tulane University, 1995).

56. As the PRI was the only party in government for more than sixty years, it is important to note that in Mexico's political culture, until recently, the boundaries between the PRI, government, and the state were quite blurred, if perceivable at all. Thus the expectation was that if the state was being criticized or threatened, the PRI could and would defend it through electoral or policy punishment or concessions.

57. Sara Lovera, personal communication, 10 October 1997.

58. Mercado and Tapia, "Primeras reflexiones."

59. Kathleen Bruhn, *Taking on Goliath: The Emergence of A New Left Party and the Struggle for Democracy in Mexico* (University Park: Penn State University Press, 1997).

60. Luz Rosales, interview with Linda Stevenson at the office of the Movimiento Ciudadana por la Democracia (MCD), Mexico City, 13 July 1995.

61. Thomas Carothers, "The Observers Observed," *Journal of Democracy* 8, no.3 (July 1997): 17–31; Neil Nevitte and Santiago A. Canton, "The Role of Domestic Observers," *Journal of Democracy* 8, no. 3 (July 1997): 47–61.

62. Susan B. Hansen, "Talking about Politics: Gender and Contextual Effects on Political Discourse," *Journal of Politics* (February 1997): 73–103.

63. Comision de Población y Desarrollo, "Resumen de conclusiones de la consulta legislativa, 'Una perspectiva sobre el desarrollo de la mujer' en Relación con la posición del pueblo de México frente a la Cuarta Conferencia Mundial de la Mujer en Beijing, China" (1995, mimeograph).

64. United Nations, *Beijing Declaration.*

65. María de los Angeles Moreno, former president of the Institutional Revolutionary Party (PRI), "An Agenda for the Future of Women in Mexican Political Life" (Presented at the Women in Contemporary Mexican Politics II: Participation and Affirmative Action conference at The Mexican Center of Institute for Latin American Studies, University of Texas at Austin, (12–13 April, 1996).

66. María Elena Chapa, "Partido Revolucionario Institutional, Congreso de Mujeres por el cambio: Propuesta de trabajo para 1996" (1997 mimeograph).

67. The text of the PRI's recommendation differs from that of the PRD as it does not specify which places on the electoral lists the women candidates should be. The PRD's mandate designates that at least every third place on the list should be occupied by a woman, so at least some women get elected even if the party may not do well. But in the other recommendations the party can put the women's names anywhere it decides— including at the botton of the list, so that the women candidates will only win positions if the party does well overall.

68. Federal Electoral Institute, *Código federal de instituciones y procedimientos electorales y otros ordenamientos electorales* (Mexico City: Instituto Federal Electoral, 1996).

69. Clara Jusidman de B., "Las mujeres: una mayoría tratada como minoría," *Este País* (September 1997): 16–19.

70. Sonia del Valle, "Las mujeres, pujantes protagonistas de cambios políticos fundamentales Parte II," in *Servicio Informativo de CIMAC* [electronic bulletin board] (Mexico City: CIMAC, August–September 1997): 1–4; available from cimac@laneta. apc.org, or http://www.cimac.org; INTERNET; Sonia del Valle, "En el norte se modifica la Constitución y en el sur el código electoral estatal: En Oaxaca y Chihuahua aprue ban el sistema de cuotas de representación para no exceder el 70% de un sólo sexo," *Servicio Informativo de CIMAC* [electronic bulletin board], (Mexico City: CIMAC, October 1997): 3–4; available from cimac@laneta.apc.org, or http://www.cimac.org, INTERNET.

71. As only a quarter of all the Senate seats were up for election in 1997, Table 3.3 has been added to show the numbers and percentages of the total Senate for the new legislative period. In total, 20 of the 128 seats are occupied by female senators, or 15.7 percent.

72. The *Asamblea Nacional de las Mujeres* was formed in October 1996 to try to work by consensus on the follow-up of the recommendations that came back from the Beijing conference; it is a key player in promotion of gender and equity issues in Mexican politics at many levels. This group has a special focus on support for gendered legislation and public policy in the Congress.

73. To Kingdon's metaphor of "streams" I would add the image of the policy entrepreneurs working to try to block or dam up certain flows of the tributary streams in order to make the three larger streams run together. Policy making does not occur "naturally."

74. Procuduría General de Justicia en el Distrito Federal, "Acciones."

75. John W. Sloan, *Public Policy in Latin America: A Comparative Survey* (Pittsburgh, Penn.: University of Pittsburgh Press, 1984).

76. Merilee S. Grindle, *Bureaucrats, Politicians, and Peasants in Mexico: A Case Study in Public Policy* (Berkeley and Los Angeles: University of California Press, 1977).

77. Sloan, *Public Policy in Latin America,* 148.

78. I plan to carry out interviews of people in the agencies, those they serve, and the proponents of the plans in order to deepen an evaluation of the implementation of the reforms in these agencies.

79. Juan Carlos Gamboa, "Media, Public Opinion Polls, and the 1994 Mexican Presidential Election, in *Polling for Democracy: Public Opinion and Political Liberalization in Mexico,* ed. Roderic Ai Camp (Wilmington, Del.: Scholarly Resources, 1996).

80. Tribunal Electoral del Poder Judicial de al Federación, *Instructivo de medios de impugnación jurisdiccionales* (Mexico City: Gama Sucesores, S. A. 1997).

81. María Luisa Tarrés, "Espacios privados para la participación pública. Algunas rasgos de las ONGs dedicadas a la mujer," *Estudios Sociologicos* XIV, no. 40 (Jan.–April 1996): 7–32.

82. Asamblea Nacional de Mujeres, meeting of assembly members with female Congressional deputies, 1 October 1997, in the Fonda Santa Anita, Mexico City.

4

THE RESURRECTION OF THE MEXICAN LEFT IN THE 1997 ELECTIONS

IMPLICATIONS FOR THE PARTY SYSTEM

Kathleen Bruhn

For many, the biggest surprise of the 1997 Mexican elections was not that the ruling Partido Revolucionario Institucional (PRI) lost Mexico City, or even that it failed to win a congressional majority for the first time since its foundation in 1929. Both possibilities had been discussed widely at least since the peso devaluation of 1994 accelerated the long-term decline in support for the PRI. However, the conservative National Action Party (PAN) expected to benefit most. In January 1997 observers still spoke of the left's challenge as "accumulating sufficient votes to maintain its role as third option."[1] Meanwhile, the PAN talked boldly about seizing a congressional majority, setting the stage for a PAN candidate to win the presidential election in 2000.[2]

Instead, the much maligned and often-dismissed Mexican left staged a dramatic comeback, second only to the watershed 1988 presidential election which first proved that the left could win popular support. The election also represented a personal comeback for the left's living icon: Cuauhtémoc Cárdenas. In 1987 Cárdenas bolted from the ruling party which his father had participated in founding, launched an independent campaign that mobilized unprecedented popular enthusiasm—and won 31% of the official vote. After the election, the Cardenistas merged

88

with the Mexican Socialist Party to create the Party of the Democratic Revolution (PRD), today the main party of the Mexican left. Yet Cárdenas's failure to defend the 1988 vote against fraud, compounded by his failure to get more than 17% in the much cleaner 1994 presidential election, left him a two-time loser, publicly discredited and unable to assume formal leadership in his party due to statutes prohibiting reelection to the party presidency. After the 1994 debacle, his own campaign press secretary wrote a tell-all book, arguing that Cárdenas should retire from politics and PRD leadership, acting only as a spiritual and moral leader to Perredismo.[3]

Thus, it was doubly sweet when the 1997 electoral returns began to come in, showing not only major advances for the PRD, but a personal victory for Cárdenas as the first-elected mayor of Mexico City. Riding his electoral coattails, the PRD won thirty-eight of the forty plurality districts in Mexico City's Asamblea de Representantes (the equivalent of a city council),[4] raised its share of the congressional vote from 16.2% in 1994 to 25.7%, and increased its share of congressional seats from 14.2% to 25%.[5] With 125 seats in the new Congress, the PRD displaced the PAN (with 122) as the largest opposition bench. Finally, when the four opposition parties with congressional seats banded together to oust the PRI from formal leadership of the Congress, they elected a PRD member, Porfirio Muñoz Ledo, as its first opposition head. In a single election, the PRD had won control of the top position in the Mexican Congress and the mayoral position considered so powerful and sensitive that it had been filled by presidential appointment for more than sixty years.

In this chapter I focus on the surprising resurrection of the left rather than the decline of the PRI per se, a task undertaken by Beatriz Magaloni's chapter. My question is this: Granted that such factors as the economic crisis, corruption scandals, the decay of corporatism, the lingering Chiapas crisis, and long-term voting trends had undermined the PRI, why did opposition voters unexpectedly reverse the pattern dominant since 1988 of supporting the PAN and vote for leftist candidates again? Although the PRD's rise did not bother Wall Street—Mexican stocks rose in the days after the election—it raises concerns about prospects for effective governance in a system experiencing divided government for the first time. Indeed, the Mexican Congress must not only function without a PRI majority but also with an opposition bench nearly equally divided between two parties on opposite sides of the ideological spectrum. This poses challenges more akin to European coalition building than to U.S. two-party divided government. However, most European countries in this position function under a parliamentary system (not a presidential system, like Mexico), and under electoral systems that have encouraged responsible, disciplined parties, which Mexico also lacks. The PRD in particular has a reputation for disorganization, divisions, and refusal to compromise, which makes it harder to predict a stable coalitional outcome.

On a more abstract level, the fact that the PRD could surge so quickly suggests the possibility of fundamental instability in the Mexican party system. The PRD's rise could indicate increasing polarization between conservative PAN voters and a radical left. It could also indicate high volatility, low partisan loyalty, and a weak ideological basis for voting. This might empty voting of its representational meaning, reward populist appeals, and put pressure on parties to bid up budgets in ways that undermine economic recovery.

On the other hand, the PRD's rise could result from ideological movement toward the center—a successful appeal to moderate voters. This would suggest much more positive conclusions about the Mexican party system: that existing incentives encourage centripetal competition and that parties respond to electoral preferences. This in turn suggests that the PRD's elevation to governing responsibility should further moderate the party, as it realizes that future electoral gains depend on convincing voters that it can govern effectively. Alternatively (or additionally), the PRD's improvement could reflect organizational development. The consolidation of the PRD as an institution would also augur well for its likely performance in Congress and coalitional reliability.

Thus, while no one can predict with certainty how the 1997 election will affect governance in Mexico, some clues may lie in sorting out the reasons for the resurrection of the left. One hypothesis points to organizational improvements making the PRD a more competitive party. A second hypothesis points to ideological change. The most likely versions of this story argue that either the PRD moved to the center, or the electorate moved left. If this ideological story is not compelling, one might look at voters' strategic reasons for choosing the PRD. A third hypothesis looks at how the dynamics of the party system affected campaign strategies. Finally, one could look at institutional reason for changing voting preferences, particularly the effects of electoral reforms.

In this chapter I examine these hypotheses and make four principal claims. First, while PAN strategies changed little, the PRD modified its positions and campaign strategies to attract voters that previously supported other parties, moving outside its loyal voter base more aggressively and effectively than in previous elections. Second, I found little evidence that ideological changes in the electorate explain PRD improvement. These two points suggest that the Mexican party system has not become substantially more polarized. However, there is indirect evidence of volatility and strategic voting, as well as personal response to Cárdenas over a less-appealing PAN candidate. The PRD success in 1997 probably represents less a mandate for the left or rejection of the PAN than confirmation of trends suggested in Domínguez and McCann: that, "the question of the ruling party's future was the central decision facing each voter. First and foremost, the voter asked, 'Am I for or against the PRI and the president?'"[6]

Third, and less promising, I found little evidence that the PRD changed organizationally, except in terms of campaign strategy. It still suffers from divisions, relatively low institutionalization, and personalism. Its strategy to attract outside allies left it with an odd coalition in both Congress and the Mexico City Asamblea. Some problems in cooperation and negotiation within the PRD can be expected due to lack of party identification and ideological differences among its elected officials.

Finally, improvements in PRD performance reflect system-level change, like the economic crisis, party system dynamics, and electoral reform. The economic crisis was a necessary condition for dramatic PRD improvement but not a sufficient one; between 1994 and 1997, the PAN received most of the protest vote. The success of electoral reform is a very positive sign for democracy, though more remains to be done.

The dynamics of the party system also led to generally positive results, though less clearly so. The PRI gambled that it could keep its congressional majority by splitting the opposition vote. Yet despite losing its majority, the PRI won many districts that it would have lost to a united opposition (a united PRD-PAN candidate would have beaten the PRI in 44 percent of the districts the PRI won in 1997), and it avoided the worst case scenario of a PAN majority.[7] The PRI now faces an opposition "majority" that is unlikely to hold together on major substantive issues because of ideological differences. As of this writing, the PRI has already split the majority once to pass—with PAN support—a budget which essentially follows presidential prescriptions. Thus, the PRI may keep the initiative and choose allies depending on the issue. The PRI congressional bench is nearly twice the size of its closest competitor, and it controls the Senate, which as in the United States must reject or approve initiatives passed in the lower house. President Zedillo used this weapon to block a reduction of the value added tax passed in December 1997 by the opposition majority in the Cámara de Diputados.[8] The split opposition may actually leave the Cámara *less* vulnerable to deadlock than if the PAN had won a larger share of the vote, since shifting majorities can form depending on the issue. This depends, however, on the ability of the PRI to hold together, the will to compromise, and the ability of opposition leaders to cooperate to seize the initiative. I address these points in the conclusion to this chapter.

AND LAZARUS CAME FORTH

The PRD's rise in 1997 was led by the effective campaign of Cárdenas for mayor of Mexico City. Close to 20 percent of Mexico's population lives in

Mexico City and its surrounding suburban zone, and 11.2 percent of the nation's registered voters live in Mexico City itself.[9] This magnifies the national impact of defeat—or victory—in Mexico City.

However, a careful examination of congressional district results reveals a surprisingly thorough defeat for the PRI—in stark contrast to 1988, when PRI candidate Carlos Salinas could still count on a massive (though partly fraudulent) rural vote to balance the sheer number of opposition votes in Mexico City, and even to the much cleaner 1994 election. Using the categorization developed by Gómez and Bailey,[10] district competitiveness rose dramatically in 1997, as Table 4.1 below shows.

In some ways, the 1997 election represents an even sharper departure than 1988. First, the number of opposition victories was much greater, due in part to the unification of the left in the PRD. In 1988 the parties that supported Cárdenas ran few joint candidates for the legislature and as a result lost many seats to the PRI in districts that Cárdenas won. Second, while the PRI still dominated more than a third of all districts in 1988, it fell below 70% in every district in 1997 and finished at least forty points ahead of its nearest rival in only three districts. Electoral competition is far from an exclusively urban phenomenon. Finally, the PRI faced competition from *more than one* party in nearly three-fourths of the districts it did win. In 19% of the districts, three parties won at least 20% of the vote each. This testifies not only to the impact of a revitalized left but also to the continuing strength of the PAN. In fact, the PAN won a higher percentage of the congressional vote in 1997 than in 1994 and qualified for two more seats. In any other year, the PAN's results would have been seen as a triumph, not a disappointment.

The tripartite nature of competition also shows up in analysis of the order of finish in electoral districts.[11] Since 1985, the PAN and PRD have grown at the expense of the PRI and the tiny parastatal parties which allied themselves with the PRI. The PAN, PRI, and PRD placed in the top three spots more than 90% of the time in both 1994 and 1997. However, the left went from placing first or second 5.3% of the time in 1985, to 30% of the time in 1994, and an astonishing 51.6% of the time in 1997. The PRI fell to third place in only eight districts in 1997 and remains the party to beat throughout Mexico.

Yet overall, the 1997 election left the PRI in even worse shape than in 1988. Meanwhile, and not coincidentally, the PRD found itself in its best position since 1988, and the PAN held its own. This came after years of admittedly self-serving PRI diagnoses which nevertheless won a fair degree of consensus: that the PRD had failed "basically for [being] incoherent, pretentious, obsessive, authoritarian, blackmailing, opportunistic, and worn out."[12] But who—or what—called Lazarus forth?

Table 4.1
Electoral Competitiveness: 1964–94
(Percentage of plurality electoral districts—N = 300)

Type of Competitiveness

Year	Monopoly	Strong Hegemony	Weak Hegemony	Two-party	Multiparty	Opposition Victory
1964	28.1	52.2	4.5	14.0	0	1.1
1967	24.2	61.2	3.6	9.7	0	1.2
1970	27.0	53.9	1.7	17.4	0	0
1973	18.7	51.3	4.1	21.8	1.0	3.1
1976	35.8	44.6	6.7	11.9	.5	.5
1979	9.4	48.0	12.3	6.3	22.7	1.3
1982	1.3	51.7	6.3	26.1	14.0	.3
1985	3.3	41.7	9.0	21.0	21.3	3.7
1988	1.0	19.0	15.0	8.3	34.0	22.7
1991	0	31.0	17.0	23.3	25.3	3.3
1994	0	2.3	8.3	26.0	55.3	8.0
1997	0	0	1.0	13.3	40.3	45.3

Classifications and figures for 1964–88 are from Gómez and Bailey (see note 10), as follows: monopoly, if PRI > 95%; strong hegemony if PRI < 95% but > 70%; weak hegemony if PRI < 70% but the difference between PRI and the second party is > 40 percentage points; two-party if PRI < 70%, the difference between PRI and the second party is < 40 percentage points, the second party > 25%, AND the third party < 10%; multiparty if the PRI < 70%, the difference between PRI and the second party is < 40 percentage points, but the second party < 25%, OR the third party > 10%. For 1988, opposition victories sum the votes of coalitions. 1991–97 figures calculated by author, from *Relación de los 300 distritos federales electorales* (Mexico City: IFE, 1991); *Elecciones federales 1994*; and *Elecciones federales 1997*.

THE ORGANIZATIONAL STORY

One could argue persuasively that the PRI is less effectively organized now than at any time in its post-1940 history, though this would not necessarily explain why PRI defectors should flock to the PRD rather than the PAN. It would be more difficult to claim that the PAN had become significantly less well organized between 1994 and 1997. The PAN has indeed had some trouble digesting the massive waves of new adherents and aspiring candidates, yet its institutional structure has largely survived. There is little reason for a party on the rise to introduce major reforms in organizational configuration.

This leaves the possibility that a better-organized, more institutionalized, and less-divided PRD simply put itself in a better position to compete with the PAN for wavering or alienated PRI voters. The PRD's lack of a strong party organization had caused many electoral problems.[13] Internal divisions probably cost the PRD its best chance at a governorship, in Michoacán in 1995. One contending candidate—Roberto Robles Garnica —complained that his rival—Cristóbal Arias—committed fraud to win the internal primary. Because both candidates had powerful allies at the national level, party committees designed to resolve electoral disputes failed to reach agreement on how to deal with the charges. Even after the national executive committee declared Arias the winner, largely because it was too late to hold another primary, Robles Garnica continued to challenge Arias publicly. Arias lost by just 6 percent. Robles Garnica took a position in the new PRI government. Countless similar examples could be cited, from Michoacán and Morelos to Chiapas and Veracruz. Voters were understandably skeptical that a party which could not conduct itself in an orderly way would govern effectively. Internal divisions also hindered attempts to develop more programmatic platforms, to conduct poll-watching activities, to organize campaigns, and to exercise power in government.[14]

If disorganization hurt the PRD in past elections, improved organization might explain improved electoral performance. Organizational reform could have helped the PRD conduct itself with more decorum and effectiveness, convincing voters that the PRD represented a viable alternative. Unfortunately, there is little evidence of significant organizational change between 1994 and 1997.[15] The features most relevant to *governmental* (rather than electoral) performance—including the structure of authority and decision making, the party's relations with popular movements, and its relations with its elected officials—changed least. Changes in the party's Regulations for Internal Elections did not affect the basic principles of election of candidates or party leaders. Thus, it is hard to trace changes in PRD behavior to changes in its rules and regulations.

Nevertheless, the balance of power changed within the party as a result of the conjunctural election of a new party president in 1996. This affected organization in 1997. To choose its president, the party held a national direct election involving more than 360,000 voters, instead of a convention of party leaders. This required elaborating a register of party members (mostly ignored in practice, since anyone could solicit membership and vote on the spot), as well as extensive national campaigning by all three candidates. The winner was a popular state leader and Cárdenas protege: Andrés Manuel López Obrador. Like all PRD presidents to date, the new president was a former PRI member, best known for leading confrontational mobilizations in his home state of Tabasco (against the governor and the oil company PEMEX). His election was seen as a victory for the radical wing of the PRD, against the moderate social democratic wing of his predecessor, Porfirio Muñoz Ledo. However, López Obrador presided over the biggest improvement in PRD electoral results since the party's foundation. In the first ten months after his election, the number of PRD municipalities increased nearly 50 percent, from 185 to 251.[16]

Was López Obrador primarily responsible for this? And more importantly for our purposes, did it result from organizational changes which improve prospects for good PRD performance in office? The answer to both questions is probably no. López Obrador did contribute to PRD electoral improvement, although results were already improving before he took office and would have improved no matter who led the party, especially with the Cárdenas campaign boost. His most important organizational innovation was the "Sun Brigades," which strongly resemble the "vote promoters" program operated by the PRI since 1991.[17] Both involve thousands of "volunteers" who canvass house-to-house, encourage people to register, and try to persuade them to vote for their respective parties. Eventually, the PRD claimed to employ 63,000 *brigadistas*.[18] The PAN, using a similar house-to-house program, employed 10,000 in Mexico City.[19] In conversations with this author, party activists in Mexico City credited the Sun Brigades with giving the PRD a kinder, gentler image among a population terrified by media portrayals of the PRD as a violent and antisocial party. The perceived success of this program will encourage the PRD to repeat it in future elections.

However, the Sun Brigades could not have been organized without the new funding made available by the 1996 electoral reform—a general system change.[20] The majority of brigade members were paid 600 pesos a month for their efforts, a respectable sum considering that full-time work at minimum wage would have paid approximately 792 pesos. Many were not PRD members. As PRD leader Amalia García noted, "the risk is that this structure is moved without the ethic that a commitment to a proposal implies; it is easily co-optable if someone pays more."[21] Moreover, the Sun Brigades have virtually no effect, positive or negative, on the PRD's ability to govern. They were not integrated into the party structure and largely disbanded once their electoral purpose ended.

Other strategies instituted by López Obrador, while they contributed to improved electoral results, do not represent genuine organizational innovations and depend heavily on an inevitably transient balance of power in the party. López Obrador won 75% of the vote in the internal election, giving his slate an overwhelming majority of the positions in the party's National Council. More than any previous party president, including Cárdenas, López Obrador could credibly threaten party sanctions against members who undermined electoral campaigns.[22] Similarly, he could offer more candidacies to defectors from the PAN and PRI, contributing substantially to

PRD electoral totals.[23] López Obrador's super-majority did not always prevent splits but did give him an edge. Meanwhile, the Sun Brigades blunted the damage losers could do by not cooperating with campaigns.

Nevertheless, most of these changes are not permanent. López Obrador's term ends in 1999, and he cannot run for reelection. The PRD is not institutionally committed to continue his strategies; to the extent it is informally committed, it has tried them before. In 1994, 50 percent of the party's candidacies were reserved for "external" candidates, and efforts were made to recruit defectors. But in 1994, the peso had not been devalued; Salinas had not been exposed to public contempt; and PAN candidate Diego Fernández had reduced Cárdenas to a distant third in the polls. The PRD's success in recruiting defectors in 1997 has more to do with the dynamics of the party system than with organizational change or López Obrador's persuasiveness.

More immediately, it is not clear that this strategy of candidate selection benefits the ability of the PRD to make collective decisions, to negotiate in parliament, or to govern. One must wonder whether the selection of candidates who defect from the PRI or PAN for short-term electoral gain contributes to the clarification of party programs, or party unity, or party morale. In the short run, it was electorally profitable. The PRD vote in Campeche nearly doubled after it named as its candidate for governor Layda Sansores, daughter of a prominent PRI family that had run Campeche for generations. The PRD's second most popular congressional candidate in 1997 (after the oldest son of Cárdenas) is the son of the corrupt petroleum workers' union leader Joaquin "La Quina" Hernández.[24] But in the long run, this may add to confusion between the PRD and the PRI.

The PRD also remains essentially the same party in organizational (or *dis*-organizational) terms, particularly in areas relevant to governing: party cooperation and effectiveness. In Mexico City, although Cárdenas will have a majority in the Asamblea, he may find his own party nearly as troublesome as the "opposition." When the PRD held internal elections to choose Asamblea candidates, such severe conflicts erupted that in one district, the party could not agree on a candidate until all but thirteen of the seventy-five days of the formal campaign had passed.[25] After the election, efforts to choose the leader of the PRD bench by consensus ended in failure. The PRD delegation includes at least three significant factions.[26] Few PRD *asambleistas* have any previous legislative experience; many come from movements with divergent agendas, including unions and neighborhood associations. Many do not belong to the PRD. Cárdenas will have to rely on his personal stature to persuade these diverse groups to support his proposals.

Similarly, the selection of Porfirio Muñoz Ledo as the PRD parliamentary coordinator reveals how divisions could affect performance in Congress. Muñoz Ledo was the clear front-runner to become coordinator, given his legislative experience, intelligence, and forceful personality.[27] However, he represents a minority faction within the national leadership, opposed to the faction of López Obrador and Cárdenas.[28] This not only made his selection more problematic but also may endanger cooperation within the parliamentary delegation, many of whom support the majority faction. The PRD also reserved 40 percent of its district candidacies and 12.5 percent of its PR list for non-PRD members.[29] Such *diputados* have even less loyalty to the PRD leader. Muñoz Ledo's selection as coordinator took place only after negotiation among party currents named a member of the Cárdenas/López Obrador group as vice-coordinator. This institutionalized a dual leadership and is eloquent witness to continuing divisions in the PRD.

Thus, even if organizational changes contributed to PRD success in the election, they may not enhance its effectiveness in Congress or the Mexico City Asamblea.

THE IDEOLOGICAL STORY

A second possibility is that the 1997 electoral results reflect ideological shifts, either by the parties, or the electorate. Yet the 1997 PRI electoral platform displays basic continuity with the principles of the Salinas administration, and the PAN had already made ideological moderation a reality by 1994. In both 1994 and 1997 the PAN declared itself in favor of a "human economy" based on the liberty of the individual, strong, efficient, and honestly managed public finances, price stability, and state investment in human capital.[30] The 1997 PAN platform criticizes the effects of debt, but neither its 1994 nor its 1997 platform spares more than a passing mention for NAFTA. Based on these platforms, neither the PRI nor the PAN seems to have shifted its ideological position dramatically.

This leaves the PRD. Did the PRD proposal change, becoming either more moderate (to capture voters in the center) or more radical (to take advantage of disillusionment with NAFTA)? In fact, the PRD seems to have moved toward the center; as the cover of the journal *Proceso* nostalgically remarked after the election: "On the path of pragmatism: PRD—Farewell to the left."[31] Conservative analysts of the 1997 platforms (like the Group of Associated Economists and the Financial Group Banamex-Accival—not big fans of the PRD) found "great coincidence of the PRI, PAN and PRD," with differences "only of emphasis," in their economic policies.[32] Where the PRD's 1994 electoral platform demanded renegotiation of NAFTA to exclude basic grains, permit Mexico to establish tariffs in defense of national sovereignty, revise the rules of origin (in textiles and auto parts), and exclude foreign control of transport and financial services, the 1997 platform quietly dropped these specific demands, leaving only the vague need to eliminate clauses that impede state support of agricultural or industrial productivity.[33] Cárdenas made an effort to reassure conservatives that his election would not hurt them. Not only did he meet at least a dozen times with members of the business sector [34] but also he pointedly did *not* visit Zapatista strongholds to embrace guerrilla rebels as he did in 1994; as analyst Jorge Castañeda remarked, "unlike the 1994 presidential elections . . . this year the leftist party would not touch Marcos with a 10-foot pole."[35]

Overall, the extent of ideological change from 1994 to 1997 is probably less than the change in Cárdenas's campaign style. In both 1994 and 1997, the PRD proposed to renegotiate the public debt and parts of NAFTA, to create jobs, to restore land reform, to encourage saving and investment, and to stimulate business. Cárdenas denies that he modified his ideological position, saying that what changed was the "political context."[36] He maintained rhetorical support for the Zapatistas, and participated in a Zapatista-sponsored forum in the summer of 1996 with Subcomandante Marcos. Public distancing between the party and the rebels was largely the result of rebel decisions, particularly their decision to boycott the 1997 election. Moreover, as a mayoral candidate in Mexico City, Cárdenas did not have to campaign in Chiapas or address the Zapatista question, which he clearly had to do in 1994 as a presidential candidate. The effectiveness of the PRD effort to appear more moderate had as much to do with this context as programmatic movement.

Nevertheless, the PRD did reach out to moderate voters. Its behavior suggests systemic limits to the "confrontationalism" that worried many observers of the Mexican party system during the Salinas *sexenio*. The PRD behaved according to legal norms when it expected rewards. This suggests that the PRD possesses the political will to become a more "prosystem" party if it senses that voters will reward them.[37]

I found much less evidence that the electorate has shifted to the left. Rather, there is indirect evidence of volatility and ideological flexibility. Where a candidate emerged with clear prospects of defeating the PRI, bandwagoning occurred. In this context, the charisma and attributes of candidates became important.

Vote volatility at the macro level has risen in Mexico since 1982 (see Table 4.2). Due to redistricting in 1996, it is impossible to compare 1994 and 1997 results directly to see how voting patterns changed within districts. However, an acceptable alternative at the national level is Pederson's index of volatility, identified as "the cumulated gains for all winning parties in the party system."[38] Using this index, Mainwaring and Scully put Mexico in the middle among Latin American nations in terms of volatility, though still higher than all established European party systems prior to 1977 except France.[39]

Table 4.2
Electoral Volatility in Mexico: 1982–97

	Lower-Chamber seats (A)	Congressional vote (B)	Mean volatility (A+B)/2
Mean volatility 1982–91[a]	22.4	18.5	20.4
Volatility 1991–94	14.0	18.0	16.0
Volatility 1994–97	12.8	12.6	12.7
Mean volatility 1991–97	13.4	15.3	14.4
Mean volatility 1982–97	15.7	17.2	16.5

Sources: Scott Mainwaring and Timothy Scully, *Building Democratic Institutions: Party Systems in Latin America* (Stanford: Stanford University Press, 1995), 8; Instituto Federal Electoral, *Relación de los 300 distritos federales electorales* (Mexico City: IFE, 1991); IFE, *Elecciones federales 1994: Resultados definitivos según los cómputos distritales* (Mexico City: IFE, 1994); IFE, *Elecciones federales 1997: Resultados de la elección de diputados federales por el principio de mayoría relativa* (Mexico City: IFE, 1997).
[a] Mainwaring and Scully calculate mean vote volatility from 1982–91 on the basis of presidential vote. This exaggerates volatility from 1982–91, since it includes only two elections—one of which was the extraordinary 1988 election. To capture changes on a smaller scale, I recalculated mean volatility, using valid congressional vote, for the 1982–91 period. Thus, I find an average volatility of 18.5%, instead of the 32.2% they reported. Like Mainwaring and Scully, I treat the FDN as a new party in 1988, but consider the PRD the heir of the FDN and treat the PARM, PPS, and PFCRN as separate parties in 1991. As they note, if these parties were added to the PRD in 1991, volatility would be lower for the 1988–91 period. I use their calculations for lower-chamber seats from 1982–91.

One must put this level of volatility in perspective. On the one hand, there is clearly substantial overall stability in the party system.[40] The average of 20% for the 1982–91 period is driven almost entirely by a single election (1988). At levels of roughly 14%, characteristic of the post-91 period, Mexico would fall farther toward the "stable" end of Mainwaring and Scully's ordering of Latin American party systems; only Uruguay and Colombia have smaller average volatility.[41] On the other hand, this was enough to deprive the PRI of its congressional majority in 1997 and to swing many elections. It contrasts strongly to the level of volatility registered between 1982 and 1985, before Cárdenas: a sluggish 3.5%. Such low volatility is not necessarily a good thing: democracy requires at least *some* unpredictability of results.

Volatility could also indicate a critical realignment, in which the social bases of political parties change fundamentally.[42] But was this the case in Mexico? More specifically, did the economic crisis cause a *left* reaction? Did voters blame NAFTA for their economic woes, remember that Cárdenas had criticized NAFTA, and reward him? It seems quite likely that the open hostility between Cárdenas and Salinas—which hurt Cárdenas in 1994, when Salinas enjoyed high approval ratings—stood him in good stead in 1997, when Salinas had become the scapegoat for all the broken promises. And it is true that Cárdenas criticized NAFTA.

However, prior to 1997, most electoral protest—even after the peso crisis—continued to benefit the PAN, which not only supported NAFTA, but cooperated with Salinas to pass many key reforms. In the state of Mexico, for example, the PAN won 30% of the vote as recently as the November 1996 local elections, compared to 21.6% for the PRD. In 1997 percentages reversed: the PAN won 20% of the vote, and the PRD 34.2%.[43] It strains credibility to argue that in less than twelve months, voters suddenly experienced a leftist conversion. Strategic calculations and/or coattail effects from the Cárdenas campaign account better for this change.

The Cárdenas campaign itself shows traces of strategic voting. In January 1997 polls predicted a PAN victory. In March, depending on which poll one believed, either the PAN or PRD narrowly led the opposition; the PRI's support had risen only a few percentage points. In May polls uniformly reported a PRD advantage over the PAN of between 6.6% and 25.8%; the PRI held steady. By June no poll reported the PRD with an advantage of less than 19%. Meanwhile, the PRI's numbers were virtually identical to its January results.[44] This suggests a gradual shift of opposition support from the PAN to the PRD. Lawson's panel study (in this volume) finds a more even shift of voters from both the PRI and PAN toward the PRD. In either case, the short period of the shift does not suggest intellectual enlightenment but more mundane factors like campaign styles and candidate personalities. Even on July 6, an exit poll conducted by the newspaper *Reforma* found that 44% of PRD voters identified "little or nothing" with the PRD, approximately the same percentage as those who voted for the PAN (but did not identify with it) and the PRI.[45] What united most voters was their consensus that the PRI had to go: in one poll, 68% of Mexico City citizens thought it would be better for the opposition to win, though this did not determine for whom they would vote.[46] Again, underlying stability appears—approximately half of all voters for the PRD, PAN, and PRI identified "a lot" with the party for which they voted—but enough volatility remains to change election results.[47]

Chapters by Lawson, Poiré, Magaloni, and Moreno deal more directly with the potential linkages between ideology and party support. However, my own evidence—mostly supported by theirs—suggests that the rise of the PRD does not reflect a serious polarization of the Mexican electorate. Rather, it suggests that the PRD reached out to moderate voters, while much of the electorate responded either out of previous party loyalties, candidate preferences, or strategic calculations about how to beat the PRI.

Although Mexican parties may remain more ideologically divided than their North American counterparts, there is little reason to suspect that any party has a vested interest in legislative breakdown, or that ideological interests are so incompatible as to prevent cooperation. This conclusion is bolstered by declarations from the PRD leadership that, "the great lesson of the election [is that] the citizens do not give unconditional support to anyone. If we give them good government in the Federal District and as a party we represent the citizens with dignity, we will keep on succeeding; if not, we will fail."[48]

However, if voters do not respond to ideology, they may respond to factors that do not necessarily bolster the stability of the party system, such as personalism or populist promises. Parties may find themselves in a bidding war for voter support, putting pressure on economic policy making. If one assumes that Mexico's dependence on the IMF will prevent serious budget excesses, the risk of economic destabilization falls, but the risk of political destabilization may grow, as voters become convinced that politicians cannot or will not keep their promises. Party loyalties and even support for democracy could suffer.

Finally, there is a danger that Mexico will prefer demagogues with charisma to parties with programs. The most obvious feature of the successful Cárdenas campaign was the name and personality of Cárdenas himself. Despite a notorious reputation for wooden presentations, Cárdenas has the magic name and reflected glory of his father, Lázaro Cárdenas, one of Mexico's most revered presidents. Cárdenas also kept the trust of a large sector of the Mexican public by refusing to soften toward Salinas even when the rest of the world thought him nearly perfect. In person, Cárdenas can be warm and charming and treats the humblest with respect. Mexico City voters clearly found those characteristics appealing. Nevertheless, strongly personalistic campaigns may undermine the principle that democratic choice should translate voter preferences into policy. It is not clear what—if anything—such candidates "represent." While this does not necessarily endanger governability, it may lead to less effective representation, disillusionment with the performance of expected saviours, and eventual alienation from politics.

THE STRATEGIC STORY

The national and international press attention given to the Cárdenas campaign boosted the profile of PRD candidates nationwide and had important coattail effects on other candidates, partly because of a weak tradition of ticket-splitting.[49] In Mexico City, Cárdenas won 48%; PRD congressional candidates won 45%. The twenty-nine congressional districts won by the PRD in Mexico City account for more than 40% of the total majority districts it won in 1997. In other states, awareness that Cárdenas was likely to win the mayor's race made the PRD seem a more viable alternative than in 1994, when Cárdenas trailed badly. Thus, as it has since 1988, the left depended heavily on Cárdenas to win popular support. In 1997 Cárdenas finally won, and this helped the PRD succeed as well.

Yet clearly, the "Cárdenas magic" is not always sufficient to guarantee results. In 1994 Cárdenas won no districts in Mexico City. He came in third to the candidates of both the PAN and PRI in all but one district. What changed in 1997? One key factor, of course, was the economic crisis. However, this did not mean that Cárdenas would automatically receive the support of voters angry at the PRI. Most observers assumed that the PAN would get these votes, as it did in 1995 and 1996.

Instead, strategic campaign decisions played a decisive role. Ironically, one factor that helped the PRD was the PAN's rise. In the first place, the PAN's string of local victories had left it in the less enviable position of having to defend the record of PAN governments, which had naturally made some mistakes. The PRD had little to defend. In the second place, the PAN's rise posed a direct threat to PRI control of the Congress. During the 1988–94 period, in contrast, the PRD, and especially Cárdenas, seemed to pose the bigger threat. In 1988 Cárdenas raided the PRI's own bases. More to the point, he nearly defeated Carlos Salinas, while the PAN had never threatened the PRI at the national level. As a result, Salinas tried hard to undermine the PRD, even as he accepted PAN victories. Elsewhere, I have argued that this effort was intended to channel protest votes away from the dangerous left—a goal in which the PAN coincided.[50] But by 1997 most observers felt that the PAN presented the more serious threat to the PRI.

This threat helps explain the PRI's willingness to exclude the PAN candidate from a televised mayoral debate held in late May 1997. Cárdenas demanded this for obvious reasons. He is a poor debater, and his stiff demeanor tells against him on television. He also hoped to avoid a repetition of the disastrous 1994 presidential debate, when—before a national television audience—PAN presidential candidate Diego Fernández de Cevallos vigorously attacked Cárdenas and his past in the PRI. After the debate, Cárdenas fell from second to third place in the polls, where he stayed.[51] He was determined not to let the PAN and PRI gang up on him again. He also took the 1997 debate more seriously, prepared more thoroughly, and performed much better.

Meanwhile, the PRI could position Cárdenas as the real alternative to the PRI in Mexico City by accepting the exclusion of the PAN from the debate. This had the foreseeable effect of siphoning away support from the PAN in the largest electoral jackpot in the country. Mexico City contains 10 percent of all majority districts. Even if they went to the PRD; losing them left the PAN in worse position to grab control of Congress.[52]

The PAN, meanwhile, selected a candidate who proved a much easier mark for Cárdenas than the charismatic and dynamic Diego Fernández de Cevallos, whom he faced in 1994.[53] It is unclear why Fernández de Cevallos declined to run for mayor. However, once he dropped out, the PAN fell back on its immediate past president, a Yucatán native widely hailed for his effective party leadership. Although a gifted writer who contributes frequently to national newspapers, Carlos Castillo Peraza never really caught on with the people of Mexico City, many of whom do not read the papers. His acerbic and intellectual style does not have the common touch, and he sometimes comes off in public appearances like Richard Nixon under attack: rigid, defensive, and acidic. He also chose rather strange issues, including one diatribe against condoms as—of all things—an *environmental* problem (the disposal of so much latex). By the end, even the PAN gave up on Castillo Peraza. In the last week of the campaign, the PAN spent "not one cent" promoting his image; evidently, they did not expect to enhance the PAN vote by reminding voters that he was the candidate. Meanwhile, the PRD spent more than a third of its money promoting Cárdenas.[54]

Political learning in the PRD also led to changes in the party's campaign strategy. Three decisions in 1994 had attracted the most critical attention as responsible for the PRD's disappointing showing: the debate, the decision to visit Marcos in the jungle, and an unsophisticated campaign style which focused on hundreds of rallies in small towns while virtually ignoring mass media as a way of reaching voters. I have already discussed how the PRD changed the impact of the first two factors (by limiting and better preparing for the debate, and by avoiding Marcos); the third deserves some elaboration as well.

According to Adolfo Aguilar Zínser, media coordinator for the 1994 Cárdenas campaign, Cárdenas at first agreed to use polls and media consultants in 1994, but quickly reverted to a more comfortable style after his dismal performance in the debate. Cárdenas disliked the notion of "tailoring" his speeches to what polls suggested the public wanted to hear and felt uncomfortable on television.[55] Instead, he focused on rallies in small-town plazas, which had worked in 1988 to attract attention despite a virtual media blackout. High attendance at PRD rallies led Cárdenas to believe that going "full out [to mobilize] his fundamental base of support," would—as in 1988—bring success.[56] However, this meant abandoning the majority, which did not attend rallies, to the more sophisticated mass media campaigns of the PRI and the PAN. Cárdenas also attracted criticism for his somber demeanor. Much of the blame for these problems fell on Cárdenas, who controlled his own campaign team largely without interference from the party leadership.

In 1997 Cárdenas again coordinated his own campaign but had learned some valuable lessons. The change that attracted the most comment was undoubtedly the success of Cárdenas's handlers in getting their candidate to smile, frequently, and in public. The campaign material was also more upbeat. All over the city, one could see posters bearing the smiling face of Cárdenas and the slogan. "Now it's time for the sun to come out." As Moreno's chapter notes, this was by far the most memorable slogan of any of the three campaigns, at least in terms of correctly identifying the party with its slogan, probably in part because of its reference to the "sun"—the PRD symbol, which appears on all electoral ballots. Moreover, in contrast to 1994, the party invested more than 70 percent of its media resources in 1997 in professionally produced radio and television spots.[57] The PRD used focus groups and private polls to test the penetration and design of its electoral campaign, selecting three themes that got the most response to focus their advertising.[58] Its ads strongly attacked both the PRI and the PAN, while associating the PRD with light, peaceful images to counteract popular images of the party as violent and disorderly. The PRD used the Sun Brigades to spread this message on videotapes and in printed literature in Mexico City neighborhoods. Where Cárdenas told his campaign adviser in 1994, "we're going on instinct," party leaders in 1997 talked about the lesson, "There is no room for improvisation . . . we decided to give the specialists an opportunity."[59] And—according to Lawson's chapter—people's image of the PRD did change.

If these factors did play a role in the PRD's improvement in 1997, what are the implications for governability and the party system? First, I think, there is encouraging evidence of learning. Not all of the PRD's choices were "democratic." The exclusion of the PAN from the mayoral debate stands out as a strategically wise but not particularly democratic outcome. Nevertheless, for a party which had been viewed as incorrigibly confrontational, this showed clearly that the PRD does respond to electoral incentives.

Second, as the PRI tried to achieve its objectives by splitting the opposition (here, by encouraging Cárdenas to split the opposition vote), it seems likely to behave similarly in Congress: working with different parties on issues where the PRI has greater coincidence with one opposition party than the opposition parties have with each other. They might cooperate, for instance, with the PRD on social reform and the PAN on economic issues.

However, party dynamics also suggest that incentives for cooperation clash with incentives for confrontation. On the one hand, both the PRD and PAN have been skeptical about a permanent opposition coalition, for reasons that go well beyond their ideological differences. In an environment where they compete with each other for anti-PRI votes, they cannot afford too close an association. PRD advertising made a great deal of political hay out of cooperation between the PAN and PRI during the Salinas *sexenio*, as "proof" that the PAN did not constitute a genuine alternative to the PRI. On the other hand, both parties see the PRI as their ultimate rival and have incentives to take advantage of anti-PRI sentiment by confronting the government. Shifting coalitions represent the most viable solution to these dual incentives, permitting all parties successively to cooperate and confront their rivals. However, although the general desire to avoid total breakdown should limit clashes to some extent, internal party conflicts could cause problems for all three parties and make shifting coalitions less than smooth.

THE INSTITUTIONAL STORY

Many of these changes in campaign style would have been impossible without the electoral reform passed in 1996. The 1996 Código Federal de Instituciones y Procedimientos Electorales (COFIPE) contained far-reaching reforms negotiated by the three major parties, including the first direct election of Mexico City's mayor. Minority access to the Senate expanded via the introduction of thirty-two proportional representation seats.[60] The composition of the General Council of the IFE also changed, further limiting PRI influence and removing the interior secretary, a presidential appointee, as titular head of the IFE.[61] These changes enhanced the credibility and impartiality of the electoral process, though some complained that the IFE's local and regional structure was, according to one electoral councillor, "the same as when we arrived," and that as a result, "the citizens have formal control of the elections in the General Council ... but the execution of its tasks is in the hands of personnel linked in many ways to the government."[62]

The 1997 COFIPE also dramatically expanded access to radio and television and increased the public financing available to parties. In 1997, as in 1994, each party got the right to fifteen minutes of television time and fifteen minutes of radio time per month. In 1994, this increased during electoral periods, "proportional to [each party's] electoral force," giving the PRI more than half of the additional time.[63] In contrast, the 1997 COFIPE provides 250 *hours* of radio time and 200 *hours* of television time for parties during a presidential campaign and half that amount for congressional elections. Parties without representation in the Congress can use up to 4 percent of this time; of the rest, 30 percent must be distributed *equally* among all parties, while the other 70 percent is distributed proportionally. In addition, the IFE can distribute up to ten thousand promotional spots on radio and four hundred on television, lasting twenty seconds each, until it has spent the equivalent of 12 percent of the total public financing for parties.[64] This still gives an advantage to the PRI. Regular news coverage, while more equal in terms of time than in the past, also tends to favor the PRI. Nevertheless, the new law represents a huge advance in opposition access to mass media.

A more complex and contentious issue was the amount of public financing for political parties. Both the 1994 and 1997 electoral codes specify that total public financing is based on IFE calculations of the "minimum costs of a campaign." However, in 1994, 20 percent of public financing went to parties in the first year after an election, 30 percent in the second year, and 50 percent in the third year, when the next federal election would take place. In 1997 this provision disappears. Instead, annual funding for the "ordinary, permanent activities" of the parties is based on extraordinary campaign expenditures. During an election year, this doubles, to cover campaign expenses.[65] In addition, the IFE naturally relies on the parties for estimates of the cost of a campaign. In 1997 the parties negotiated a price to propose to the IFE, but at the last minute, the PRI proposed a much higher amount based on figures from the 1994 election, even though the 1997 election did not involve a presidential campaign. For opposition parties, an additional carrot was a change in the distribution of funding, from completely to partially proportional, in a formula identical to the distribution of media time. As a smaller party, the PRD benefited more than the PAN from this new less proportional distribution of funds. Nevertheless, the PAN and PRD both opposed the increase.[66] The PRI approved the proposal alone, raising the cost from 2.5 pesos per registered voter to 20.

This led to huge increases in public financing for parties. The PAN, for example, received 70 million pesos in 1996 from public sources; in 1997, it got 520 million pesos.[67] The PRD expected to receive 388 million pesos— more than three times the *total* public financing it received from 1989–96.[68] They planned to spend some of it on a fund for the families of assassinated PRD activists, some on new textbooks which they distributed free in PRD *municipios,* and some on scholarships and small business credits. Many of these programs had electoral implications not unlike the "Solidarity" expenditures of the Salinas government. The rest of the money went to pay for professional ad campaigns, television time, private polls and focus groups, and programs like the Sun Brigades. Thus, improvements in PRD campaign strategies depended heavily on the financial base offered by institutional change. The PAN also rejected some of its allotted subsidy, but returned it to the government instead of spending it on constituent service, like the PRD.

Finally, although it had little to do with electoral results in 1997, I cannot end without referring to another institutional story: the story of how congressional and municipal institutions may tie the hands of the newly elected opposition representatives. This subject deserves a more extended analysis than I can undertake here. Yet it is worth remembering that the weakness of Congress did not result entirely from PRI control. Its new leaders swiftly found they would have to rewrite congressional regulations designed for a PRI majority. Congress lacks adequate staffing and research support because it was never considered necessary for PRI legislators to duplicate the work of the executive. Constitutional prohibitions against re-election also make it difficult for legislators to accumulate experience. In municipal government, lack of resources, authority, and trained personnel make many opposition experiences frustrating. Local governments need the tolerance or aid of higher levels to perform well. When help is lacking, an administration may fail to convince voters to support the opposition in the next election. Innovative governments with party-building strategies can get around these constraints. However, municipal government chal-lenges the credibility of the opposition as an alternative.

Few *municipios,* if any, present quite the challenge of Mexico City. The city's critical problems include rising crime, pollution, joblessness, housing and service deficits, and a decaying transportation infrastructure. No municipal government could possibly hope to resolve all these problems, even given adequate resources and authority, which the Cárdenas govern-ment certainly will not have. The best he can hope for is success in a few high-profile programs and avoidance of major missteps. The danger for him, and the PRD, is that his victory has raised expectations which even limited successes cannot meet.

CONCLUSIONS

Underlying all of these stories is the economic crisis which probably turned many voters against the PRI. In 1991, and even in 1994, many voters believed that despite growing dissatisfaction with Mexican "democracy," the PRI remained the best option for managing economic policy. The com-bination of economic recovery and PRI governing experience (particularly contrasted with opposition inexperience) proved too strong for risk-averse voters, as Cinta's chapter suggests. Barely a month after the 1994 election, the murder of a top PRI official revived concerns, first sparked by the assas-sination of the PRI's presidential candidate in March, that the PRI was dis-integrating internally. Even so, not until massive peso devaluation of December 1994 did many voters lose confidence in the government's com-petence. Almost immediately, PRI support suffered a drastic decline. The economic crisis (or a similar discrediting of the PRI) was probably a neces-sary condition for the PRD's rise. However, it was not sufficient. As late as November 1996, the *PAN* got the benefit of the so-called "punishment vote." My chapter has tried to analyze the bases of this second surprise and their implications for governability in Mexico.

I find hopeful signs in the evidence examined here. First, there is little evidence that polarization has increased dramatically. Instead, the PRD seems to have moved toward the center, a factor which may account in part for its improved electoral results. None of the parties has demonstrated a desire to provoke breakdown in the institutional order. Second, strategic dynamics in the party system tend to encourage shifting coalitions rather than fixed, polarized coalitions. Third, although electoral volatility has increased enough to change electoral outcomes, it has not reached the extreme levels characteristic of highly unstable party systems. Fourth, electoral reforms helped reorient party strategies and reduce confrontational behavior.

More troubling signs also turn up, however. The first and most important is the relative lack of institutional and organizational consolidation in the major parties. According to one commentator, "for the party system to be stable . . . it is necessary for the PRI, PAN and PRD to be equally stable. In short, the system cannot be stable if its parts are not. . . . Everything indicates that none of the three major parties can be characterized as stable."[69] I would not go this far; I think system stability is consistent with substantial internal disorder in the political parties. However, disorder in the major parties may undermine incentives toward coalition building and hurt performance in government. In order to build shifting legislative coalitions, for example, the parties will have to hold together as delegations. Even in the PRI—which has far more mechanisms of internal control—the recent rebellion of a group of PRI senators demanding more influence over parliamentary strategy demonstrates that this may not be easy.

Second, although electoral reform has helped, it still falls short of establishing conditions for free and fair elections.[70] Equally important, institutional norms do not yet give opposition governments sufficient tools to implement independent policy. Further reform could enhance the parties' ability and incentive to provide effective government.

Finally, there is a tendency toward personalism and populism. At the local level, most investors have concluded that this cannot harm macroeconomic policy, which is probably true. Yet even if one assumes that no Mexican government under the supervision of the IMF can follow in the footsteps of Alan García, the former Peruvian president, it seems to me that a pattern of pledging results that cannot be delivered could pose a danger to the credibility and legitimacy of democracy. One can already see in the antiparty, antipolitics discourse of groups like the Zapatistas and many popular movements the seeds of a rejection of all parties and politicians, not just the PRI. Representative democracy can certainly withstand some level of personalism, populism, and broken promises. However, in the long term, if it becomes a persistent pattern, in the context of a severe backlog of social demands, frustration seems likely to rise. When the PRI/anti-PRI division is eventually superseded—perhaps if the PRI loses the presidency in 2000—the importance of this factor may rise.

NOTES

1. Jorge Alcocer V., "El olmo del PAN, las peras del PRD," *Proceso,* no. 1053 (5 January 1997): 38.

2. See, for example, Alvaro Delgado, Fernando Mayolo López, Raúl Monge, and Francisco Ortíz Pinchetti, "Diversos, democraticos, anticentralistas, perseverantes, los panistas sienten que está por llegar el tiempo de la cosecha," *Proceso,* no. 970 (5 June 1995): 20, 22–27.

3. Adolfo Aguilar Zinser, *¡Vamos a ganar! La pugna de Cuauhtémoc Cárdenas por el poder* (Mexico City: Oceano, 1995), 467.

4. Cecilia González, "'Salen' pluris de ALDF," *Reforma* (Mexico City), 8 July 1997: 3B.

5. *Elecciones federales 1994: Elección de diputados federales por el principio de mayoría relativa* (Mexico City: IFE, 1994); *Elecciones federales 1997: Resultados de la elección de diputados federales por el principio de mayoría relativa* (Mexico City: IFE, 1997); Mireya Cuellar and Nestor Martinez, "Profundas Inequidades," *La Jornada,* 23 October 1994: A1.

6. Jorge I. Domínguez and James A. McCann, "Shaping Mexico's Electoral Arena: The Construction of Partisan Cleavages in the 1988 and 1991 National Elections," *American Political Science Review* 89, no. 1 (March 1995): 41; also see Jorge I. Domínguez and James A. McCann, *Democratizing Mexico: Public Opinion and Electoral Choices* (Baltimore: Johns Hopkins University Press, 1996).

7. Calculations by author, from *Elecciones federales 1997.*

8. The value added tax (IVA) was raised from 10 to 15 percent shortly after the peso crisis, in order to raise funds for a cash-strapped government and to encourage savings. The highly unpopular measure became one of the opposition's most effective campaign issues—both the PAN and PRD promised to lower the IVA if elected. However, Zedillo rejected even their compromise proposal of a reduction to 12 percent as dangerous to continued economic recovery. The PRI-controlled Senate obediently blocked the initiative.

9. *Elecciones federales 1997.*

10. Leopoldo Gómez and John Bailey "La transición política y los dilemas del PRI," *Foro Internacional 31,* no. 121 (July–Sept. 1990): 57–87.

11. All calculations based on official voting results, from the Registro Nacional de Electores (1985) and the Instituto Federal Electoral (1991–97).

12. See Francisco Gil Villegas M., "¿Por qué ganó el PRI?" *Examen,* no. 64 (September 1994): 9.

13. Kathleen Bruhn, *Taking on Goliath: The Emergence of a New Left Party and the Struggle for Democracy in Mexico* (University Park: Penn State University Press, 1997).

14. For specific examples of all these phenomena, see Bruhn, *Taking on Goliath.*

15. The only modification to the party's relationship to its elected officials was a requirement fixing their minimum dues at 10 percent of their salary (previously, the statutes required only "a significant quota"). Other modifications included the requirement that party executive committees have at least one member under thirty; the creation of a "youth wing"; expansion of the National Executive Committee from fifteen to twenty-one members; and a requirement that 30 percent of public financing received by the national party be transferred to states, and 50 percent of public financing of state parties be transferred to municipal committees. With expanded state financing from the 1996 electoral reform, all levels of the party ended up with more money than before despite this change. See *Estatutos y reglamentos* (Mexico City: PRD, 1996).

16. Miguel Angel Juárez, "Supervisará PRD a sus munícipes," *Reforma* (Mexico City), 10 July 1997: 6A.

17. He first implemented the concept in local elections in Tabasco, encouraged the expansion of the Sun Brigades to all 300 electoral districts (from 150 "priority districts" originally planned), and monitored them closely during the 1997 campaign.

18. Gerardo Albarrán de Alba, "El PRD, ante su nuevo reto: convertirse en un verdadero partido de centro-izquierda, con vocación de gobierno," *Proceso,* no. 1081 (20 July 1997): 21; Gerardo Albarrán de Alba, "PRD: Una campaña profesional y 63,000 brigadistas en acción, casa por casa," *Proceso,* no. 1074 (1 June 1997): 13.

19. Antonio Jáquez, "Entre tensiones internas, el PAN recompone la campaña de Castillo Peraza," *Proceso,* no. 1073 (25 May 1997): 18.

20. For example, Rosario Robles, PRD Secretary for Organization, recognized that "resistences that existed in various regions [to the idea of expanding the Sun Brigades] were overcome in large measure with a centralized management of resources." Also Albarrán de Alba, "El PRD, ante su nuevo reto," 21.

21. Ibid., 23.

22. For example, López Obrador allegedly headed off a party split during nominations for municipal elections in Nezahuacoyotl by threatening audits if local divisions cost the PRD the election. They did not split, and the PRD won the largest *municipio* it had controlled up to that time. See Rosa Icela Rodríguez and Alejandra Gudiño, "Las tendencias favorecen al PRD in varios municipios, dijo López Obrador," *La Jornada* (Mexico City), 7 November 1996: 5.

23. In contrast, when Cárdenas encouraged his old ally, Rodolfo González Guevara, to defect from the PRI and run for senator in 1991, he failed to head off an internal primary, which González Guevara lost. López Obrador could prevent such humiliating disasters, making his offers more attractive.

24. Jorge Camargo and Daniel Moreno, "Votación plural," *Reforma* (Mexico City), 9 July 1997: 4A.

25. Alonso Urrutia, "Podrían los perredistas alcanzar el control de la Asamblea de Representantes," *La Jornada* (Mexico City), 5 July 1997: 57.

26. Of the majority legislators, sixteen come from the Corriente por la Izquierda Democrática; ten from the Corriente por la Reforma Democratica (which controls the Mexico City municipal committee), and six from a neighborhood association called the Asamblea de Barrios (plus six more "from different groups"). Cecilia González, "Disputan grupos liderazgo en ALDF," *Reforma* (Mexico City), 9 July 1997: 4B.

27. Muñoz Ledo is widely acknowledged as one of Mexico's most intellectually gifted politicians and has more experience in national government than virtually any other Perredista. He served as secretary general of the Mexican Institute of Social Security (1966–70), and in the government of Luis Echeverría as secretary of the Ministry of Labor. He directed the presidential campaign of José López Portillo, was briefly president of the PRI in 1976, then became López Portillo's secretary of the Ministry of Public Education. He later served as Mexico's ambassador to the United Nations. He was a cofounder of the Democratic Current in the PRI, and left with Cárdenas in 1987. In 1988, he became one of the first four opposition senators and served with such enthusiasm that he holds the record for most speeches made in the Senate. When elected president of the PRD in 1993, he became the only Mexican to have served as president of two major political parties.

28. Usually, Muñoz Ledo was identified as a member of the "moderate, social-democratic, and pro-negotiation" faction, while López Obrador and Cárdenas stood for

confrontational behavior toward the state and alliance with the Chiapas rebels. This exaggerates their real differences, but the two groups did clash repeatedly over party strategy. Muñoz Ledo and Cárdenas also have a long-standing personal rivalry. Muñoz Ledo challenged Cárdenas for the mayoral candidacy, rejecting suggestions that he withdraw for the sake of party unity, until he lost the internal election.

29. Rafael Hernández Estrada, "El perfil de los candidatos a diputados federales del PRD," internal party document (Mexico City: Secretaría Electoral del PRD, 1997), 2–3.

30. *Plataforma legislativa federal 1997–2000* (Mexico City: PAN, 1997), esp. 45–46; *La fuerza de la democracia: Plataforma política 1994–2000* (Mexico City: PAN, 1994).

31. *Proceso*, no. 1085 (17 August 1997).

32. Carlos Acosta Córdova and Fernando Ortega Pizarro, "Ante las eleciones, en materia económica, no hay alternativa: PAN y PRD ofrecen lo mismo que el PRI," *Proceso*, no. 1075 (8 June 1997): 23.

33. See *Cuauhtémoc Cárdenas 94: Plataforma electoral* (Mexico City: PRD, 1994), esp. 35–39; *Plataforma electoral 1997* (Mexico City: PRD, 1997), esp. 38–39.

34. Gerardo Albarrán de Alba and María Scherer, "Seguro de que 'arrasará' y pondrá fin al 'mito del bipartidismo,' el PRD no prevé resbalones, caídas o cambios de estrategia," *Proceso*, no. 1073 (25 May 1997): 21.

35. Jorge Castañeda, "Chiapas 'War' Ends in a Whimper," *Los Angeles Times*, 15 September 1997: B5.

36. Alonso Urrutia, "PRI y PRD, en escenarios políticos sin precedente," *La Jornada*, 5 July 1997: 54.

37. It also suggests that cooperativeness could vanish if rewards vanish too. However, this analysis connects confrontational behavior to a rational response to incentives, rather than irrational "character."

38. Mogens Pedersen, "Electoral Volatility in Western Europe, 1948–1977," in *The West European Party System*, ed. Peter Mair (Oxford: Oxford University Press, 1990): 199.

39. Pedersen, "Electoral volatility," 202.

40. If Lawson's results hold up, underlying instability at the level of the individual voter may be much higher, with changes in individual preferences either random or canceling each other out. However, relative stability at the macro level remains an important consideration, which may create more continuity in policy, gives voters more information about existing parties, and gives parties incentives for parties to take good care of their reputations since they expect to continue to compete in future elections.

41. Even if the higher 1982–97 figure is used, Mexico still ranks at approximately the same level as Costa Rica and Chile. Scott Mainwaring and Timothy R. Scully, *Building Democratic Institutions: Party Systems in Latin America* (Stanford: Stanford University Press, 1995): 8.

42. Walter Burnham, *Critical Elections and the Mainsprings of American Politics* (New York: W. W. Norton, 1976).

43. Mireya Cuéllar, "En 95 y 96, los descalabros electorales más grandes del PRI," *La Jornada* (Mexico City), 23 December 1996: 4; José Ureña, "Se mantiene el PRI como primera fuerza," *La Jornada* (Mexico City), 17 November 1996: 5; *Elecciones federales 1997*.

44. "Tendencias de enero a junio," *La Jornada* (Mexico City), 7 July 1997: 60.

45. Rafael Giménez and Vidal Romero, "Avala ciudadanía elección," *Reforma* (Mexico City), 8 July 1997: 4B.

46. Jorge Alcocer, "Prospectiva electoral," *Proceso*, no. 1077 (22 June 1997): 44.

47. This contrasts with results for the Green Ecology Party (PVEM), which won a

surprising 8.6% in Mexico City. Only 35% of its voters identified "a lot" with the PVEM. Giménez and Romero, "Avala," 4B.

48. Albarrán de Alba, "El PRD, ante su nuevo reto," 24.

49. Lawson's panel study finds some evidence of higher ticket-splitting at the individual level, but this behavior, if confirmed, does not appear to produce consistent calculations which affect overall results in any particular direction. On the contrary, party results at all levels usually are close to identical.

50. Bruhn, *Taking on Goliath.*

51. On May 2, a *New York Times* article gave him "a better chance of winning than any opposition candidate since 1929," and placed him "clearly ahead of the other opposition candidates, including Diego Fernández de Cevallos of the conservative National Action Party." In a poll taken June 3–5, shortly after the debate, Fernández de Cevallos headed voter preferences at 31%, with Zedillo at 23%, and Cárdenas trailing badly at 14%. See Anthony DePalma, "Mexican Seriously Challenging Long-Ruling Party," *New York Times,* 2 May 1994: A4; "Instantaneas: Hacia las elecciones," *Este País,* no. 40 (July 1994): 2. Interestingly, Poiré's chapter suggests that the impact of the debate on Cárdenas may not have been as negative as virtually all observers assumed. However, *Cárdenas* and most of his advisers considered the debate to have cost them, which affected their calculations of what to do regarding the 1997 debate.

52. The PAN candidate complained about a PRI-PRD alliance to undermine the PAN well before the debate. Carlos Castillo Peraza, "Priísmo de todos los tiempos," *Proceso,* no. 1064 (23 March 1997).

53. See chapter by Lawson for additional evidence on the impact of candidate evaluations on the vote.

54. These figures were calculated by the Mexican Academy of Human Rights, reporting cost of television spots, including those paid for by the Federal Electoral Institute, in the Mexico City campaign. Triunfo Elizalde, "Gastan partidos $48 millones en una semana," *La Jornada* (Mexico City), 4 July 1997: 7.

55. Aguilar Zinser, ¡*Vamos a Ganar!,* esp. ch. 4.

56. Aguilar Zinser, ¡*Vamos a Ganar!,* 345.

57. The rest went to such items as posters, flyers, bumper stickers, and promotional items. Gerardo Albarrán de Alba and María Scherer, "Armada con estadística y propaganda profesional, toda la estructura perredista está volcada en las campañas," *Proceso,* no. 1073 (25 May 1997): 23; Albarrán de Alba and Scherer, "Seguro de que 'arrasará,'" 21.

58. These themes were "economic policy has not worked"; honesty versus the corruption of the PRI; and the need for a change. Albarrán de Alba, "PRD: Una campaña profesional," 12.

59. Aguilar Zinser ¡*Vamos a Ganar!,* 110; Albarrán de Alba and Scherer, "Armada con estadística y propaganda," 23. The election of López Obrador encouraged these changes. Unlike the voices that had encouraged Cárdenas in 1994 to adopt the same changes, López Obrador was both strong enough in his own right to carry considerable weight, yet loyal enough personally for Cárdenas to trust.

60. Thus, as of 1997, sixty-four seats were awarded by plurality in Mexico's thirty-two states; thirty-two to the second-place party in each state, and thirty-two by proportional representation. In 1994 three of four Senate seats went to the first-place party, and thirty-two to the first minority. COFIPE, (Mexico City: Instituto Federal Electoral, 1994), Article 11; COFIPE (1997), Article 11.

61. In 1994, the General Council of the IFE included four councillors from the legislature, six "citizen councillors," and representatives of the political parties. The interi-

or secretary presided. Two of the legislative councillors represented the majority party. This left the PRI with considerable influence. In 1997 the legislative councillors include one from each chamber for each parliamentary group and have no vote. The head of the General Council is elected by two-thirds of the Chamber of Deputies, a body which the PRI has not controlled by two-thirds since 1985. Eight "electoral councillors," also elected by a two-thirds majority in the Chamber of Deputies, must have a professional title and "knowledge of political-electoral subjects." They cannot have been a leader or a candidate of any political party for at least five years. The electoral councillors and the president of the General Council have seven-year terms. See COFIPE (1994), Article 74; and COFIPE (1997), Article 74.

62. "La estructura operativa del IFE, formada por priístas y exfuncionarios públicos," *Proceso*, no. 1075 (8 June 1997): 12.

63. COFIPE (1994), Article 44.

64. COFIPE (1997), Article 47. Regulation of the time that parties can *buy* continues (candidates cannot buy time individually); however, this also limits the ability of rich parties to crowd out poorer ones by buying up available time.

65. COFIPE (1997), Article 49.

66. See, for example, Gerardo Albarrán de Alba and Fernando Mayolo López, "La propuesta oficial de financiamiento a los partidos, 'derroche inmoral' y 'asalto escandaloso' en beneficio del PRI, advierten PAN y PRD," *Proceso*, no. 1043 (27 October 1996): 6–9.

67. Gerardo Albarrán de Alba and Fernando Mayolo López, "A propósito de 'deshonestidad': PAN y PRD recibirán 350 millones de pesos menos que el PRI," *Proceso*, no. 1054 (12 January 1997): 15.

68. Albarrán de Alba and Mayolo López, "A propósito de 'deshonestidad,'" 17.

69. Jorge Alcocer, "Tripartidismo," *Proceso*, no. 1069 (27 April 1997): 38.

70. While I focused in this paper on changes with a positive impact, not all changes were positive. The 1997 COFIPE does *not* include a section on the conditional registry of parties (making it more difficult for new parties to get registry). It raised the floor for keeping registry and qualifying for PR seats in the Congress from 1.5 percent of the national vote to 2 percent, and requires all parties that lose their registry in one election to wait until another federal election has passed before reapplying. It created the category of "national political groups," which require only 7,000 members but qualify for public funding and can run candidates under the registry of any political party. The parties denounced this as an attempt to "divide society and weaken the political parties." Finally provisions restricting the formation of electoral coalitions remained in place, partially relaxed in the case of congressional and Senate elections, but pointedly excluding presidential campaigns. COFIPE (Mexico City: Instituto Federal Electoral, 1997); see also Fernando Mayolo López, "Con las nuevas agrupaciones políticas, el gobierno busca dividir a la sociedad y debilitar a los partidos," *Proceso*, no. 1043 (27 October 1997): 8.

5

CAMPAIGN AWARENESS AND VOTING IN THE 1997 MEXICAN CONGRESSIONAL ELECTIONS

Alejandro Moreno

Do political campaigns matter in Mexico? Characterized by broad media campaigning, the 1997 election process raised the question of who was and who wasn't affected by the campaign information. The campaign process was innovative in that all relevant political parties had a strong presence in the mass media, not only through news coverage but also through paid political advertising. Changes in election laws regarding campaign finance allowed the three major parties in the country to spend considerable and comparable amounts of money, especially in television and radio advertisements. This innovative way of campaigning in Mexico was accompanied by other more traditional and less mediated ways to approach the voters; massive mail advertising, door-to-door campaigning, and the delivery of campaign souvenirs by the parties and candidates were only some of the many stimuli to which voters were exposed.

The historical loss that the Institutional Revolutionary Party (PRI) suffered in this election as well as the substantial gains by other parties leads us to ask whether these losses and gains were partly due to political campaigns; that is, whether short-term campaign influences account for some of the variance in electoral choice. The questions that this chapter addresses are the following: Who are the most likely voters to be affected by the campaign process? And who are the least likely to be affected by it? How is the vote affected by campaign stimuli?

This chapter focuses on the audience's side of the political campaign process, rather than on the political messages or their sources. For that reason, it explores the explanatory potential of some of the voters' characteristics in how they receive and process campaign information and political events. Some of those characteristics include media exposure, political attentiveness, campaign awareness, vote consistency, the intensity of party identification, and personal contact with the political campaign. The task is to elaborate a useful frame of analysis of campaign effects that help us complement the picture that studies about public opinion and electoral behavior in Mexico have produced.

The main argument in the chapter sustains that the level of awareness is an intervening variable that affects the ways in which individuals perceive politics and behave politically. In this chapter I address several issues that show these differences, in many of which the role of awareness is a matter of degree. In doing this research, I was particularly interested in assessing the role of awareness in making voters more likely or less likely to be affected by political campaigns. The findings suggest that, in general, awareness makes voters more resistant to changing their political views and choices when they have partisan affinities but makes them more open to change their political views if they are not partisan. If there are any campaign effects among the more aware, then they tend to favor opposition parties. Given the campaign's information flow, and the variation in the voters' awareness, the PRI benefits from low campaigning and low awareness. This finding suggests that intense campaigning definitively increases the level of competition, and awareness has a twofold role, reinforcing the partisan vote and making the nonpartisan vote more volatile. This chapter aims to bring these findings to a broader consideration by researchers on Mexican electoral behavior.

THEORETICAL FRAMEWORK

Individuals differ from each other in the ways they receive, process, understand, and react to political stimuli and attempts at persuasion. Voters not only differ in their levels of attentiveness to political campaigns but also in terms of the previous information and predispositions that help them accept or reject new information. Political campaigns are a matter of new information, or at least that is what they are expected to be: "Political campaigns are expected to inform voters about issues of the day, to reduce their dependence on simplistic labels, and to enable them to reach reasoned choices."[1] But new information is not the only aspect there is in people's minds when they form an opinion or shape a preference: "Every opinion is a marriage of information and predisposition: information to form a mental picture of the given issue, and predisposition to motivate some conclusion about it."[2]

The differences between voters—their exposure to new information, their capacities to process it, and their previous ideas and orientations—make them react differently to campaign information. Thus, campaigns may have different effects.

Of course, I am assuming that campaign information may actually have some effects. I am also assuming that political campaigns and political messages are precisely that: messages. Ansolabehere and Iyengar mention that, although it is expected from political campaigns to be informative, "even as candidates have become increasingly reliant on television advertising, the information function of political campaigns has fallen into disrepute. Campaigns appear all too superficial, and the question naturally arises whether superficial campaigns breed superficial voters."[3] Evaluating how informative or how substantial those messages are is a task beyond this chapter's purposes.

The way information is accessed and processed varies from voter to voter, ranging from those who accumulate a considerable amount of information to those who have only some pieces of information. But, how necessary is information to reach conclusions or to make choices? How much information is needed? Ignorance and poor political attention have been seen as a sickness to democratic politics. However, most voters in a democracy tend to pay little attention to political events, and it is true that they do not have to know everything in order to make a decision. Getting information has high costs and brings low benefits; thus, ignorance is to some extent rational.[4]

In addition, people are more interested in some things than in others. Specializing in some particular information forms different *issue publics* in society—those sectors of the public that are especially interested in a particular issue and therefore pay more attention to it than to other issues.[5] Thus, attention can be selective in a way that it is likely to be domain-specific: "The more relevant some domain is to the individual, the higher the level of information concerning that domain."[6]

To summarize the double way in which information is distributed among the electorate, we may simply say that "the mean is low and the variance high."[7] In other words, people differ greatly in their attentiveness to political campaigns, but the average level of attentiveness is quite low.

Previous political knowledge is an important aspect that influences the reception and processing of political information. For example, "getting the news"—or the ability to recall news stories—is a function of the level of previous political knowledge that people have.[8] Perhaps, in the same way, "getting the campaign" messages is a function of the awareness and knowledge that people have previous to or develop during the campaign itself. None-theless, getting the campaign message and being able to recall it does not mean that only those who are attentive to the campaign are the most likely to be affected by it when making their political choices. Individual sophisti-cation is complex and it is not easy to accept that only the well informed can be persuaded by the campaigns because they are the ones who are aware of them. In fact, the more sophisticated and knowledgeable individuals tend to have more information bases that allow them to see and understand politics more ideologically.[9] Therefore, it seems unlikely that they are the ones who may be more greatly affected by campaign stimuli. Zaller illustrates this point: "[T]he people who know most about politics in general are most heavily exposed to the incumbent's self-promotional efforts. Yet, as political sophisticates, they are also better able to evaluate and critically scrutinize the new information they encounter. So, in the end, highly aware persons tend to be little affected by incumbent campaigns."[10]

On the other hand, less-sophisticated individuals should be more likely to be affected by the campaign information; but, how can the least aware to political campaigns be affected if they do not even pay attention to them? Following Popkin,[11] we may argue that, among these voters, only "bits" of information or cues about political candidates and parties may be enough information to reach conclusions. If this is true, campaign events should have significant effects in shaping unaware people's choices. I will return to this below.

That hypothesis is complemented by another component: the voters' predispositions that lead them to accept, reject, and process new infor-mation. In this chapter, I will pay special attention to party identifica-tion—and its *intensity*—as a key determinant of the vote as well as a strong predisposition that "filters" the campaign's new information. A voter views candidates from the party with which he or she identifies dif-ferently to candidates from other parties. The partisan views tend to be more favorable. Therefore, if the questions are who is most affected by political campaigns and how, then it is important to consider the voters' loyalty to a political party as a potential obstacle to persuasion and cam-paign effects.

The argument in this chapter is that campaigns are more likely to affect those individuals who *do not identify* with a political party and are open to different voting options, and less likely to affect those individuals who *do identify* with a specific party and are more resistant to cast their vote for a different party. As party identification intensifies, the persuading potential of campaigns diminishes, and the likelihood of voting in a more partisan way increases.

We must consider also another goal of campaigning. I have assumed that political campaigns seek to persuade voters to vote for a specific party or candidate and not for another. This includes the possibility of reaching out to new potential voters as well as the possibility to reinforce the "usual" or more partisan voters. Thus, both partisans and nonpartisans are subject to potential campaign effects in one way or another. The only possibility left out is campaigning to persuade voters to vote. Given the data available for this research, this last option is not addressed here.

Successful campaigns may not only be those that *attract* voters to vote for a candidate or party but also those that reinforce the voters' previous decisions. In other words, we cannot limit our view of campaign effects to voters who switch their votes as a consequence of political campaigns; we must also consider the way voters' decisions are reinforced by the process itself.

The levels of information and campaign awareness vary by party identification and this makes the relationships stated here more complex. Popkin[12] suggested that party identification is an information shortcut because it substitutes or complements the lack of information about political campaigns and any other political events. When they evaluate a party or a candidate, voters lower the costs of information by just evaluating them in terms of the perceived affinities with one's party identification. "Party identification, viewed from the perspective of low-information rationality, is an informational short-cut or a default value, a substitute for more complete information about parties and candidates."[13]

In general, the more a voter identifies with a political party, the less information he or she needs to make political decisions. This, of course, is not true in all cases. We may find very aware party identifiers as well as very aware nonpartisans. Additionally, we may find very unaware party identifiers as well as very unaware nonpartisans. Who among all of them is more likely to be affected by political campaigns is the question this chapter addresses.

THE DATA

The data used for this research is rather limited for many of the questions asked. However, the data offer an opportunity to set the basis for substantial inquiry into who reacts to political campaigns in Mexico and how. Empirical evidence draws from a 1997 national postelection survey of 1,243 respondents eighteen years of age or older, 1,001 of which said that they voted in the July 6 elections. The percent of sample voters relative to the total sample overestimates by 23 percent the actual turnout (80 percent of sample voters versus 57 percent of actual voters).

Regarding the vote, the official numbers for Congress were well reflected by the survey's reported vote: among the subsample of voters, the PRI obtained 37% of the sample's effective vote, versus 39.1% in the official valid vote; the National Action Party (PAN) obtained 28.8% in the sample, versus 26.61% of the actual vote; the Party of the Democratic Revolution (PRD) got 28.4% in the sample, and 25.71% officially; the Mexican Green Ecologist Party (PVEM) got 2.7% of the sample vote, and 3.81% officially; the Labor Party (PT) got 2.3% in the sample, and 2.58% in the actual vote; finally, the other three parties, Cardenista (PC), People's Socialist (PPS), and Mexican Democratic (PDM), did not reach the electoral threshold of 2% to keep their official registration and represented 0.8% of the sample's effective vote. The sample numbers reflect the parties' positions in the total vote share, with the PRI having the greater number of votes, followed by the PAN, the PRD, the Greens, and the PT, in that order. For this reason, the data are reliable to analyze the voters' behavioral aspects in the 1997 elections. The survey design was carried out by researchers at the Instituto Tecnológico Autónomo de México (ITAM), and the fieldwork took place two weeks after the election during seven days. Fieldwork was carried out by a Mexico City-based polling company, Result Analysis on Communication and Public Opinion (ARCOP).

Some Concepts and Their Operationalization

Before getting to the analysis, it is necessary to define the main concepts and explain the way in which they were operationalized.

As defined by Zaller, *political awareness* is the "extent to which an individual pays attention to politics *and* understands what he or she has encountered" (italics in original).[14] Zaller operationalizes this concept using basic measures of knowledge about political facts. Borrowing from this definition—but unable to affirm with the data at hand that there is a true "understanding" of the encounters—I will refer to *campaign awareness* as the extent to which an individual pays attention to political campaigns during an election process and recalls substantial facts from it. I operationalize this concept using measures of association of campaign slogans with their respective political parties. In the construction of the *campaign awareness index* I employed seven slogans widely used in the mass media during the 1997 campaign process: five from the political parties that achieved Congress representation; one used by the election authority, IFE (Federal Electoral Institute); and one used by the federal government during the process of campaigns. The seven slogans are listed in Table 5.1 in the next section.

The resulting index of campaign awareness is a scale from 0 to 7, where "0" means that the respondent was unable to associate any slogan with its respective political institution and "7" means that the respondent was able to associate all seven slogans with their respective institutions. The index seems to reflect relatively well what we are trying to measure: reliability analysis gives us a Cronbach's alpha equal to 0.68.

Due to the total sample size (n = 1,243) and the subsample of voters (n_v = 1,001), in some cases it was necessary to collapse the 7-point index into three categories (High, Medium, and Low campaign awareness), and in some cases even into two categories (High and Low). Otherwise, the small number of cases would have made it impossible to analyze the data and reach some conclusions about it.

Media exposure

This refers to the extent to which an individual uses different mass media to obtain information about the parties and the campaigns. Respondents were asked how much they relied on television, radio, the press, and friends and family for information about the campaigns and the parties. The response options for each medium were "a lot," "some," "little," or "not at all." Based on the combination of the four categories in each of the four media variables, I constructed a composite index by adding the four variables. The resulting scale had a range from 4 (for those who do not rely at all on any of the four media to get information about the campaigns) to 16 (for those who rely a lot on all four media for such a purpose). The Cronbach's alpha in this case is 0.73.

Campaign contact

As stated at the beginning of the chapter, media campaigns are not the only way to approach voters. Thus, it is necessary to evaluate how other ways of campaigning, such as personal contact with the voter, affect him or her to vote in a certain way. By *campaign contact* I refer to the personal contact that the voter had with the campaign process other than exposure to media information. I use measures of whether voters received mail from parties or candidates, were visited by candidates or parties in their homes, or were given campaign souvenirs by the candidates or parties. The index scale goes from 0 to 3, where "0" means no campaign contact at all (that is, none of the three aspects mentioned happened to the voter), "1" means the voter experienced at least one type of contact, "2" means two types of contact, and "3" means the voter experienced all three types of contact measured in the survey. The Cronbach's alpha in this case equals 0.58.

Vote consistency

This is a very important concept for this analysis, but at the same time, a very limited variable. The noted variable serves as a proxy to evaluate vote patterns using a one-shot survey. By *vote consistency* I refer to voting for the same party in different elections. I do not refer to voting for the same party for different offices during the same election. Instead, I refer to the extent to which a voter votes for the same party in different elections separated by a time span. To some extent, this tells us whether campaigns are relevant to voters because they change their political preferences. Whether campaigns reinforce rather than change the voter's preference, will be assessed by controlling for party identification.

A panel survey design would allow us to follow the patterns of preference among several respondents and to determine the degree of stability and change in vote intentions during a campaign process. However, using a one-shot survey we are limited to the reported patterns of the vote. For this, I used a measure of vote consistency constructed by matching the same party from two voting questions: whom respondents voted for in 1994 (asked verbally at the beginning of the questionnaire) and whom respondents voted for in 1997 (asked at the end of the questionnaire using a secret ballot method). The code "1" was used for all matching pairs of parties and "0" for all nonmatching pairs of parties.

There are great risks in considering this measure as good enough to assess campaign effects. The simplest one is that the 1994 vote was to elect a president and the 1997 vote was to elect representatives to the Chamber of Deputies: the nature of the election may be a sole reason for some people to vote for different parties in each election without any campaign effects taking place. Ignoring this fact would be the same as denying the voting decisions that produce divided governments: that people reason their votes differently for different levels of government. However, for the one-shot survey evidence used here, vote consistency is our best proxy.

The intensity of party identification

This refers to how strongly or weakly voters identify with a political party, or whether they identify with one at all. So, while the *party identification measure* used here refers to strong and weak Panistas, Priístas and Perredistas, as well as nonpartisans, the *intensity of party identification* refers to a composite variable in which all strong partisans, no matter what party they identify with, are placed into the same category, and so are the weak partisans and the nonpartisans in their respective categories.

The rest of the variables are simple and self-explanatory. A list of survey questions can be found in the Appendix.

POLITICAL ADVERTISING AND VOTING

Not all campaign slogans are recognized and associated with their respective political parties or candidates. In some cases they are associated—logically or illogically—with the wrong party or candidate. Additionally, recognition and association do not necessarily affect the voters' choices.

The postelection data show some variation in the vote by recognition and association of slogans and parties. Table 5.1 shows that eight out of ten respondents correctly associated the PRD's slogan ("It's time for the sun to

Table 5.1
Political Advertising and Awareness

Could you tell me what party or political institution comes to your mind with the following phrases? (Percent)

Slogan / Party or Institution	Correct Association	No Association	Incorrect Association*
"It's time for the sun to come out" / PRD *Ya es tiempo de que salga el sol*	78	14	1 (PT)
"Don't vote for a politician, . . ." / PVEM *No votes por un político***	53	29	4 (PRI)
"Because you are Mexico, Mexico is first" / PRI *Porque México eres tú, México es primero*	49	26	8 (PAN)
"For the Mexico we all want to see" / PAN *Por el México que todos queremos ver*	37	24	19 (PRI)
"The choice is yours" / IFE *La elección es tuya*	32	34	12 (PRI)
"A turn . . . on your behalf" / PT *Un giro . . . a tu favor*	22	42	15 (PRD)
"Mexico is its people" / Federal Government *México es su gente*	10	39	24 (PRI)

Source: National Post-Election Poll, n=1,243.
* The percent shown in this column only refers to the most commonly mentioned incorrect party or institution.
** This slogan had the subsequent phrase "vote for an ecologist," which was not offered to the interviewee because it was redundant with the party's name.

rise") with that party. This was by far the most recognized political slogan and perhaps the most successful in reaching the voters' minds—which is a necessary but not a sufficient condition to get their votes. The slogan has different and interesting symbols, the most important of which is the sun: the PRD's logo is an Aztec-style sun and that may explain the direct association of slogan and party. The second most recognized and correctly associated slogan with its party was that of the Greens (PVEM). This was so despite the fact that the questionnaire only presented half the slogan ("Don't vote for a politician, . . ."), for the simple reason that the whole slogan would have been redundant with the party's name (" . . . vote for an ecologist"). Half of the sample correctly associated this slogan with the

PVEM. Neither of the two slogans was significantly associated with any other political party or institution, while other party slogans were attributed to the wrong parties. The associations shown in Table 5.1 suggest that the PRD's and the PVEM's slogans were exclusive of their parties.

In contrast, the PRI slogan was associated with both the PRI and the PAN in a ratio of 6 to 1; the PAN slogan was associated with both the PAN and the PRI in a ratio of 2 to 1; and the PT slogan was associated with the PRD almost as much as with the PT. One of the main slogans used by the Federal Electoral Institute (IFE) was also associated with the PRI in a ratio of 3 to 1; and finally, the slogan used by the federal government during the campaign process was mostly associated with the PRI in a ratio of 1 to 2, even though the commercials did not make any explicit reference to that party, except that the PRI uses the same colors of the Mexican flag, which are also commonly used in government logos.

The least successful slogans in terms of recognition and correct association were the PAN's (which was very strongly associated with the PRI) and the PT's (which was very strongly associated with the PRD). Also, it is certainly suggestive that the IFE's and the government's slogans had very high proportions of nonassociation with any institution as well as a very significant association with the PRI.

In order to see how this was linked with the vote, Table 5.2 presents the vote shares for Chamber of Deputies by association and no association of party slogans with their respective parties. The data show that the vote for the PAN was much higher among those who correctly associated the PAN slogan with that party. This probably measures two distinct phenomena. First, being exposed and being able to recall the party's advertisements was a cause of voting for that party; in other words, the vote is the dependent variable. Second, because we are using postelection data, it is possible that the measure reflects selectively attentive parts of the electorate; because an individual voted for the PAN, that individual was more likely to recall the PAN advertisement than people who did not vote for the PAN (selective partisan attention).

Whichever the direction of causality is, recalling the PAN slogan was positively correlated with the vote for the PAN; and this also happened, to a greater or lesser extent, for the rest of the parties. Thus, there is a relationship between voting for a party and the ability to recall that particular party's ads.

Voting for the PRI was more likely among those segments of the electorate who were not capable of recalling or associating the opposition slogans. The PRI benefited from the vote of those who were relatively less aware of the opposition's media advertisements. The lesson is that the PRI gets more votes from those segments of the electorate that pay little attention to politics. Something similar happened with the PAN, whose pro-

Table 5.2
Awareness, Political Advertising, and Voting

Percent of People Voting for a Party by Association of Slogans with the Corresponding Parties or Institutions

	\multicolumn{6}{c}{Vote for Chamber of Deputies}
	PAN	PRI	PRD	PVEM	PT	n
Total sample of voters	29	37	28	3	2	925
Association of PAN ad with PAN	36	30	29	3	2	360
No association	24	42	28	3	2	565
Association of PRI ad with PRI	26	38	29	2	3	477
No association	31	36	28	3	2	448
Association of PRD ad with PRD	27	35	31	3	3	745
No association	36	43	18	1	1	180
Assoc. of PVEM ad with PVEM	30	31	32	4	3	504
No association	28	44	24	2	2	421
Association of PT ad with PT	20	32	37	3	1	219
No association	31	38	26	3	1	706
Association of IFE ad with IFE	30	30	32	4	3	316
No association	28	41	26	2	2	609
Association of Govt. ad with Govt.	35	27	35	3	0	100
No association	28	38	28	3	2	825

Source: National Post-Election Poll. Respondents who said they did not vote and those who did not give an answer to the vote question were excluded, n = 1,001.

portion of votes from those who were not aware of the PRD's ads was much higher than the proportion of votes among those who were aware of it.

Recognition of both the IFE's and the federal government's ads was related with a higher vote for the opposition and a lower vote for the PRI. The PRI vote was underrepresented by seven points among those who recognized the IFE slogan and by ten points among those who recognized the federal government's slogan. These associations raise the paradox that potential free-ride advertising for the PRI was actually very costly for that party. The recognition of the federal government's slogan took away 10 points from the PRI and the lack of recognition only added one point to that party. In contrast, recognition of the federal government's slogan over-represented the PAN and the PRD by 6 and 7 points respectively.

The IFE advertisement also had a similar effect: while its recognition implied more votes for the opposition and less for the PRI, its lack of recognition overestimated the PRI by four points. Nonetheless, the differences made by the IFE ad are smaller than the differences made by the government's ad.

CAMPAIGN AWARENESS

Some individuals are able to recognize all political ads, while some others do not recognize any of them. It was suggested earlier that more sophisticated people are less likely to be affected by political campaigns, but in fact there are very few sophisticates. Figure 5.1 shows the distribution of the campaign awareness index constructed with the measures of slogan recognition and association. The data show that most individuals have low and

Figure 5.1
Distribution of the Campaign Awareness Index: 1997

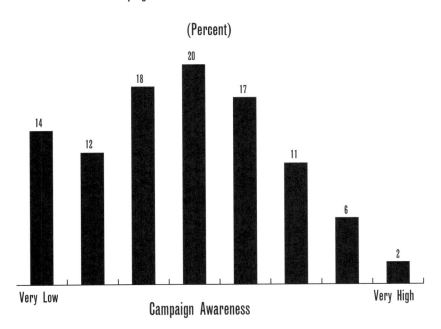

Source: National Post-Election Poll, n=1,243.
The index goes from 0 to 7, where 0 means that the respondent was not able to associate any of the slogans with their correct party or institutions and 7 means that the respondent associated all slogans with the correct party or institution. Total sample's mean: 2.8; standard deviation: 1.8.

Figure 5.2
Levels of Campaign Awareness by Social Group

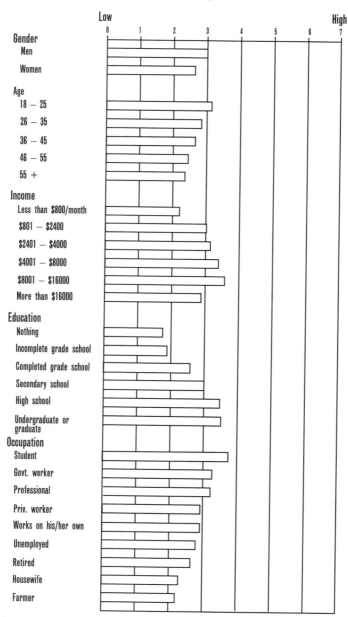

Source: National Post-Election Poll, subsample of voters.

middle levels of campaign awareness while very few individuals have high levels of awareness.

So, if the hypothesis that states that the individuals more likely to be affected by political campaigns are those with low and middle levels of campaign awareness, the distribution of awareness shown in Figure 5.1 suggests that the part of the electorate subject to campaign effects is much greater than the part of the electorate in which campaign effects are potentially minimal. The average level of campaign awareness for the whole sample is 2.8 (in a scale from 0 to 7), with a standard deviation of 1.8. In other words, on average, Mexicans recognized almost three out of seven campaign slogans (two of which were supposed to be nonpartisan). Whether this is low or high is something we cannot tell, given the lack of comparable measures for other societies or measures for other campaign processes.

However, we can definitively see who is more aware and who is less aware of political campaigns among different segments of Mexican society. Figures 5.2 to 5.4 show the average levels of campaign awareness by different groups of individuals. Figure 5.2, for example, shows that men are more aware than women. Awareness is higher among younger individuals and tends to decrease as age increases. Also, awareness tends to increase as we move upward in an income scale. Very clearly, the more education, the more campaign awareness. Among occupation strata, students are the most attentive, followed by government workers and professionals. Retired individuals, housewives, and farmers are the least attentive of all.

Figure 5.3 shows the levels of campaign awareness by interest in political advertisements, media exposure, and news broadcasts that respondents watch. Campaign interest is definitively a very strong correlate of campaign awareness: the more interested, the more attentive. Attentiveness also increases with the levels of media exposure. Among television news viewers, the *Hechos*'s audience is more politically aware than the *24 Horas*'s viewers; this may reflect the different profiles of channel audiences.

Political orientations and predispositions also reflect different levels of campaign awareness. Individuals who place themselves on the political left of a left-right scale show the highest level of awareness, while those who place themselves on the right show the lowest level of awareness. Labor Party voters (only twenty-two in the sample) show the highest levels of campaign awareness among all voters, followed by the PRD and the Green voters. The PAN voters are relatively less aware and the PRI voters are the least aware of all. This is consistent with the fact that the PRI vote is overrepresented not among voters who are aware to the PRI's advertisements, but among voters who are not aware of the opposition ads.

The levels of campaign awareness by party identification are highly suggestive. One might think that strong party identifiers tend to be the most interested and concerned with what happens in politics and elections.

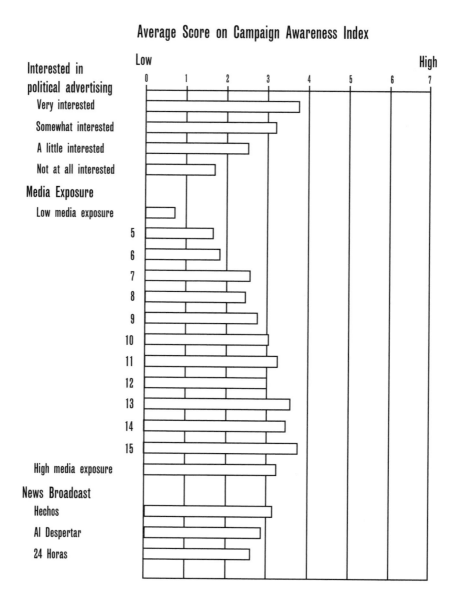

Figure 5.3
Levels of Campaign Awareness by Interest in Political Advertisements
and Media Exposure

Average Score on Campaign Awareness Index

Low

High

Interested in
political advertising
Very interested
Somewhat interested
A little interested
Not at all interested

Media Exposure
Low media exposure
5
6
7
8
9
10
11
12
13
14
15
High media exposure

News Broadcast
Hechos
Al Despertar
24 Horas

Source : National Post-Election Poll, subsample of voters.

Figure 5.4
Levels of Campaign Awareness by Political and Ideological Orientations

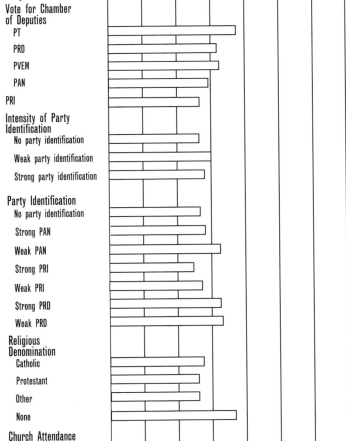

Average Score on Campaign Awareness Index

Source : National Post-Election Poll, subsample of voters.

However, the average level of awareness among strong party identifiers is lower than that of the weak partisans. In fact, with the exception of the strong PRI identifiers, those who do not identify with any political party are the ones who show the lowest levels of campaign awareness. These differences suggest that, while it is true that in general partisans are more aware than non-partisans, as partisanship gets stronger the levels of awareness tend to decrease. This leads us to think that strong partisan orientations really become an information shortcut, a conclusion we may reach given the lower levels of awareness among strong partisans compared to weak partisans. In other words, strong partisans pay less attention to political campaigns than weak partisans, suggesting that strong party identification may provide them with the sufficient elements to make political choices. This is especially notable among Panistas and Priístas, but not so much among Perredistas, who regardless of the intensity of partisanship tend to be relatively more aware than the other partisans.

Finally, secularization seems to strengthen campaign awareness. Individuals who do not belong to a religious group tend to pay much more attention to campaigns than religion affiliates. Also, on average, the more often one goes to church, the lower the level of campaign awareness one has.

The single categories illustrate who is more aware and who is less aware but do not tell us what really determines campaign awareness. Table 5.3 shows a regression model of campaign awareness. In order to explain the level of awareness, the model includes sociodemographic variables, variables of interest in campaign and media exposure, and measures of ideological predispositions.

Education plays a key role in making individuals more aware of political campaigns. Naturally, education provides the voters with a greater ability to follow, understand, and recall political information. Moreover, the process of education itself contributes significantly in making individuals more aware politically. While some specific occupations, such as being a government employee or professional, show high average levels of awareness, being a student contributes positively and significantly to pay more attention to campaigns. Although there are clear differences between their respective categories, gender, age, and income levels are not strong predictors of awareness, as the multivariate model shows.

Because Mexico City bears a great deal of the weight in the flow of information regarding national political campaigns, and because most of the national media are based there, it was important to include a dummy variable for the Federal District to assess its role in the levels of awareness. The assumption is not that Federal District dwellers are qualitatively distinct from other urban Mexicans, but that the Federal District has a special centrality in the flow of campaign information. The regression coefficient for this variable shows that the levels of awareness tend to be higher in

Table 5.3
Determinants of Campaign Awareness in the 1997 Mexican Elections
(OLS Regression Estimates)

Variable	b	se
Constant	2.65	(.51)***
Demographics		
Gender (female)	−.16	(.12)
Age	−.00	(.01)
Income	−.01	(.07)
Education	.20	(.06)***
Student	.43	(.20)*
Federal District dweller	.51	(.18)**
Interest and Media		
Interest in political advertising	.47	(.07)***
Media exposure	.07	(.02)**
Ideological Predispositions		
Left-Right self-placement	−.21	(.07)**
Intensity of party identification	−.09	(.09)
Religiosity	−.09	(.04)*
R^2	.22	
Adjusted R^2	.21	

Source: National Post-Election Poll, n=682 (list-wise deletion of missing data). b=coefficient; se=standard error.
Significance levels: *** $p<.001$; ** $p<.01$; * $p<.05$

Mexico City than in the rest of the country, either urban or rural. Data not included in Table 5.3 show that in a few specific cities the average level of awareness is higher than in Mexico City. However, those few cities are scattered in different regions of the country and do not constitute a single regional cluster.

The levels of interest in political campaigns and the levels of media exposure are strongly related to campaign awareness. We would expect that media exposure precedes campaign awareness: an individual cannot be very aware of campaign slogans if he or she is not exposed to them first. Having interest in campaigns increases the probability to pay attention to them and therefore raises the levels of awareness. Thus, in political campaigns both exposure to and interest in information increase the levels of awareness and the probability of recalling campaign events and information.

Some ideological predispositions are very strongly linked with the

Figure 5.5
Economic Performance and Awareness

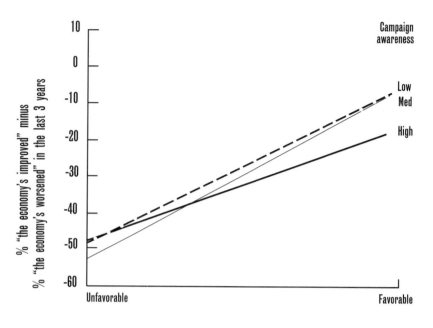

Opinion about President Zedillo's job
handling the economy

Source: National Post-Election Poll, n=1,243. A negative percent represents the case where respondents who think that the economy has worsened outnumber respondents who think the economy has improved.

individuals' awareness of campaigns. Based on the coefficient and the statistical significance of the ideological left-right measure, we may conclude that ideology is a strong predictor of awareness, with the politically leftist more aware and the political right less aware of political campaigns. Unlike left and right predispositions, the intensity of party identification per se does not explain the variance in awareness; though, the religious-secular dimension does in fact contribute significantly to the variance encountered.

In summary, education, interest, media exposure, ideology, and religiosity all contribute significantly to explain why some individuals are more aware of campaigns than others. Also being a student or living in Mexico City offers greater chances to pay more attention to national campaigns.

PRESIDENTIAL APPROVAL AND EVALUATION OF THE ECONOMY
BY LEVELS OF AWARENESS

The variation in levels of awareness may determine how individuals perceive and evaluate political information. Before we get into the voting analysis, let us take a look at how more aware and less aware people evaluate the economy and the president's performance. Figure 5.5 shows the relationship between opinions about how the president is handling the economy and perceptions about the country's economic situation in the last three years. Opinions about presidential performance were collapsed into favorable and unfavorable, and the general perception of the country's economic situation was calculated as the proportion that says it has improved minus the proportion that says it has worsened. The negative numbers in the resulting scale show that the number of people who think that the economy has worsened is greater than those who think it has improved.

In every case, the proportion of individuals who think that the economic situation has worsened outnumber those who think that it has improved. Among the individuals who approve of the president's job handling the economy, the gap between those who perceive economic improvement and those who perceive economic worsening is relatively small. In contrast, among those who disapprove of the president's economic performance, the gap between those opposite views is much greater. In other words, the perception of the economic situation is much more pessimistic among those who disapprove of the president's job than among those who approve of it. This is observed by the inclination of the lines in Figure 5.5.

Observing the different views about the economy by levels of awareness, that is, by looking at the difference between the three lines in Figure 5.5, we find some variation in how the economic situation is perceived: the data show that the more aware individuals have more moderate views about the economic situation, while the less aware tend to magnify the worsening or improvement of it. In other words, the perceptions of the less aware are more positive when they approve of the president and more negative when they disapprove of him. This is graphically seen by the lines' slopes: the slope for the more aware is smaller than the slope for the less aware, which means that the more aware hold more moderate views and the less aware hold more extremist views.

In this particular case, among those who disapprove of the president's job, the gap between highly aware and poorly aware is 4 points, with the poorly aware being more pessimistic about the economic situation. Among those who approve of the president's job, the gap between highly aware and poorly aware is 12 points, with the unaware being more optimistic about the economic situation.

This finding may raise the claim that it is not awareness but real economic conditions which cause different views about the economy. This would be true if there was a relationship between personal economic experience and the correlates of awareness, so that the more aware had less drastic economic circumstances, while the less aware had a more difficult economic situation.

The data at hand show that this is not the case. The mean scores on the awareness index of those who think that their personal economic situation improved, remained the same, or worsened in the last three years are 2.8, 2.8, and 3 respectively. This shows us that individuals who reported relatively worse personal economic situations had a higher average level of awareness than those who reported economic improvement: exactly the opposite expectation. Thus, we may suggest that awareness moderates opinions, while the lack of awareness tends to magnify perceived situations.

VOTE CONSISTENCY BY PARTISANSHIP AND LEVELS OF AWARENESS

If the levels of awareness filter the way political events are perceived, it is likely that political behavior also varies by the levels of information and awareness that characterize different individuals. To test this expectation, and to address the question about who is more likely to be affected by campaign information, this section focuses on the chances of voting for the same party in different elections, or what I call *vote consistency.*

The relationship between campaign awareness and vote consistency will not be assessed alone. A measure of the intensity of party identification has been added to the analysis, for the simple reason that the likelihood of vote consistency increases as party identification becomes more intense. After all, nonpartisans are more likely than partisans to switch their votes from one party to another.

Figure 5.6 shows these relationships. The data in this figure show that the likelihood of voting for the same party in different elections—given by the percent of vote consistency—is greater among partisans than among nonpartisans, and it is greater among strong partisans than among weak partisans. So, there is a monotonic relationship between the intensity of party identification and vote consistency. In other words, the stronger the party identification, the greater the likelihood to vote for the same party in different elections.

The variation by levels of campaign awareness shows two phenomena. On the one hand, the more aware partisan voters have higher levels of vote consistency than the less aware partisan voters; in other words, among partisans the higher the level of awareness, the higher the probability of voting for the same party in different elections. On the other hand, awareness makes nonpartisan voters more likely to change their political preferences than the less aware nonpartisan voters; in other words, among nonparti-

Figure 5.6
Vote Consistency, Intensity of Party Identification, and Campaign Awareness

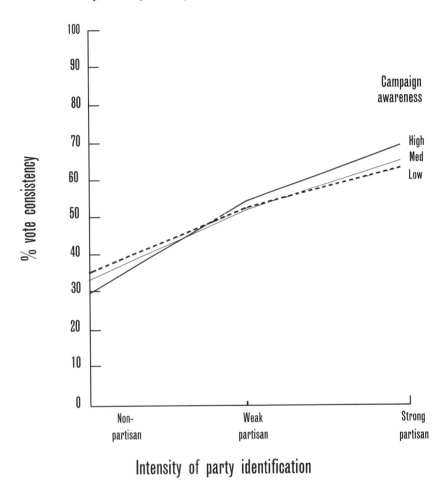

Source: National Post-Election Poll, subsample of voters, n=1,001.

sans the higher the level of awareness, the lower the probability of voting for the same party in different elections.

The aggregated variable called "intensity of party identification" indicates that the stronger the partisanship, the more likely it is to vote for the same party in different elections. It also shows that the high levels of awareness increase vote consistency among partisans. However, when we disaggregated that variable by party labels we find an exception: in 1997 the highly aware weak Panistas expressed lower levels of vote consistency than the poorly aware weak Panistas, as it can be seen in Figure 5.7. This finding will be addressed below.

Figure 5.7 shows the levels of vote consistency by party identification and levels of campaign awareness. PRI identifiers show the higher levels of vote consistency, which increase as awareness increases. The Panistas show relatively lower levels of consistency than the Priístas, but higher than the Perredistas. This suggests that either the vote may have been more volatile among opposition identifiers than among PRI identifiers, or that the opposition vote of today was in fact the PRI vote yesterday, which is actually the case among many opposition voters. In other words, dealignment from the PRI has been strong, and the opposition has attracted many former PRI voters—the PRI vote was around 61 percent in 1991, around 50 percent in 1994, and around 39 percent in 1997. However, realignment in favor of an opposition party has not been so strong.

Strong and weak partisans show higher levels of consistency as aware-ness increases. This supports the assertion that awareness becomes an obstacle to campaign persuasion especially among partisans. As mentioned above, the only exception is the weak identification with the PAN, where vote consistency decreases as awareness increases. In other words, weak Panistas who were highly aware were also more likely to vote for a different party than weak Panistas with low awareness. What this may suggest is that many weak PAN identifiers probably weighted the chances of the PAN to win in the 1997 elections, and if the chances weren't high, then weak Panistas preferred to vote for another party with higher chances to win. Awareness may have contributed to evaluate the party's chances to win as low. In Mexico City's mayoral race, for example, in the weeks immediately before the election, the PAN candidate did poorly in the polls published by the media. This probably contributed to the consideration of others and not him as the likely winners, and this perception should be more common among more aware voters than among less aware voters. However, the effects that the Mexico City race may have had on national elections is a question for elsewhere.

The fact that the phenomenon just described only happened among weak Panistas does not mean that weak Panistas are more volatile than weak Perredistas, for example. In fact, even though weak Panistas' vote con-sistency decreased as they became more aware of the campaigns, their level of consistency remained higher than that of the weak Perredistas. A possi-ble explanation of this may be the political parties' time in the electoral arena: from the older PRI and PAN to the newer PRD, the older the party, the higher the level of vote consistency among its partisans. But, again, this reflects the effects of more recently developed PRD partisan affinities, in

Figure 5.7
Vote Consistency, Party Identification, and Campaign Awareness

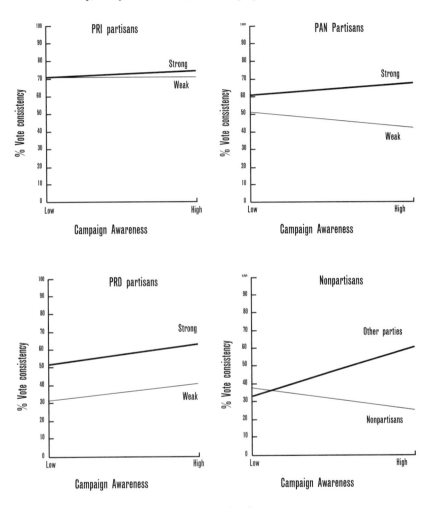

Source: National Post-Election Poll, subsample of voters, n=1,001.

the sense that many people who voted in 1997 for that party had voted for a different party in 1994: the 1997 PRD vote was around 10 percent higher than it was in 1994. This includes new voters as well as people who voted for a different party. This is the reason why opposition partisans show lower levels of vote consistency than PRI partisans: a lot of people who voted for the PRI in 1997 also voted for that party in 1994, while several people who voted for the PAN or the PRD in 1997, had probably voted for the PRI in 1994 (or Panistas who voted for the PRD, and so on).

Finally, nonpartisans show very low levels of vote consistency, which is even lower as nonpartisans become more highly aware. This leads us to conclude that, while partisans are relatively more stable in their political choices and awareness reinforces stability, nonpartisans are less stable in their political choices and awareness increases instability. In other words, campaign "switching" effects are potentially greater among nonpartisans who pay more attention to campaigns.

THE EFFECTS OF PERSONAL CONTACT

Massive political advertising through radio and television was an important means of campaigning in the 1997 elections. However, parties and candidates also employed more traditional canvassing methods to approach the voters, such as sending mail information with the voters' names and addresses, making home visits, and distributing campaign souvenirs in their rallies and visits. This section focuses on how these forms of campaigning affected the voters and their levels of campaign awareness. The analysis suggests that awareness mediates the relationship between more direct and personal forms of campaigning and the vote.

The first three columns in Table 5.4 show data about the relationship between personal campaigning and the vote. The other six columns show that relationship by levels of awareness. The columns with the total vote show that the proportion of votes for the PAN and the PRD were much higher among those who received mail from those parties respectively: the proportion of the PAN vote was 11 points higher than the actual vote in the sample, and the proportion of the PRD vote was 22 points higher. Among those who received mail from the PRI, the vote for both the PAN and the PRI was lower, while the vote for the PRD was higher. This, rather than showing the effects of these types of campaigning, probably reflects campaign tactics: perhaps the PAN and the PRD target their own followers more than the PRI, that is, that they send letters to the areas or districts where they have won elections.

Controlling by levels of awareness, the situation is similar among highly aware voters, but the vote for both the PRD and the PAN was somewhat higher. Nevertheless, among the poorly aware voters, the PRI vote was not as low and the opposition vote was not as high. In other words, campaign letters and mail hurt the PRI, but the damage was not as bad among voters with low levels of awareness as among the highly aware. The government party seems to benefit from low information, while the opposition benefits from making people more aware of the political events in the campaign.

Unfortunately, our measures of home visits and souvenirs did not reg-

Table 5.4
Campaign Contact, Campaign Awareness, and Voting

| | Total Vote | | | Vote by Levels of Campaign Awareness | | | | | | |
| | | | | Low | | | High | | | |
	PAN	PRI	PRD	PAN	PRI	PRD	PAN	PRI	PRD	n
Received mail from										
PAN	40	18	27	39	27	20	41	10	33	120
PRI	22	28	33	20	36	26	24	20	41	256
PRD	13	25	50	10	31	48	15	17	52	110
Received mail										
Yes	26	26	32	25	32	27	28	19	38	359
No	27	39	23	26	41	22	28	35	26	642
Received a home visit										
Yes	26	34	27	26	37	24	25	29	33	389
No	27	35	26	26	39	23	29	28	29	612
Received a souvenir										
Yes	26	31	28	25	37	23	27	22	35	256
No	27	35	26	26	38	24	28	30	29	745
Campaign contact index*										
No contact	26	38	23	26	41	21	28	33	26	416
Low contact	27	36	28	25	38	28	29	31	30	286
Med. contact	31	27	30	32	32	26	29	21	35	179
High contact	21	29	28	20	35	21	22	20	40	120

Source: National Post-Election Poll, subsample of voters, n=1,001.
Note: The subsamples of low and high awareness are given respectively by the codes 0 to 3 and 4 to 7 from the campaign awareness index.

ister what party they came from. So, in the analysis I used a composite measure of campaign personal contact constructed with all three variables. The distribution of the contact index is shown in the last four rows in Table 5.4. The data confirm that the PRI was hurt as campaigning became more intense, while the opposition benefited, especially the PRD.

The damage for the PRI was more significant among the highly aware voters than among the poorly aware. Among the highly aware, the vote for the PRI decreased as personal campaigns became more intense, but the vote for the PRD increased. The vote for the PAN was only higher in the middle levels of personal campaigns. The best scenario for the PRI—where the vote for that party was significantly higher than its average vote—was among voters with low levels of awareness that had no personal contact with the campaign. In other words, the PRI benefited from low awareness and low campaigning. This finding suggests that campaigns offer more information and open more options to Mexican voters, thereby helping to increase the vote for parties other than the PRI. Nonetheless, as it has been argued along this chapter, campaign effects are mediated by awareness.

PREDICTORS OF VOTE CONSISTENCY

As mentioned earlier, volatility in electoral choice is partly explained by a gradual process of dealignment from the PRI during the last fifteen years. Voting for the same party in different elections, or vote consistency, is a particular phenomenon of individual political behavior that has implications for the party system. In this analysis, I have focused on vote consistency as a measure to assess the possible campaign effects in 1997. Nevertheless, vote consistency is a much broader phenomenon that deserves a final note in this chapter. In this section I develop a multivariate analysis showing that campaign awareness does not have a significant effect as a predictor of vote consistency. This is a logical finding given the twofold role that awareness has on the vote depending upon what voters we take into account: partisans or nonpartisans. As shown earlier, awareness reinforced the partisan vote in 1997 and made the nonpartisan vote more volatile. However, awareness seems to make a difference in the role that other determinants of vote consistency have. In this section we go further into the role of awareness, as well as into the determinants of why Mexicans vote for the same party in different elections.

Because the role of campaign awareness is mediated by party identification, awareness itself does not have a direct influence on vote consistency. The first column of logit coefficients in Table 5.5 shows this fact. The dependent variable in Table 5.5 is our measure of vote consistency. Because this variable is dichotomous, with the value "1" for vote consistency and "0" for inconsistency, I considered it appropriate to use logistic regression estimates. The explanatory variables were grouped into four categories: (1) sociodemographic measures, which provide the profile of voters who tend to vote for the same party in different elections and those who do not; (2) information variables, which provide measures of how the voters were exposed to, aware of, and contacted by the campaigns; (3) retrospective variables, which provide an explanation of why voters vote for or against the government party given its performance in office; and (4) a set of variables that measure the voters' political predispositions and ideologies; in this latter group I originally included a measure of left-right self-placement, which was omitted later because it considerably increased the number of missing data.

Table 5.5 has two models. The first model is shown in the first column

Table 5.5
A Model of Vote Consistency
(Logistic Regression Estimates)

	Total Voter Sample		Subsample with Low Awareness		Subsample with High Awareness	
	b	se	b	se	b	se
(Constant)	−3.84	(.68)****	−3.20	(.86)****	−5.38	(1.24)****
Demographics						
Gender (fem.)	.08	(.08)	.14	(.11)	−.02	(.14)
Age	.03	(.01)****	.03	(.01)**	.02	(.01)*
Education	.08	(.08)	.14	(.10)	−.00	(.14)
Income	-.08	(.09)	−.09	(.12)	−.01	(.15)
Student	−1.03	(.17)****	−1.23	(.33)****	−1.02	(.22)****
Mexico City dweller	−.24	(.13)*	−.32	(.21)	−.23	(.18)
Information						
Media exposure	.10	(.03)***	.05	(.04)	.22	(.06)****
Awareness	.08	(.05)	—	—	—	—
Campaign contact	−.01	(.08)	−.05	(.10)	.07	(.13)
Retrospective evaluations						
Presidential approval	−.02	(.10)	.02	(.13)	−.10	(.16)
Personal economic cond.	−.29	(.14)**	−.35	(.18)*	−.31	(.23)
Country's economic cond.	.10	(.14)	.04	(.18)	.26	(.22)
Predispositions						
Party identification	.67	(.12)****	.55	(.16)****	.88	(.20)****
Church attendance	−.10	(.06)**	−.12	(.07)*	−.05	(.09)
Percent correctly predicted	68.15		66.36		72.31	
n	1,001		619		382	
Missing data	260		185		75	
Cases included in analysis	741		434		307	

Source: National Post-Election Poll.
Note: The dependent variable is vote consistency, with the value "1" for voters who voted for the same party in 1994 and 1997, and "0" for voters who voted for different parties in both elections. b=coefficient; se=standard error.
Significance levels: **** p<.001; *** p<.01; ** p<.05; * p<.10.

of coefficients, which includes the variable of campaign awareness and the total voter sample. The second model, shown on the third and fourth columns of coefficients, omits the campaign awareness variable, which was in fact not significant in the analysis. The second column of coefficients included only the voters with low awareness and the third column of coefficients included the highly aware voters.[15]

As mentioned above, the model using the total voter sample shows that awareness has no direct effect on vote consistency; however, the model also shows that media exposure did have a significant effect on it. This finding suggests that information plays a role in the vote choice, and that the reason awareness was not significant is that it plays a role mediated by partisanship. As expected, party identification is a strong predictor of vote consistency. Also, age appears as a very strong determinant of vote consistency, in the sense that older voters are more likely to maintain their political preferences through different elections, while younger voters are more likely to switch their votes from one party to another.[16] This is confirmed by the fact that the likelihood of voting for the same party in different elections decreases among students. The model also shows that vote consistency was less likely in Mexico City, where there has been a great deal of electoral volatility, and among the more secular voters. In other words, religiosity—as measured by church attendance—seems to reinforce the partisan vote in Mexico: the more religious the voter is, the more likely it is for him or her to vote for the same party in different elections.

The role of these variables is confirmed by using the subsamples of low and high awareness: their statistical significance is only reduced in some of the variables due to the smaller number of cases included in the analyses. This is especially the case of age and the dummy variable for Mexico City. However, there are also some variables that kept their statistical significance in one of the smaller samples and not the other. The question is whether this fact is due to differences between the aware and the unaware voters. In the case of media exposure it is definitively a difference between both types of voters, because there is no reason to think that such a significance level would be present only in the relatively smaller sample of highly aware voters and not in the relatively bigger one.

It may seem reasonable to think that personal economic conditions and religiosity may play a significant role among unaware voters but not among aware voters, for the simple reason that it does not require a great deal of information to make evaluations about one's personal economic conditions and because religiosity is an information shortcut. However, the differences in statistical significance may just be caused by the sample sizes: the unaware subsample is relatively bigger than the highly aware one.

CONCLUSION

Campaign awareness is an intervening variable in the possible effects that campaign information has on voters. The variance on how people receive, understand, and recall campaign information is relatively high, ranging from a significant number of individuals who are unable to recall specific campaign facts to a reduced number of individuals who actually show very high levels of attentiveness.

Voter awareness is a factor that helps to explain why some people are more affected by political campaigns than others. Operationalized with measures of campaign awareness, political attentiveness is an intervening variable on how individuals view politics and behave politically. Party identification increases the likelihood of voting for the same party in different elections, but voter awareness affects that likelihood: it makes highly aware partisans more resistant to campaign effects than the less aware partisans; and it also makes the more aware nonpartisans more likely to change their political preferences than the less aware nonpartisans. In other words, awareness reinforces the partisan vote, but makes nonpartisans more likely to change their political preferences.

Vote consistency is a relevant concept to the patterns and dynamics of competition in future elections and it is important to understand what determines the likelihood of voting for the same party in different elections. Of course, party identification is an aspect that theoretically explains vote consistency, and the data used here have confirmed its role in Mexico. Age also seems to account for partisan loyalties: older voters show higher levels of vote consistency, suggesting in fact that the strongest partisan ties are among the older electorate, and that younger voters tend to be more volatile. Whether today's younger voters will keep being volatile in the future or develop some new partisan ties is also a relevant question for the dynamics of the Mexican party system. In any case, understanding how partisan loyalties develop in the Mexican context is an open task for research in Mexico. The data used here also show that the younger electorate tends to be the more informed and aware of political campaigns. Competition seems to have opened a window for political interest in Mexico.

Elections have become much more competitive in Mexico and the role of political campaigns has changed. Their role is to distribute more information to the electorate about the different political options. In the process of increasing political competition that Mexico is undergoing, if campaign information is not necessarily about specific policy proposals and programs, it is definitely about the presence and strength of opposition parties. The lack of this information obviously limited the voters' political options before 1997. However, in the 1997 elections we may have witnessed an increase on the average levels of information to which the Mexican electorate was exposed, especially from the major opposition parties.

APPENDIX

List of variables from the ARCOP National Post-Election Poll, with the item number from the original questionnaire, and the variable name as used in this chapter in capital letters.

A. GENDER. (Coded without asking: 1=Male; 2=Female.)

B. AGE. How old are you? (Coded textually.)

5. VOTE IN 1994. In the 1994 presidential elections, which party did you vote for? (Codes: 1=PAN/Diego Fernández de Cevallos; 2=PRI/ Ernesto Zedillo; 3=PRD/Cuauhtémoc Cárdenas; 4=Other; 5=Don't remember; 6=Didn't vote; 7=No answer.)

9. PRESIDENTIAL APPROVAL. In general, do you approve or disapprove of the way President Zedillo is governing? Do you (approve/disapprove) totally or somewhat? (Codes: 1=Approve totally; 2=Approve somewhat; 3=Neither approve nor disapprove; 4= Disapprove somewhat; 5=Disapprove totally.)

11. PERSONAL ECONOMIC SITUATION. Comparing your current economic situation with the one you had three years ago, would you say that it is better now, worse now, or is it about the same? Is it a lot (better/worse) or somewhat (better/worse)? (Codes: 1=A lot better; 2=Somewhat better; 3=About the same; 4= Somewhat worse; 5= A lot worse.)

12. COUNTRY'S ECONOMIC CONDITIONS. Now, compared with three years ago, would you say that the country's economic situation is better now, worse now, or is it about the same? Is it a lot (better/worse) or somewhat (better/worse)? (Codes: 1=A lot better; 2=Somewhat better; 3=About the same; 4= Somewhat worse; 5= A lot worse.)

26. PARTY IDENTIFICATION. No matter whom you have voted for in the past, which political party do you like (*simpatiza*) the most? (If respondent named a party, s/he was asked whether s/he like it a lot or some.) (Codes: 0=None; 1=PRI a lot; 2=PRI some; 3=PAN a lot; 4=PAN some; 5=PRD a lot; 6=PRD some; 7=Another party; 8=No answer.)

33. NEWS BROADCAST. Which television news program do you watch the most? (Codes: 1=*Hechos*; 2=24 *Horas*; 3=*Al Despertar*; 4=Other; 5=None.)

34. MEASURES OF MEDIA EXPOSURE. During the last electoral season, how much did you get to know about the political parties' campaigns through (. . .), A lot, some, little, or nothing?

    a. Television
    b. Radio
    c. Newspapers
    d. Family and friends

37. INTEREST IN POLITICAL ADVERTISING. How interested were you in the political advertising that has been showing on radio and television during the last months, would you say that you were very interested, somewhat interested, little interested, or not at all interested?

38. CAMPAIGN SLOGANS. Could you tell me what party or political institution comes to your mind with the following phrases? (Response codes not offered: 1=PAN; 2=PRI; 3=PRD; 4=PT; 5=PVEM; 6=IFE; 7=Government; 8=None.)

        a. "Don't vote for a politician, . . . " ("No votes por un político . . .")

        b. "For the Mexico we all want to see" ("Por el México que todos queremos ver")

        c. "Because you are Mexico, Mexico goes first" ("Porque México eres tú, México es primero")

        d. "A turn on your behalf" ("Un giro a tu favor")

        f. "It's time for the sun to rise" ("Ya es tiempo de que salga el sol")

        e. "The choice is yours" ("La elección es tuya")

        g. "Mexico is its people" ("México es su gente")

39. RECEIVED A HOME VISIT/ RECEIVED A SOUVENIR. During the political campaigns that just ended . . . (Codes: 1=Yes; 2=No.)

        a. Were you visited at home by people representing a political party?

        b. Did you get a souvenir from a political party?

        c. Did you place a bumpersticker from a political party in your car or home? (Not used in the analysis.)

40. RECEIVED MAIL. During the political campaigns, did you receive any personalized mail from a political party? Which party? (Codes: 1=Mentioned; 0=Not mentioned.)

        a. Did not receive any

        b. Yes, from the PAN

        c. Yes, from the PRI

        d. Yes, from the PRD

        e. Yes, from the PVEM

        f. Yes, from another party

53. LEFT-RIGHT SELF-PLACEMENT. In politics, people talk about left and right positions. In a 10-point scale, where 1 means being on the left in politics, and 10 means being on the right, where would you place your own views?

57. CHURCH ATTENDANCE. How often do you attend church services? (Codes: 1=At least once a week; 2=Once a month; 3=On special occasions; 4=Almost never/never.)

58. RELIGIOUS DENOMINATION. Which religious group do you belong to? (Codes: 1=Catholic; 2=Protestant; 3=Other; 4=None.)

C. EDUCATION. Which was the last grade of school that you studied?

D. INCOME. Approximately, what is the monthly income in your household?

E. OCCUPATION. What is your main occupation?

I. VOTE IN 1997. In the July 6 elections for federal deputies, for which party did you vote? (Asked at the end of the interview with a secret ballot method; codes in the ballot: 1=PAN; 2=PRI; 3=PRD; 4=PVEM; 5=Partido Cardenista; 6=PDM; 7=PT; 8=PPS.)

NOTES

1. Stephen Ansolabehere and Shanto Iyengar, *Going Negative: How Political Advertisements Shrink and Polarize the Electorate* (New York: The Free Press, 1995), 37.

2. John Zaller, *The Nature and Origins of Mass Opinion* (Cambridge: Cambridge University Press, 1992).

3. Ansolabehere and Iyengar, *Going Negative,* 37.

4. Anthony Downs, *An Economic Theory of Democracy* (New York: Harper and Row, 1957).

5. Philip E. Converse, "The Nature of Belief Systems in Mass Publics," in *Ideology and Discontent,* ed. David Apter (New York: The Free Press, 1964), 206–61.

6. Shanto Iyengar, "Shortcuts to Political Knowledge: The Role of Selective Attention and Accessibility," in *Information and Democratic Processes,* ed. John A. Ferejohn and James H. Kuklinski (Urbana: University of Illinois Press, 1990), 160–85.

7. Philip E. Converse, "Popular Representation and the Distribution of Information," in *Information and Democratic Processes,* ed. John A. Ferejohn and James H. Kuklinski (Urbana: University of Illinois Press, 1990), 369–88.

8. Vincent Price, and John Zaller, "Who Gets the News? Alternative Measures of News Reception and Their Implications for Research," *Public Opinion Quarterly* 57 (Summer 1993):133–64.

9. Converse, "The Nature of Belief Systems in Mass Publics."

10. Zaller, *The Nature and Origins of Mass Opinion,* 19.

11. Samuel Popkin, *The Reasoning Voter: Communication and Persuasion in Presidential Campaigns* (Chicago: The University of Chicago Press, 1991).

12. Ibid.

13. Ibid., 14.

14. Zaller, *The Nature and Origins of Mass Opinion,* 21.

15. The subsample of low awareness included the codes 0 to 3 from the campaign awareness index, and the subsample of high awareness included the codes 4 to 7 from the same index.

16. Age is a strong sociodemographic predictor of vote consistency. The relationship between age and vote consistency is that older voters are more likely to vote for the same party in different elections, while younger voters are more likely to change their party preferences from one election to the next. In this case, the measure of vote consistency may not be reflecting the fact that the youngest voters did not vote in 1994 and were coded as "0." Excluding respondents age eighteen to twenty (those who did not vote in 1994 because of their age, given that Mexico's minimum voting age is eighteen) from the regression equation did not cause significant variations.

6

WHY CÁRDENAS WON

THE 1997 ELECTIONS IN MEXICO CITY

Chappell Lawson

On May 15, 1997—less than two months before the July 6 *elections*—
Reforma newspaper reported that the bottles of water being distributed by
ruling party activists at campaign stops in Mexico City contained roughly
190 times the acceptable level of certain microorganisms. The bacteria in
question caused no serious illnesses, only nausea and mild intestinal problems. In other words, observers joked at the time, the symptoms were
essentially indistinguishable from the feeling one normally gets after
attending a ruling party rally (with or without the bottled water): queasi-
ness, slight discomfort, and the nagging sensation that one has recently
been exposed to local parasites.

But the incident was more than just an amusing piece of campaign gos-
sip; rather, it highlighted the basic dilemma that confronts Mexico's long-
standing "official" party (the Institutional Revolutionary Party, or PRI).
Although dependent on pork-barrel spending to maintain its political base,
the PRI has been forced by financial crisis to abandon its free-spending
ways—both in government and on the campaign trail. In the past, the PRI
was able to compensate for temporary losses in electoral support through
manipulation of the mass media, repression of the opposition, and electoral
"alchemy" (i.e., fraud). Unfortunately for the ruling party, its recent financial woes came at precisely the time that Mexico's slow-motion process of
democratization prevented it from relying on traditional measures. The

political reforms of 1995–96—negotiated by the leadership of Mexico's main political parties during the first half of President Ernesto Zedillo's administration—effectively guaranteed electoral integrity and opposition access to the media during political campaigns. Furthermore, a general climate of social mobilization and civic pressure ensured that these reforms would, in fact, be observed. In this political context, Mexican voters would decide who won Mexico City.[1]

By an overwhelming margin, they chose Cuauhtémoc Cárdenas, standard-bearer of Mexico's left for the past decade, and son of revered former president Lázaro Cárdenas. In Mexico City, Cárdenas's Party of the Democratic Revolution (PRD) captured 28 of 30 single-member congressional districts and 38 of its 40 plurality-winner seats on the city council. The party also did well nationally, winning 26% of the vote and thus the second-largest representation in Mexico's lower house of Congress. But Cárdenas's victory as Mexico City's first elected mayor had the greatest symbolic importance, as the contest was widely viewed as a dry run for the presidential elections of 1997. The Mexico City elections of 1997 thus signaled the revitalization of Mexico's left and the political renaissance of its leader.

Why did the PRD do so well in Mexico City, instead of the conservative National Action Party, which had benefitted from antigovernment sentiment in the past? How did Cárdenas win such a decisive victory in a race that was essentially tied between the three major candidates in March? Why did opinion shift so strongly in favor of Cárdenas and his party? And what does this shift reveal about voting behavior in Mexico in general?

This chapter relies on data from a three-round panel survey of Mexico City voters in 1997.[2] It begins by reviewing the principal arguments regarding Mexican voting behavior. It then analyzes voter choices in Mexico City, which generally support earlier research into how Mexicans vote. Next, it examines the shift toward Cárdenas during the campaign (which is particularly pronounced in the panel sample). I argue that Cárdenas won because he simultaneously converted a range of voters to the PRD and tapped a strong current of anti-PRI sentiment.

1. MEXICAN VOTING BEHAVIOR

During the last several years, political scientists have assembled a fairly comprehensive picture of the Mexican electorate.[3] Though analysts have sometimes emphasized slightly different determinants of electoral preference—including regional, ideological, sectoral, attitudinal, class, and gender variables—recent scholarship has tended to confirm and reinforce earlier research. In general, scholars agree on three basic facts.

First, the dominant cleavage in Mexican politics pits the country's political opposition against a crumbling authoritarian regime and its electoral arm, the PRI.[4] The progovernment side includes the principal beneficiaries of clientelism and one-party rule in Mexico: government employees, owners of large businesses, members of the PRI's state-corporatist organizations, and peasants in villages traditionally favored by the government. On the opposition side lie the professionals, small- and medium-sized businessmen, independent unions and peasant organizations, and other groups that have traditionally been abused by Mexico's authoritarian system. In general, opposition voters tend to be better educated, more engaged in politics, more urban, and younger; by contrast, the PRI's core supporters remain, in the words of one presidential adviser, "the old and the ignorant."

Second, analysts have noted a pronounced and persistent regional cleavage that divides the country roughly in half.[5] In the North, West, and the state of Yucatán—areas where the Catholic Church remains influential and local business elites have long opposed centralized control from Mexico City—the country's conservative National Action Party constitutes the main opposition force. In the poorer, more rural South, the leftist Party of the Democratic Revolution remains the principal challenge to PRI rule. Mexico thus comprises a pair of essentially two-party systems—PRD-PRI in the South, PAN-PRI in the North. Only in the capital and a handful of provincial areas does competition regularly take on a multiparty character.[6]

Third, scholars generally agree on the existence of a "floating" opposition vote, which may fall to either the PAN or the PRD.[7] In the presidential elections of 1988 and 1994, for instance, the total opposition vote remained roughly the same, at least according to official figures. But the distribution of that vote among opposition parties varied dramatically. In 1988, the bulk of it fell to leftist candidate Cuauhtémoc Cárdenas; in 1994 it was captured by Diego Fernández de Cevallos of the PAN. This finding mirrors electoral swings in certain states, such as San Luis Potosí and Baja California, where the anti-PRI appeared to slosh between different opposition parties.[8] The existence of this floating opposition vote tends to reinforce Mexico's regional divide, as anti-PRI voters in historically pro-PAN areas support that party, while those in regions where the PRD is strong tend to favor it.

These general conclusions find abundant support in aggregate-level electoral returns. What is missing from existing analyses of Mexican voting behavior, however, is insight into individual attitudes and behavior. Salient political cleavages may exist, but do voters fall decisively on one side or another of these divisions? Are voters' sentiments actually stable, or do aggregate figures mask volatility at the individual level? Where shifts in attitudes and partisan support occur, are these the results of strategic voting, real attitude change, or random fluctuations among people with little political interest and commitment? In short, how do Mexicans really think and act about politics? To address these questions, I first review the principal determinants of partisan support in Mexico City and then analyze shifts in this support over the campaign.

2. EXPLAINING THE MEXICO CITY VOTE

In general, familiar predictors of partisan loyalties explain most of the vote for the major parties in Mexico City in 1997. All parties drew support from those who held higher opinions of that party and from those who had voted for that party in the past. As in previous elections, PRI voters tended to be less educated, more rightist ideologically, more concerned about crime in their neighborhoods, and less disposed to political change.[9] Presidential approval,[10] lack of political interest,[11] favorable impressions of the PRI's mayoral candidate Alfredo Del Mazo, optimistic assessments of the economy, and government employment were also associated with PRI support, though these variables were not significant in all models. In contrast to what some analysts have found in other elections, fear of political violence was not related to support for the PRI.[12] But overall these findings essentially confirm existing research.

Support for the major opposition parties also followed expected trends. In broad terms, PAN voters tended to be ideologically centrist or rightist, better educated, and more likely to approve of the president's performance.[13] In logistic regression models, the most important variables predicting a PAN vote for Congress were education, a (positive) opinion of the party, and a (negative) opinion of the PRD.[14] A richer picture of the party emerges when opinion of the PAN,[15] rather than voting behavior itself, is taken as the dependent variable. In this case, five factors contributed to a positive evaluation of the party: (1) favorable attitude toward the party's mayoral candidate, Carlos Castillo Peraza; (2) education; (3) a preference for democracy over authoritarianism;[16] (4) church attendance; and (5) conservative ideology. Occupational, class, and income variables played little role. This picture of PAN support is illuminating, as it calls attention to the religious dimension of PAN support—a dimension that many observers have noted but has yet to show up consistently in statistical analyses of Mexican voting behavior.[17] These findings also confirm conventional wisdom that the PAN draws its support from a more educated and conservative constituency.

By contrast, PRD supporters tended to come from lower-class backgrounds and be more skeptical of economic reforms (though attitudes toward economic policy were not significant in all models). Perhaps the most salient finding regarding PRD voters, however, was the strength of the relationship between PRD support and antigovernment sentiment. Virtually all indicators of opposition to the government were statistically significant predictors of PRD support. These included not only negative feelings about the PRI but also a positive impression of the PAN, a preference for democracy over authoritarianism, disapproval of the president, left-wing ideology,[18] and a favorable attitude toward political change in Mexico. The strength and consistency of these relationships is impressive; collectively, they indicate that the PRD drew support from those with a pervasively negative view of the government. Because PAN support in 1997 was not correlated with antigovernment sentiment while PRD support was, it seems that the PRD became the home for the most strongly committed members of Mexico's political opposition in the Federal District.

Findings from the 1997 campaign in Mexico City, then, generally parallel what has become conventional wisdom among analysts of Mexican voting behavior. As in other elections, the prototypical PRI voter was a housewife with limited education; the classic PAN supporter an educated Catholic; and the paradigmatic PRD voter a politically engaged member of the working class. The principal exceptions in 1997 were the relatively narrow PAN base, which left it with more Catholic and conservative support, and the relatively broad base of the PRD, which included a greater range of voters than in 1991 or 1994.[19] (See Appendix B.)

3. EXPLAINING SHIFTS

Why did the PRD enjoy particularly broad support in 1997? The PRD's appeal was not immediately obvious at the start of the campaign; the campaign itself produced marked shifts in public opinion and partisan support. While the three major party candidates for mayor were essentially tied in March, PRD candidate Cuauhtémoc Cárdenas finished more than 20% ahead of PRI candidate Alfredo Del Mazo, with PAN nominee Carlos Castillo Peraza a distant third. This trend is magnified in the sample analyzed here, in which Cárdenas increased his vote share by 26 points in the course of the campaign. The PRI and the PAN, by contrast, lost a roughly equal portion of voters each (12% and 14% respectively).[20]

Who switched to the PRD? In broad terms, the Cardenistas lured three categories of voters. First, and least numerous, were undecided voters who actually turned out and voted for Cárdenas. This group composed 4 percent of the sample (or twice that if one includes voters who initially refused to state their preferences and those who originally did not intend to vote). Second, and much more important, were PRI supporters who changed their minds in the course of the campaign and voted for the PRD. This group composed about 8 percent of the sample. Finally, comprising just under 10 percent of the sample, were initial PAN supporters. The PRD thus lured away supporters from two other major parties while retaining party loyalists and strengthening its position among undecided and uncommitted opposition voters.

The nature of these trends becomes clearer if we analyze changes in overall opinion toward the major parties, rather than voting intention. Shifts toward the PRD reflected real changes in attitudes toward that party and, to a lesser extent, increasing skepticism of the PAN. Though the PAN began the race with the highest average rating, by June the PRD had surpassed it.[21] In fact, the PRD's aggregate score increased by approximately 1.5 on a scale of 1 to 10—an improvement of 27%. Meanwhile, the PAN lost ground slightly (falling from 5.74 to 5.57), and the PRI stagnated (improving its rating by a statistically insignificant 0.09 on the same scale). The campaign thus produced an impressive shift in sentiment toward the PRD that paralleled the shift in voting preference.

The Cárdenas Message

Two general factors seem responsible for the shift toward Cárdenas. First, the campaign appears to have boosted the PRD's appeal across the population in general. Although the PRD's overall score improved, the variance in respondents' evaluations of the party increased only slightly. In other words, the campaign did not polarize supporters for and against the PRD; it shifted the mean.[22] The campaign thus appears to have erased the effects of anti-Cárdenas propaganda during the Salinas administration (1988–94) and rehabilitated the image of the PRD in the minds of most Mexico City voters.

Second, the PRD increased its support among its "natural" base. Opposition to neoliberal economic policies, lower-class status, perceptions of rising street crime, disenchantment with existing institutions, and a preference for democracy over authoritarianism were all associated with improved opinions of the PRD. In this sense, the campaign awoke, crystallized, and reinforced underlying pro-Cárdenas preferences.[23]

This same process worked in reverse as well. Women warmed to the PRD much less than men in the course of the campaign, reinforcing the notion that the PRD faces a persistent gender gap.[24] In this case, it seems likely that the PRD's association with violence and provocation—an association exploited by PRI propaganda but not entirely without foundation contributes to the greater skepticism with which women view the party.

Finally, the PRD seems to have picked up support from those most and least engaged in the political process. Both newspaper readership and *lack* of interest in politics predicted increased support for the PRD. Together, these two contradictory effects suggest that the PRD simultaneously tapped voters who were previously politically disengaged and voters who followed the campaign closely. Media effects and political mobilization thus worked together to activate potential supporters.

Why the PAN lost

Though Cárdenas's ascendance is the most dramatic story of the 1997 mayoral campaign, changes in support for the PAN and the PRI are also illuminating. Together, they support the notion that the campaign reinforced cleavages in the electorate. In other words, they reveal substantial shifts in individual-level attitudes despite limited aggregate changes in evaluations of the two parties. They also suggest why the PAN fared so badly during the campaign.

In general, changes in attitudes toward the PAN were a function of four factors: ideology; support for democracy; church attendance; and fear of political violence. Education and (higher) social class also appeared to be associated with increased support for the PAN, though these variables failed to reach statistical significance in most models. In other words, as with the PRD, the PAN's natural supporters tended to like the party more over the course of the campaign. Not only did more religious, conservative, and democratic-minded citizens tend to favor the PAN initially but also they tended to like it more as time went on. Those concerned about the risks of political transition also warmed to the party during the campaign.

These findings also shed light on the causes of the PAN's collapse into third place. Why did the PAN lose so badly when it began the campaign with relatively high levels of support? One tempting explanation is that the PAN's loss was inevitable: the party may have been too Catholic and too attached to neoliberal policies for most voters (especially opposition voters). In other words, perhaps the PAN's natural constituency was simply too small in comparison with the PRD's, and the party thus lost ground as opinion coalesced. While plausible, this explanation is not supported by the data. Mexico City voters in general—and the sample of them analyzed here in particular—are ambivalent about neoliberal reforms and not particularly ill-disposed toward the PAN. Most are also churchgoers who would not necessarily have been put off by the party's religious orientation. In other words, the crystallization of ideological and religious sentiment does not appear to have damaged the PAN.

A second explanation is that the PAN lost because of its candidate, Carlos Castillo Peraza. Both anecdotal evidence and survey data suggest that Castillo was a poor choice and cost the party dearly. Castillo's ratings were significantly lower than his party's (0.3 points on a 0-to-10 scale, while Del Mazo's were significantly higher (0.4 points) than the PRI's and Cárdenas's identical to the PRD's.[25] Nevertheless, these findings fail to explain why the *party's* reputation, as well as Castillo's vote share, dipped in the course of the campaign.

One final explanation is that the PAN lost because it failed to articulate a clear message that would tap intense antigovernment sentiments. This claim is supported by the data, which clearly show that antipathy toward the PRI was associated with growing support for the PRD but not for the PAN. Consequently, the PRD, rather than the PAN, became the party of those who wished to punish the government and the ruling party. If this explanation is correct, the PAN's crucial debility was not its ideology, its policies, its religious orientation, or even its candidate. Rather, it was a legacy of past collaboration with the PRI, combined with a poor campaign strategy that failed to produce a simple, coherent, antigovernment message. Cárdenas, not the PAN, capitalized on widespread public discontent with the ruling party.

PRI Support and the Presidential Pull-through

At an aggregate level, opinion of the PRI changed very little if at all from March to July. The party began the mayoral race with low ratings, which the campaign itself failed to alter. Nevertheless, this overall trend conceals a few nuggets of information about Mexican voting behavior.

Besides initial opinion of the PRI, only two factors affected changes in voters' opinion of the party. The first was ideology, which exercised a powerful influence on respondents' attitudes. In general, each step to the right on a 7-point ideological scale was associated with an increase of around 3 points (on a 10-point scale) in support for the PRI. The second was presidential approval, as measured by average support for Ernesto Zedillo over three waves of the sample.

The role of presidential approval probably reflects the fact that the president campaigned aggressively for the PRI. Those who approved of his performance might thus be expected to like the ruling party more. Though Zedillo's prestige was not sufficient in the Federal District to redeem the party or raise popular opinions of the PRI above those of its competitors, the president clearly helped his party within a section of the population.

The impact of ideology is less easy to explain. In left-right terms, the PRI is an amorphous political coalition, comprised of pork-barreling populists, technocratic economic reformers, and everyone in between. Though the last three presidents have advocated market-oriented reforms, the party has simultaneously supported targeted subsidies and a variety of welfare-state programs. Moreover, the PRI's mayoral candidate in 1997, Alfredo Del Mazo, was clearly identified with the party's populist wing. Why, then, should conservative ideology be so strongly associated with increased support for the PRI?

The answer to this puzzle lies in the nature of ideology in Mexico. As hinted above, left-right redistributive issues do not represent the dominant political cleavage in Mexico. Rather, the most salient division is between the government (as represented by its electoral arm, the PRI) and the opposition. Ideological self-identification appears to tap this dimension, and only secondarily (if at all) the redistributive dimension.

Table 6.1
Principal Correlates of Ideological Self-Identification

Correlate	Bivariate Correlation
Opinion of the PRI	.40
Presidential approval	.33
Support for political change	−.29
Opinion of the PRD	−.28
Opinion of the PAN	.15
Left-Right index	−.12
Support for democracy	.06

Table 6.1, above, shows the main correlates of ideology in Mexico (where a higher score indicates rightism). As the data indicate, ideology is most strongly related to opinion of the PRI and attitudes toward political change. It is much more weakly correlated with an index of traditional left-right attitudes (where higher scores indicate leftism), and even this weak correlation disappears once opinion of the PRI is taken into account.[26] In other words, Mexicans view "right" as indicating a favorable opinion of existing government institutions: the ruling party, the president, and so forth. They view "left" as signifying a favorable attitude toward political change. From this perspective, the PRD lies on the left, the PRI on the right, and the PAN (perhaps surprisingly) in the center-right.[27]

Importantly, ideological self-identification correlates only weakly (−.06) with a preference for democracy in the abstract. The dimension it taps thus concerns attitudes about the pace of political change, not necessarily the ultimate value of democracy as a form of government. Support for democracy was associated with support for both the PAN and the PRD, but only the PRD was viewed as a thoroughgoing opponent of "the system." On the question of how much of the existing system to dismantle and how fast to do so, the PAN was viewed as moderately rightist. Presumably as a result of its collaboration with the PRI during the Salinas years, the PAN remains associated in the public eye with gradualism and ambiguous opposition.

Summary

In general terms, the campaign of 1997 had two major effects. First, it raised the standing of the PRD among broad sections of the population. Second, it polarized public opinion toward political parties along ideological and attitudinal lines. Leftists and hard-core members of the opposition gravitated toward the PRD; those who favored democracy but were concerned about political violence warmed to the PAN; and those who supported existing institutions tended to like the PRI more in the course of the campaign. The PRD thus won the support of those Mexico City voters who favored rapid political change. In 1997 this group was a decisive plurality. (See Appendix C.)

4. IMPLICATIONS FOR MEXICAN VOTING BEHAVIOR

Apart from the outcome of the elections in Mexico City, the dynamics of the 1997 campaign suggest three general conclusions about Mexican voting behavior. First, they paint an interesting picture of campaign effects in Mexico, suggesting that attitude change is at least as important as strategic voting in determining electoral shifts. Second, they suggest that the apparent stability of political opinions indicated by aggregate level data masks substantial volatility at the individual level. Third, they suggest that existing models of voting behavior may require reconceptualization to take into account attitude change and instability.

Campaign Effects

In general terms, the 1997 campaign in Mexico City had three important effects. First, it crystallized existing cleavages within the population. As discussed above, Mexico's major parties and their "natural" constituencies found each other in the course of the campaign. Second, the campaign produced real shifts in attitudes that reflected campaign messages and dynamics. Those who perceived street crime as increasing sharply in their neighborhoods, for instance, tended to like the PRD more in the course of the campaign. In part, this shift probably reflects class cleavages, as street crime was worst in poorer neighborhoods. But it also reflects the fact that Cárdenas made crime one of the central issues of his campaign. Similarly, both the PAN and the PRD increased their standing among those who favored democracy—a pervasive theme of opposition advertisements and speeches. In other words, voters appear to have understood and responded to broad campaign messages. Third, the campaign had a thoroughly positive impact on opinions of Cárdenas. The PRD and its leader increased their standing across the political spectrum and within diverse segments of the electorate.

For this reason, it is intriguing to consider what would have happened if the campaign had not taken place, or if it had occurred in a much more constrained political environment. Could the PRD have rehabilitated its image without a campaign? Would Cárdenas have won the election had he not been able to get his message out to the voters? The findings presented here suggest that the answer to both questions is probably no—people's attitudes and opinions might have remained much the same as before the campaign, and the lingering effects of years of anti-PRD propaganda would have remained dominant in their minds. This does not mean, of course, that the PRD was exclusively dependent on the mass media to boost its support. But the general context of the campaign—the combination of grassroots mobilization, mass media coverage, campaign propaganda, and greater attention to politics—did have an important influence on voters' opinions of the major parties.

It is important to stress that these campaign effects are different from the strategic voting that other political observers have noted.[28] In the 1997 mayoral election, strategic voting played a negligible role. Virtually every voter in the sample voted for the party they claimed to like most (as opposed to the one they liked second most). It might be argued that Cárdenas was widely viewed as the favorite by election day, thus strategic voting was not necessary. But even at the early stages, when the outcome was by no means certain, evidence of strategic opposition voting is scanty. Not only did respondents express their intention to vote for the party they rated highest but also ticket-splitting did not appear to follow the logic of strategic voting. If voters were to behave strategically, then they would be much more likely to vote for their second-favorite opposition party for mayor (which was decided by plurality winner) than for Congress (which was determined by a combination of plurality winner and proportional representation). In March, however, only six of the seventy-nine respondents who favored the PAN for Congress also favored the PRD for mayor. This was essentially the same ratio as those who favored the PAN for mayor but the PRD for Congress (eight of eighty-two).[29] In other words, people did not seem to split their ballots in a way that indicated strategic opposition voting.[30]

To summarize, real attitude change rather than strategic voting seems to have determined the shift toward Cárdenas in 1997. A range of voters, especially opposition voters, liked the PRD more as the campaign progressed. As a result, Cárdenas, not Castillo Peraza and the PAN, captured their support.

More generally, the 1997 Mexico City elections suggest that political campaigns in Mexico have at least four separate effects. First, as scholars have already noted, they may encourage floating opposition voters to throw their lot with the opposition candidate that appears most likely to win (strategic voting). Second, they may crystallize existing sentiments and mobilize "natural" supporters for each party. Third, they may prime particular political issues, thus encouraging support for the parties that seem to represent the people's views on those issues. Fourth, they may persuade people previously opposed to a party about its relative merits. During 1997 the last three effects were dominant. In the future, therefore, analysts will thus have to take seriously the possibility that campaign dynamics are driving real shifts in voters' opinions of the main parties.

Table 6.2
Vote in July by Voting Intention in March

Actual vote in July	Voting Intention in March		
	PAN	PRI	PRD
PAN	7%	6%	8%
PRI	7%	26%	3%
PRD	46%	36%	64%
Other	13%	6%	5%
Didn't vote	20%	23%	12%
Didn't answer	6%	3%	9%

Minimalism in Mexico

Thus far, my findings have concentrated on the causes of shifts in political attitudes. But they have focused on the portion of these shifts that can be explained by demographic and attitudinal variables. What they have not stressed is the tremendous volatility of individual-level opinions. In general, my findings indicate that voting preferences in Mexico are not particularly stable or consistent at the individual level. Rather, aggregate trends in voting behavior and partisan support mask substantial underlying fluctuations in the population.

This can be seen most clearly in voting preferences. Table 6.2, above, summarizes the final decisions in July of respondents who originally declared their intention to vote for one of the three major parties in March. As Table 6.2 indicates, voting intention in March was an exceedingly poor indication of how people actually voted four months later. Though the relationship between voting intention at the beginning of the campaign and actual voting in July was not entirely random, it was quite weak. Initial PAN supporters, in particular, ended up no more likely to vote for the PAN than initial supporters of other parties. Inconsistency was also pronounced for evaluations of the main parties, presidential approval, ideological self-identification, and other political attitudes. In all these cases, opinions at one time were a poor predictor of opinions only a few months later. Table 6.3, below, shows the correlations over time for presidential approval, evaluations of the main political parties, and ideological self-identification.

These data suggest three basic conclusions. First, there does appear to be some degree of "real" public opinion that is consistent over time. All the correlations presented in Table 6.3, for instance, are statistically significant at the 1% level. But, there also appears to be a great deal of apparently random change within the population.[31] The bulk of these changes in attitudes is not explicable in terms of demographic, opinion, or other variables.

Table 6.3
Attitude Consistency

	Correlations of:		
	March with July	March with June	June with July
Presidential approval	.32	.38	.35
Opinion of PRI	.42	.34	.41
Opinion of PAN	.28	.28	.37
Opinion of PRD	.26	.33	.52
Ideology	.24	.40	.44

Models of the change in opinions about the major political parties, for instance, explain at best 20% of the variation from March to July. Moreover, fluctuations are just as pronounced in variables that would not be expected to change much in the course of the campaign (such as ideology) as they are in opinions of the major parties or the president.

Second, attitude stability appears to deteriorate over time. In general, the correlations on the right of the table (where observations were separated by only a month) are stronger than those on the left-hand side (which were separated by four months). This deterioration probably reflects real political learning in the course of the campaign that stabilized public opinion between June and July. But it may also be the result of contamination effects from the survey itself. Respondents who have no firm political attitudes may be more likely to recall what they told pollsters one month earlier than four months earlier.

Third, certain types of attitudes appear to be more stable than others. Most obviously, opinions of the PRI show a divergent trend from opinions of the other parties. Consistency is both higher over the course of the campaign and *less* likely to deteriorate over time. This finding is hardly surprising, as the PRI is the most well known of Mexican parties and respondents have had decades to appraise its national-level track record. Opinions are likely to remain relatively fixed—though it must be stressed that "relatively fixed" in this context is still quite variable.

What causes the instability of political attitudes in Mexico? As in other contexts, education appears to be the most important factor in giving opinions a measure of consistency.[32] To illustrate this relationship, I segmented the sample into four groups, based on education. In general, those with higher levels of education held more consistent political views about the president, the major parties, and other attitudes.[33] Table 6.4, below, shows the correlations of opinions in March with those in July, by educational level.[34] As the data suggest, only those with college education (and, to a lesser extent, those with preparatory education) held firm ideological

Table 6.4
Education and Opinion Stability (March–July)

	Ideology	Presidential approval	Opinion of PRI	Opinion of PAN	Opinion of PRD
Primary school (N=82)	−.08	.08	.39	.31	.30
Secondary school (N=105)	.18	.26	.25	.26	.32
High school (N=107)	.27	.41	.41	.29	.45
College or more (N=84)	.54	.47	.67	.28	.30

positions throughout the campaign. They also tended to have more stable opinions of the president and, to a lesser extent, the main political parties.[35]

Furthermore, a greater component of the change among educated voters appears to be related to genuine shifts in attitudes than to random fluctuations. To illustrate this finding, I analyzed shifts in opinions of the PRD from March to July for each educational subsample. For those with some college education and above, variables like occupation, ideology, hostility to neoliberal policies, prospective sociotropic evaluations of the economy, political interest, church attendance, newspaper readership, and attitudes toward the PAN all explained shifts toward Cárdenas. This segment of the sample thus appeared to have clear, coherent reasons for changing their opinion of the PRD. Their motivation was sophisticated, prospective, and programmatic. For those with only a primary school education, by contrast, only two other variables even approach statistical significance: attitudes toward democracy and retrospective evaluations of respondents' personal economic situation. To the extent that there was any real content to opinion shifts within this cohort, then, it was limited to broad, unambiguous political messages and specific economic grievances—in this case, a sort of primitive punishment vote.

To summarize, the data suggest that there is a great deal of inconsistency in the Mexican electorate. Respondents frequently changed their minds about what they thought of the major political parties and which ones they intended to support. Inconsistency, however, is not evenly distributed across the population. Educated Mexicans hold more stable opinions, and when their opinions do change, this change is more likely to be the result of real attitude shifts. By contrast, much of the change in opinion among Mexicans with limited education appears to be the product of random fluctuations.

In the aggregate, of course, random fluctuations among voters with few fixed political views tend to cancel each other out. As a result, inconsistency is not directly observable from the previously available data on Mexican voting. But the panel data analyzed here demonstrate that attitude instability is real, and a satisfactory model of Mexican voting behavior will have to take it into account.

Modeling Mexican Voting Behavior

These findings have clear implications for the most well-known explanation of Mexican voting behavior: the so-called two-step model.[36] According to Domínguez and McCann, Mexican voters first decide whether they support the ruling party or not. Their decisions are based not only on social and demographic factors, but also on perceptions of the economy and concern about political change. Those who decide to oppose the PRI then choose between the country's opposition parties based on a familiar set of regional, religious, and ideological variables. But a substantial portion of these individuals, Domínguez and McCann argue, vote strategically in the sense that they simply cast their ballots for the opposition party with the best chance of defeating the PRI. Can this model explain election dynamics in 1997, in which the PRD drew substantial support from previously committed PRI voters and shifts in electoral support were the result of attitude change or random fluctuations rather than strategic voting?

The two-step model makes three implicit claims about individual-level voting. First, it implies that opposition voters who switch their allegiance should be more likely to switch to another opposition party than they should to switch to the PRI. This claim was basically confirmed by panel data: of initial PAN and PRD voters who switched their party allegiance in the course of the campaign, 16% switched to the PRI and 84% switched to another opposition party. If these opposition switchers had simply behaved as though they had no secondary partisan attachments, 30% would have switched to the ruling party.[37] Thus, opposition voters were substantially more willing to cross the left-right ideological cleavage (from PAN to PRD and vice versa) than to cross the opposition-government divide.

Second, the two-step model implies that PRI voters should be simply less likely to switch their allegiances than supporters of the PAN and PRD. A comparison with PRI switchers also supports this contention. Only 26% of initial PRI supporters switched to one of the main opposition parties in the course of the campaign, against 38% of initial PRD and PAN supporters. In other words, PRI voters were substantially less likely to change allegiance than opposition voters.

Third, the two-step model suggests how citizens should split their ballots. Specifically, it implies that voters who split their ballots should do so between rival opposition parties or, conceivably, between major parties and ideologically proximate minor parties.[38] In 1997 Mexico City voters cast four ballots: mayor, lower house of Congress (Chamber of Deputies), upper house of Congress (Senate), and city council (the Asamblea). Approximately one-quarter of the voters in the sample split their ballots in one way or another. Some of these voters appeared to follow a clear logic, dividing their ballots between two major parties or one major party and the Green Party; others sprinkled their votes across as many as four competing factions. To simplify analysis, I have divided ticket-splitters into three groups: (1) those who voted for the PRI and at least one of the two major opposition parties; (2) those who cast ballots for both of the two major opposition parties but not the PRI; and (3) those who voted only for one major party and one or more minor parties. If the two-step model is accurate, the first group—those who cross the opposition-PRI divide—should be small relative to the other two.

This prediction, however, does not appear to hold up. Voters who split their ballots appear about as likely to do so between the PRI and the major opposition parties (32% of splitters) as they do between major and minor parties or between rival opposition groupings (37% of splitters). In other words, the opposition-government divide did not appear particularly wide to ticket-splitters.

The findings presented here thus offer only mixed support for the two-step model. They suggest that the opposition-PRI divide is hardly absolute. Most voters perceive a greater ideological distance between the PRI and the main opposition parties than they do between rival opposition groups, but some do not.

Why is empirical support for the two-step model weak? One possibility is that Mexicans never really voted as the two-step model implied. In other words, the model offered a useful heuristic for predicting aggregate-level returns, but it did not capture the way Mexicans actually vote. An equally plausible interpretation, however, is that the two-step model was once an accurate depiction of Mexican voting behavior, but emerging partisan cleavages are finally eroding the old logic.[39] If this interpretation is correct, even further erosion of two-step voting is to be expected in the future. As political cleavages crystallize, the partisan affiliations of opposition voters are likely to become more pronounced. In addition, as democratization proceeds, the issue of political change should ultimately lose its salience. Two-step voting makes some sense in a system governed by one ruling party; once that party no longer rules, Mexicans may behave in a more typical way. Sincere preferences should supplant strategic voting.

The data presented here suggests one further ingredient that models of Mexican voting behavior will have to address—apparent random switching by people with little political interest or information. Current models of voting behavior assume that Mexicans must have real political opinions and must hold these opinions consistently over time. My findings suggest that many do not. Attitude instability is a real phenomenon in Mexico, and it represents an important caveat to the two-step model—or any other model of voting behavior premised on the existence of abiding political attachments.

Conclusions

The panel data analyzed here have a number of implications for the study of Mexican voting behavior. They indicate that political cleavages in Mexico do exist but are not absolute, and that many voters regularly cross those cleavages in the course of a campaign. Most of this shifting can be attributed to attitude instability in the electorate, but a portion appears to be the result of real attitude change provoked by electoral competition. Future models of Mexican voting behavior will have to explain both types of change.

APPENDIX A

The panel study analyzed here consists of three waves: in March (with 798 respondents) after candidates were announced but before the official beginning of the campaign; in early June (with approximately 500 respondents) shortly after the mayoral candidates' debate; and after the elections in July (with approximately 400 respondents). The first and third rounds took approximately one week to administer; the second lasted approximately two weeks. All surveys were carried out by pollsters from *Reforma* newspaper, working in pairs, under the direction of Rafael Gímenez, director of research at *Reforma.*

In all, the survey contains approximately 135 items, designed by the author with considerable input from the polling staff at *Reforma,* other leading pollsters, and several scholars of voting behavior. The questions cover demographics, evaluations of the economy, political attitudes, political interest, media use, impressions of the leading parties and candidates, voting preferences, perceptions of corruption, and related topics. Certain key questions—media use, ideology, partisan evaluations, presidential approval, and voting preference—were repeated in different rounds.

Because of attrition, the final sample of 402 respondents is not representative or random. In broad terms, it underrepresents men and the wealthy and overrepresents 1997 PRD voters. Because the first-round preferences of the surviving respondents are roughly equivalent to the preferences of all those polled in the first round, however, the sample effectively overrepresents those who switched to the PRD. In other words, the data capture in bold relief the main shift in the 1997 Mexico City elections.

The following are frequencies for selected variables in the survey.

Gender

Men:	45%
Women:	55%

Age

18-22:	22%
23-29:	29%
30-45:	25%
46 or older:	24%

Education

None:	2%
Primary:	20%
Secondary:	26%
High school:	27%
College or more:	21%
Didn't answer:	4%

Monthly household income

0–1000 pesos	18%
1001–2000 pesos	26%
2001–3000 pesos	24%
3001–4000 pesos	12%
4001+ pesos	17%
Didn't answer:	3%

Class

Lower:	12%
Working/lower-middle:	29%
Middle:	54%
Upper-middle:	3%
Upper:	1%
Didn't answer:	1%

Occupation

Housewife:	37%
Student:	17%
Shopkeeper/Salesman/Vendor:	10%
Professional/Technical/Managerial	6%
Government employee:	6%
Factory worker:	5%
Teacher:	2%
Unemployed:	2%
Retired:	2%
Other:	9%
Didn't answer:	1%

Vote/Voting intention

	Presidential Contests		Mayoral Contest (1997)		
	1988	1994	March	June	July
Didn't/Won't vote:	14%	13%	8%	5%	17%
Too young:	24%	17%	—	—	—
Didn't answer:	2%	2%	6%	6%	6%
Undecided:	—	—	10%	12%	—
PAN:	15%	18%	21%	14%	10%
PRI:	22%	27%	22%	17%	13%
PRD:	14%	17%	25%	36%	46%
Other:	3%	4%	8%	10%	8%

Do people feel free or afraid to express themselves about politics?

People feel free:	35%
People feel afraid:	62%
Didn't know/It depends/Didn't answer:	3%

APPENDIX B

Table 6.5
Principal Determinants of Support for Major Mexican Parties

Generic Model		Dependent Variable	
	Opinion of PRI	Opinion of PAN	Opinion of PRD
Constant	1.96	1.96*	7.03**
New party in power? (1=yes)	−1.06**	.25	.31
Democracy? (1=yes)	.03	.34*	.41*
Social class	−.16	.05	−.26*
Education	.01	.21*	−.16
Ideological self-identification	.19*	.15*	−.26**
Left-Right Index	.05	.03	.31
Gender (female)	−.25	−.01	−.64**
Retrospective evaluation of crime in neighborhood	.27**	−.04	.18*
Presidential approval	2.56**	.49	−.60*
Age	.00	−.01	−.06
Political interest	−.06	.07	.02
Opinion of PRD	−.05	.22**	N/A
Opinion of PRI	N/A	.13**	−.04
Opinion of PAN	.19**	N/A	.25**
Church attendance	−.00	.19*	.05
Adjusted R-squared	.39	.14	.20
N	297	297	297

*Significant at the 5% level
**Significant at the 1% level

APPENDIX B (continued)

Table 6.6
Party-Specific Models

	Dependent Variable		
	Opinion of PRI	Opinion of PAN	Opinion of PRD
Constant	.67	2.45**	3.16**
New party in power? (1=yes)	−.89**	—	.35**
Democracy? (1=yes)	—	.37**	.26*
Social class	—	—	−.15
Education	.05	.12	—
Ideological self-identification (higher is right)	.16*	—	−.14**
Left-Right Index (higher is left)	—	—	.21
Gender (female)	—	—	−.18
Age	—	—	−.00
Political interest	.05	—	—
Opinion of PRD	—	.14**	—
Opinion of PRI	—	.10**	—
Opinion of PAN	.10	—	.16**
Church attendance	—	.15*	—
Opinion of Cárdenas (June)	—	—	.47**
Opinion of Castillo Peraza (June)	—	.34**	—
Opinion of Del Mazo (June)	.41**	—	—
Newspaper readership	—	−.05	—
Retrospective evaluation of crime in neighborhood	—	—	.06
Presidential approval	1.61**	—	−.53**
Adjusted R-squared	.59	.37	.59
N	319	367	338

*Significant at the 5% level
**Significant at the 1% level

APPENDIX C

Table 6.7
Changes in Support for Major Parties

	Dependent Variable		
	Opinion of PRI (July)	Opinion of PAN (July)	Opinion of PRD (July)
Constant	−.10	1.87	5.17**
Opinion of party in March	.24**	.19**	.19**
Age	.00	−.01	−.00
Presidential approval	1.98**	.34	−.95*
New party in power? (1=yes)	−.05	.57*	.14
Social class	.03	−.06	.25
Retrospective evaluation of crime in neighborhood	.05	—	.23*
Democracy? (1=yes)	−.01	.49*	.51*
Education	.01	.20	−.01
Newspaper readership	—	—	.06
Gender (1=female)	−.13	−.23	−.50*
Ideological self-identification (higher is right)	.22*	.12	−.06
Left-Right Index (higher is left)	.13	.09	.88*
Political interest	.05	—	−.19
Opinion of PAN	.31**	—	.09
Opinion of PRI	—	.17**	−.03
Opinion of PRD	−.03	.12	—
Church attendance	—	.28**	—
Fear of political violence (1=yes)	—	.48*	—
Government employee? (1=yes)	.47	—	—
Adjusted R-squared	.27	.16	.12
N	359	354	359

*Significant at the 5% level
**Significant at the 1% level

APPENDIX C (continued)

Table 6.8
Party-Specific Models of Change during Campaign (March—June and June—July)

	Opinion of PRI (June)	Opinion of PAN (June)	Opinion of PRD (June)	Opinion of PRI (July)	Opinion of PAN (July)	Opinion of PRD (July)
Constant	.74	3.42**	8.65**	−.16	.10	3.10**
Opinion of party in March	.14*	.16**	.21**	—	—	—
Opinion of party in June	—	—	—	.12	.31**	.29**
Opinion of Del Mazo in June	—	—	—	.20**	—	—
Opinion of Castillo Peraza in June	—	—	—	—	.09	—
Opinion of Cárdenas in June	—	—	—	−.26**	−.18**	.18*
Age	—	−.01	−.02	—	.00	.01
Presidential approval	2.30**	.47	−.31	1.77**	.34	—
New party in power? (1=yes)	−.28	.31	.33	−.40	.03	.11
Social class	—	−.02	−.47**	—	−.10	−.20
Retrospective evaluation of crime	.30*	—	.17	.07	—	.18*
Democracy? (1=yes)	—	−.01	.35	—	.58**	.45*
Education	—	−.02	−.22	—	.18	.08
Gender (1=female)	—	−.21	−.88**	—	−.20	−.27
Ideological self-ID (higher is right)	.38*	.07	−.23*	.15	.12	.01
Left-Right Index (higher is left)	—	−.09	.08	—	.10	.70*
Political interest	.04	—	−.02	.10	−.10	−.14
Radio listenership	.08	—	—	.05	—	—
Opinion of PAN	−.01	—	—	.34**	—	—
Opinion of PRI	—	.13*	—	—	.11	—
Opinion of PRD	.00	.24**	—	.19	.38*	—
Church attendance	—	.22*	—	—	.22*	—
Fear of political violence (1=yes)	—	−.21	—	—	.55*	—
Adjusted R-squared	.22	.11	.16	.31	.27	.29
N	342	295	306	339	297	312

*Significant at the 5% level
**Significant at the 1% level

NOTES

1. Neither coercion nor heavy-handed clientelism played a significant role in the vote in Mexico City. Not only did a decisive majority of voters choose the opposition, those voters who did favor the PRI appear to have done so based on their personal preference. In the sample analyzed here, only ten respondents (2.5% of the sample) stated that they felt "obliged" to vote for a particular political party or refused to answer whether they felt obliged or not; of those ten, only half voted for the PRI. The data further suggest that "captured" voters—those whose well-being depends directly on the PRI and would be at risk if they voted for the opposition—represented a negligible portion of the Mexico City electorate in 1997. In the sample analyzed here, there was no correlation between being a member of a labor union and voting for the PRI, nor was there any relationship between receiving a gift from the PRI and voting for the ruling party. In other words, voters in Mexico City in 1997 appeared to support the party of their choosing and to choose that party in an atmosphere of political pluralism and vigorous electoral competition.

2. For further detail, see Appendix A. Analysis presented in this paper is based only on those respondents (N=402) who participated in all three rounds. It does not rely on imputation to replace missing data, and unless otherwise stated, all linear regressions are based on list-wise deletion of data.

3. See, in addition to other chapters in this volume, Joseph L. Klesner, "Changing Patterns of Electoral Participation and Official Party Support in Mexico," in *Mexican Politics in Transition*, ed. Judith Gentleman (Boulder, Col.: Westview Press, 1987).

4. See Alejandro Moreno, *Democracy, Economic Development, and Party Choice: Political Cleavage in Comparative Perspective* (Ph.D. dissertation, Department of Political Science, University of Michigan, 1997).

5. See Joseph Klesner, "The 1994 Mexican Elections: Manifestation of a Divided Society," *Mexican Studies* (winter 1995).

6. In the southern part of the state of Sonora, for instance, the PRD has recently discovered a previously untapped base of support in what was a PRI-PAN state. Similarly, competition has also been three-party in certain parts of Guerrero, Colima, and the north-central Bajío area.

7. See Jorge I. Domínguez and James A. McCann, *Democratizing Mexico: Public Opinion and Electoral Choices* (Baltimore: Johns Hopkins University Press, 1996).

8. See Victoria E. Rodriguez and Peter M. Ward, eds., *Political Change in Baja California: Democracy in the Making?* (La Jolla, CA: Center for U.S.–Mexican Studies, University of California at San Diego, 1994); Victoria E. Rodriguez and Peter M. Ward, eds., *Opposition Government in Mexico* (Albuquerque: University of New Mexico Press, 1995).

9. The question regarding political change was phrased as follows: "Some people say that it would be good for Mexico to have another party in power. Others say that continuity and stability are more important. Which position is closer to yours?"

10. Presidential approval was measured in each wave of the panel. Unless otherwise stated, the analysis presented here uses an average of approval from all three waves.

11. Political interest was an index based on two questions: (1) How often the respondent talks about politics with family members; and (2) How often the respondent talks about politics with friends and coworkers. Both variables were measured on the same five-point scale.

12. See chapters in this volume by Alberto Cinta, Beatriz Magaloni, and Alejandro Poiré. In my survey, fear of political violence was assessed with the following question: "Sometimes one hears talk about the political changes that are occurring in Mexico. Do you believe that these changes will be peaceful or are you concerned that they may provoke violence?"

13. As Beatriz Magaloni and others have noted, education tends to help both opposition parties, but it helps the PAN substantially more than the PRD.

14. In logistic regression models of voting for the PAN in the mayoral race, only opinion of the PAN itself was significant. In other words, Carlos Castillo Peraza appears to have lost all but the hardest core of PAN supporters.

15. Opinion of the PAN and other parties was measured on a scale of 1 to 10, with higher scores indicating a more favorable rating. Unless otherwise specified, the rating used here is an average of the respondent's rating of the party in question in each wave of the panel.

16. Support for democracy was measured by the following question: "Some people say that it is best to live in a democratic country. Others say that it is more important to have a government that guarantees stability and order, even if it is not democratic. Which position is closer to yours?" I am indebted to Alejandro Moreno of the Instituto Tecnológico Autónomo de México (ITAM) for the choice and wording of this question.

17. See Domínguez and McCann, *Democratizing Mexico*. Possibly, this dimension would have been visible earlier had "feeling thermometers" of the major parties been available in addition to data on voting intentions.

18. As discussed below, being "leftist" in Mexico means favoring rapid political change; it does not have much to do with questions of economic policy.

19. Appendix B summarizes the findings for Mexico's main parties.

20. For electoral shifts, see Appendix A.

21. Why did the PRI (and the PRD) receive a higher vote share than the PAN, given that its level of support seems lower? The main factor was the floating opposition vote, which shifted almost entirely to the PRD in the course of the campaign. Because these voters have a generally high evaluation of the PAN relative to the PRI but did not vote for it, the PAN's mass approval was higher than its vote share.

22. The standard deviation of opinion of the PRD on a scale of 1 to 10 was 2.28 at the beginning of the campaign and 2.38 at the end.

23. See Appendix C for findings for the main parties. In a regression on changes in opinion of the PRD (on a 10-point scale) from March to July, the following variables were significant at the 5% level: initial evaluations of the PRD; sentiments regarding democratization; ideological self-identification; attitudes toward neoliberal economic reforms; gender; perceptions of crime; political interest; and newspaper readership. Two other variables—social class and retrospective evaluations of one's personal economic situation—just fail to reach significance, presumably because they are highly intercorrelated with each other and with other variables in the model. Models relying on instrumental variables to replace initial opinion of the PRD and models which took opinion of the PRD in July as their dependent variable yielded similar results.

24. See Domínguez and McCann, *Democratizing Mexico,* 138. In my sample, this finding survives controls for education, political interest, religiosity, and other potentially confounding variables, suggesting that gender itself actually influences political sentiments.

25. Numbers are taken from the second round of the survey (early June)—the

only round on which candidates were evaluated. Castillo Peraza's rating was 5.5, while the PAN's was 5.8. Del Mazo's rating was 5.2, while the PRI's was only 4.8. Average ratings for both Cárdenas and the PRD were 6.5 each.

26. The left-right index was composed of answers to dichotomous questions on privatization, free trade, and redistribution. Favoring redistribution, opposing privatization, and opposing free trade were considered left.

27. This finding appears to be supported by previous data on Mexican public opinion but unappreciated by analysts of Mexican voting behavior. (See, for example, Domínguez and McCann, *Democratizing Mexico*, 90–91.) It has been noted by other Mexicanists whose work does not focus on elections. (See Denise Dresser, "Mexico: The Decline of Dominant-Party Rule," in *Constructing Democratic Governance: Mexico, Central America, and the Caribbean in the 1990's*, eds. Jorge I. Domínguez and Abraham F. Lowenthal [Baltimore: Johns Hopkins University Press, 1996], 161.)

28. Domínguez and McCann, *Democratizing Mexico*; Adolfo Aguilar Zinzer, *¡Vamos a Ganar! La Pugna de Cuauhtémoc Cárdenas por el Poder* (Mexico City: Oceano, 1996).

29. The same figures for June offer a few more signs of strategic voting: only sixteen of the seventy-one respondents who supported the PAN for Congress also intended to vote for Cárdenas. These figures are roughly comparable to the level of strategic voting that Domínguez and McCann found in previous elections. (See *Democratizing Mexico*.)

30. As a final check, I analyzed the behavior of those respondents who believed the PRI would win the mayoral contest in March but intended to vote for either the PAN or the PRD themselves. Of these fifty-four voters, only two intended to vote for the opposition party that was not their favorite. Another eight rated the PAN and the PRD equally; these split between Cárdenas and Castillo Peraza.

31. These results were so striking that my first reaction was to question the data itself. To evaluate whether the same individuals were, in fact, interviewed in all three waves, I constructed a respondent match index based on self-reported household income. (Unfortunately, respondents' gender and age were not recorded separately each round of the survey.) In all, I found approximately ninety cases in which household income varied by more than one category on a ten-category scale from March to June. Excluding these cases, however, the correlations presented above remained essentially identical. I next checked every data point for each of the first half of the sample respondents (approximately 20,000 entries); I found some minor coding and transcription errors but no serious inconsistencies. Finally, I checked to see how well past voting behavior (a question asked on the first round) predicted actual voting in July (a question asked on the third round). The correlations were weaker than what other analyses have found for earlier elections, but the bulk of this difference could be explained by the PRI's relatively poor performance in 1997. My working assumption, therefore, is that the data analyzed here are reliable.

32. The importance of education has been noted by a range of scholars. See Philip E. Converse, "The Nature of Belief Systems in Mass Publics," in *Ideology and Discontent*, ed. David Apter (New York: The Free Press, 1964). See also Paul M. Sniderman, Richard A. Brody, and Philip C. Tetlock, *Reasoning and Choice: Explorations in Political Psychology* (New York: Cambridge University Press, 1991).

33. In fact, they even hold with estimates of monthly household income. The correlations between estimated household income (on a 10-point scale) in March and June are 0.44 for respondents with primary school education, 0.47 for those with a secondary

school education, 0.50 for those with a high school education, and 0.76 for those with a college education or better.

34. The table omits those with no education (N=9) and those who did not state their education level.

35. It is worth noting that the crucial variable is education, not media use, income, or political interest. Though these variables are positively correlated with ideological consistency, the correlations disappear or weaken substantially once education is taken into account. Controlling for education, the only variable that is associated with attitude stability to a statistically significant degree is age; older people tend to hold more stable opinions.

36. See Domínguez and McCann *Democratizing Mexico.*

37. These calculations are based on a weighted average of initial PAN supporters (who made up four-fifths of opposition switchers) and initial PRD supporters (who made up one-fifth of opposition switchers). Approximately 27% of initial PRD supporters who switched moved to the PRI, against the 58% that would be expected given the parties' final share of the vote in the sample. Approximately 14% of PAN supporters switched to the PRI, against 23% that would be expected based on parties' share of the final vote in the sample. Voters who switched to and from small parties were omitted from the analysis.

38. Most small parties in Mexico are satellites of the PRI. Because these parties are typically leftist and have sometimes been allied with the PRD, however, it might also be reasonable for voters to split between the PRD and traditional satellite parties. In addition, ticket-splitting between any of the major parties and the Green Party (PVEM) would not seem to confirm or disconfirm the model, given that the PVEM has few political positions beyond its ecological stance.

39. One piece of evidence that points in this direction is the fact that the two-step model worked best in 1988 and less well in 1991. See Domínguez and McCann, *Democratizing Mexico.*

7

UNCERTAINTY AND ELECTORAL BEHAVIOR IN MEXICO IN THE 1997 CONGRESSIONAL ELECTIONS

Alberto Cinta

PRESENTATION

Why was it so natural for Mexican people to complain about their government officials and then vote for them, even when democratic and institutional opportunities for a real change exist? Why was it so common to learn that in many former socialist countries, for example, people decided to vote for well-known communist politicians who had been strongly criticized before election time? In May 1997 the PRI (Partido Revolucionario Institucional), the only party in power for the last seventy years, started its political campaign by raising the following question to Mexican voters: "Why change and risk what you already have?" Uncertainty could probably help me to better understand this puzzle. After all, "fear of change" was a vox populi argument to explain many electoral outcomes in Mexico, notably President Zedillo's electoral victory in 1994. I was surprised to learn that this idea had never been formally tested.[1]

The PRI offers the electorate a seventy-year record of its performance and actions in power, which no other party in Mexico has. As a consequence, the electorate's predictions about opposition parties' performance are more uncertain than those predictions about the PRI. Therefore, if the electorate is risk averse then, ceteris paribus, it will vote for the PRI.

In July 1997 the PRI suffered major electoral setbacks: it lost the mayoral race in the capital and the governorships of the rich state of Nuevo León and historical Querétaro. Furthermore, for the first time in its history, the PRI lost the majority in Congress. This historical episode, however, should not mask another reality: the PRI was still the main electoral force in the country, having the majority in the Senate and a plurality in the House. Actually, with the number of votes it obtained, if elections had been for president, Mexico would have (easily again) a president from the PRI. There is no doubt that the opposition gained new and very important political spaces; but, considering that Mexico was experiencing one of its worst economic crises, highlighted by political murders and outrageous corruption cases, what seems strange is that the PRI's downfall hadn't been more destructive.

This study has a limitation: 1997 midterms were not a presidential election. Speculation about the future tends to be less important in this kind of election, which has been considered more a "punishment" retrospective judgment than a prospective momentum. Still, July 1997 constituted a first good opportunity to prove empirically a new analytical framework for a type of experiment that had never been conducted before. This chapter tries both to answer a question and to present an ad hoc methodology to construct a test. I used a "rational behavior with uncertainty" model and a preelectoral poll[2] designed *ex profeso* to obtain the individual data the model needed.

I. THE ELECTORAL PARTICULARITIES OF THE MEXICAN CASE AND THE NEED OF A RATIONAL UNCERTAINTY MODEL OF ELECTORAL BEHAVIOR

> When there is uncertainty, doing things, that is, to carry out any activity, becomes a secondary role in life; the fundamental problem turns to decide what to do and how to do it.
>
> —Frank Knight

Rational Models and the Use of Information about the Past

Rational models assume that voters make their choices according to the option that gives them more benefits. Citizens' behavior is explained through theoretical constructions where voters are "rational maximizers" of their utility functions. The concept of rationality they use is the same broadly utilized by neoclassical microeconomic theory, where an individual is rational if he has an ordering of preferences that is complete, reflexive, and transitive.

One of the first scholars that introduced this perspective in voting studies was Anthony Downs, with his book *An Economic Theory of Democracy*.[3] According to this important work, the voting choice is centered upon the perception individuals have about their expected utility. As Downs put it, "the most important [reason] for taking an electoral decision is the differential between parties, that's to say the difference between the utility one received during period t, and the utility one could have received if opposition was in office during the same period."[4]

It can be inferred that the information individuals possess should play a central role in all studies that assume a "rational maximizer" conduct from the electorate. In the United States, for example, there exists a considerable literature where the "historical postures" of the Democratic and Republican parties are supposed to be known by the public, and therefore constitute a central element in the construction of electoral models.

It is said for instance, that confronted with the neoclassical dilemma of inflation and unemployment, the Democratic party has demonstrated a historic propensity for carrying out politics oriented to reduce unemployment, whereas the Republican party has shown a tendency to carry out anti-inflationary politics (this has been proved by Hibbs).[5] Many scholars have consequently developed electoral models where citizens take into account this historical record when the moment comes to choose a government. Alesina and Rosenthal, for example, explained how the "American people desire to have moderated politics," which has resulted in a particular voting strategy for having a "divided government."[6]

Such works serve to reinforce the intuitive idea that information about the past should be an important factor when modeling how "rational" people make choices. Actually, this judicious supposition is implicitly incorporated in most rational voting studies, which introduce retrospective judgments as a central part of their analysis.

Mexican Electoral History as a Reason for Electoral Uncertainty

Mexico constitutes a particular case of asymmetrical electoral information, where there is enormous public knowledge about the PRI and very little retrospective information about opposition parties. This is due to the particularities of Mexican electoral history. The Mexican "revolutionary family," that is the PRI, has been in power continuously since 1929, when President Calles assembled almost all the political and military forces of the country and gave birth to the Partido Nacional Revolucionario (PNR). A few years later, when General Cárdenas was president, this same group of power brokers changed its name in 1938 to become the Partido de la Revolución Mexicana (PRM). In 1946 Miguel Alemán, the first civilian president of Mexico, gave the party its contemporary name, Partido Revolucionario Institucional (PRI).

Without any doubt, the history of the PRI is inseparable from the stages of formation of the "new State in Mexico," particularly between 1928 and 1945. Until very recently, for many Mexicans, the PRI, the state, and the government were basically the same thing. This is understandable if we take into account that for the period from 1929 until 1988, the candidates of the PRI had won in all presidential, state, and Senate elections, and practically all the representative elections for federal and local congress, including municipalities. As Garrido[7] put it, "*there is not a similar case in the XX century, apart from the Communist Party of the Soviet Union*" (italics mine).

This study is not interested in the reasons for the PRI's dominion, but in the way this dominion can have very specific consequences in current and future electoral behavior and therefore in electoral outcomes. Effectively, as no opposition party has a historical record of its performance, neither in the executive power nor in leading Congress,[8] Mexico indeed presents an impressive case of electoral decision making with asymmetrical information flows. How do rational voting models analyze situations like this, where information about past governing performance barely exists for many of the available choices? Curiously, this possibility has almost never been formally represented.

There exist of course many sources of uncertainty that electorates around the world have to face—the complexity of making difficult evaluations, the nature of mental processes, the unforeseeable future, many forms of incomplete or imperfect information.[9] Nevertheless, the lack of information about political opposition represents a potential source of asymmetrical uncertainty, *à la Mexicaine,* that forces us to assess how the basic assumptions of rational electoral behavior have been modeled.[10]

Uncertainty and "Classical" Models of Rational Voting Behavior

Retrospective Voting à la Key

Fiorina[11] presented the three most representative theories of rational voting behavior. The first one, known as the "traditional theory" or retrospective voting à la Key,[12] considers that the voter evaluates all that has been accomplished by the incumbent party and then makes a retrospective (ex post facto) judgment to qualify it. In this model, voters either support or punish the incumbent, and elections have no other implications than the approval or rejection of the status quo. Policies are irrelevant to the voter, who decides on the basis of the results that the current administration obtained during a determined period.

As it assumes that citizens decide how to vote based exclusively on considerations about the past, this is the only theoretical approach where uncertainty about the future performance of parties is not relevant. For this particular reason, this approach cannot be applied (alone) in countries were there are reasons to believe that uncertainty affects electoral behavior.

This kind of vote assumes implicitly that there will be no important changes or risks if the opposition party wins and therefore that voters do not care about punishing their public officers.

This theory alone is only convenient in regimes with a democratic tradition. Imagine the extreme case of a "foundational" election à la O'Donnell and Schmitter[13] where the electoral result decides not only the group that will be in power but also the type of governmental structure. It seems evident that the propensity to "punish" a party is related to the cost—generally uncertain—of doing so.

Think about the Mexican case. Key's model implies that the electorate would be ready to punish the PRI at any cost, without considering the fact that "unknown" parties could win. This model is actually not adequate to explain recent Mexican electoral history. It wouldn't be able to elucidate some "postcrisis" electoral results such as the 1985 midterm election, where the PRI lost some important municipalities, but still won almost all the uninominal districts in the Congress. Key's theory could not explain the last 1997 electoral victory of the PRI,[14] obtained only two years after a crisis without precedent, and that could be reservedly summarized as a 7-point reduction of the GNP in only one year.

Retrospective-Prospective Voting à la Downs.

Another theory of voting, proposed in *An Economic Theory of Democracy* by Downs models an electoral decision-making process beyond the punishment/reward criterion formulated by Key. The vote decision depends on the differential of utility between what the individual received with one party's policies, and what he thinks he could eventually have received from another party. As Fiorina put it, this kind of retrospective vote is actually a mean for making prospective considerations.[15] In this model, policies do play a relevant role because individuals use the past as a reference guide about the policies that parties will implement in the future.

If citizens take into account past performance to forecast future performance, then in a strict sense voters in countries such as Mexico wouldn't have the chance to anticipate without uncertainty the eventual performance of the opposition in case of winning an election. This is important because, as mentioned by Magaloni, "it is then possible for the PRI to receive the vote of a core of electors that just fear to risk."[16] Surprisingly, when applied in countries such as Mexico, these kinds of voting models have not produced a systematic consideration and modeling of uncertainty.

The General Case, Retrospective, and Prospective Vote in Fiorina's Model

Finally, Fiorina's modeling tries to "combine features from both the traditional and the Downsian theories."[17] His model is a synthesis of some considerations from Key and Downs and therefore doesn't escape the criticisms applicable to the theories that inspired it. Fiorina's model notably incorporates the "subjective net utility" that a voter could have received if party X had governed instead of party Y.

This theoretical approach has a structural uncertainty problem that all rational behavior, nonpure Key models inherently have: it seems difficult to assess with certainty a "subjective net utility" of the kind where voters are supposed to assess "what would it happen if," or "what will it happen according to." Surprisingly, these models don't contemplate a method for systematically treating the uncertainty problem they create.

Effectively, even if Fiorina's model has a coefficient that is supposed to function as an uncertainty discount factor for prospective judgments, the same coefficient could be also used, as Fiorina himself suggests, as an incompetence or liability discount rate. The fact is that a simple coefficient is not appropriate for modeling uncertainty because it doesn't enrich the understanding of electoral individual decision-making processes. It doesn't help for instance to grasp the relationship between uncertainty and risk attitudes nor does it permit represention of the way different information amounts lead to different uncertainty positions. Moreover, this "uncertainty factor" appears as a fixed parameter that cannot be individually modeled, and no information is provided about how this exogenous variable could be obtained. It is understandable, then, why this idea never reemerged when the empirical proofs of the model were presented.

Uncertainty and an Empirical Study for the Mexican Case: Domínguez and McCann

Domínguez and McCann coauthored *Democratizing Mexico*, the most recent documented and complete study about the Mexican electorate. One important contribution of their work was to represent voting behavior as a two-step electoral decision-making process. Their model argues that the first selection criterion of the Mexican voter is the PRI-opposition dichotomy. According to Domínguez, this is because elections in Mexico are not just a mere competition between parties. As he explained, "Mexicans understand they are not just deciding about the fate of a simple political party." The authors then explicate that a fundamental variable for explaining Mexican voting behavior are the "ruling party factors." As it can be inferred, conclusions in this work constantly allude to the uncertainty problem, even if it is not treated formally.[18]

Note that in this case, the so-called "ruling party factors" could easily be interpreted as a fear or uncertainty measure, although as a simple parameter, it does not offer relevant information about how uncertainty operates. This exogenous significant variable is indeed similar to the theoretical "uncertainty factor" presented by Fiorina. As a matter of fact, *Democratizing Mexico* constituted a serious, open, empirically proved invitation to construct a model capable of assessing uncertainty in Mexico's electoral processes.

II. FUNDAMENTALS FOR A SURVEY STUDY ABOUT ELECTORAL UNCERTAINTY

> I feel compelled to defend the perverse and unorthodox argument
> that voters are not fools.
>
> —V. O. Key

Formalization of the Theoretical Model: Contributions for the Design and Application of an Empirical Study

Designing the Questionnaire

Until now, all the empirical electoral studies that have analyzed voting behavior with uncertainty have been based on public opinion polls.[19] This is understandable if we take into account that the model of uncertainty used by all of them needed, as presented above, the subjective opinion of voters about the policies or expected performance of their candidates. No empirical research has, until now, studied uncertainty by using questionnaires designed *ex profeso* for the occasion.

The first attempt to design an instrument for having a measure of uncertainty appeared in 1994. Alvarez and Franklin announced at that time that "it was possible to measure with opinion polls the subjective uncertainty of the interviewed people." They presented a straightforward set of questions especially conceived to obtain "direct measures of expected value and variance."[20]

> 1. In the conservative/liberal scale, what is the position of candidate (name) about the issue (issue)? (measure on mean)
> 2. How certain are you that candidate (name) holds the position (report the answer of the question above) about the issue (issue)? (measure of variance)

The structure of these questions was precisely the one I considered using in this work because it permits the use of the "microeconomic uncertainty model" presented in Appendix A. Nevertheless, some modifications had to be done to adapt them to Mexico's public opinion realities.

Particularly, I decided to transform these "issue-oriented" questions into "performance-oriented" questions. Repeating Key's words, issues are only relevant if candidates have strongly divergent positions on them. Indeed, the 1997 Mexican political campaign hadn't been too polemical so far. It seemed natural that, considering the deep crisis Mexico had been going through, all candidates concentrated on the same two issues—economy and public security—and their different positions were not generally perceptible for Mexican voters.[21] Furthermore, most of the recent empirical works[22] had suggested that Mexican voters were not issue oriented.

After some other considerations (in order to avoid biased questions, social desirability problems, clarity problems, and so forth[23]), four basic questions were formulated in order to represent the model of electoral uncertainty. All the following questions were proved in focus groups.

1. Q1. Do you think the (party) can do a good or a bad job at making things go better in this country if it wins the election on July 6?" (very good, good, bad, very bad, don't know) [Question for obtaining the mean or "expected value."]
2. Q2. How sure are you—totally, enough, little, or not at all—that (party) will do a . . . (report the answer obtained in question above) at making things going better in this country if it wins the election? [Question for obtaining the variance.]
3. Q3. With which one of the following sayings do you identify the more? ("más vale malo por conocido que bueno por conocer," o, "el que no arriesga no gana"). [Question for assessing the attitude of individuals toward risk.][24]
4. Q4. On July 6 there will be elections for representatives. If elections were today, for which party would you vote?" (PAN, PRI, PRD, PVEM, PT, PC, PPS, PDM). [Electoral question, indicates what party offers the individual the highest utility.]

Other socioeconomic questions were incorporated in the questionnaire as control variables (sex, age, gender, income, level of education, and party identification).

III. THE RESULTS OF THE SURVEY
Electoral Preferences

It must be said that the poll that generated the data for this study took place five weeks before the election it studied. This posed a problem because it is common to observe that these kinds of surveys are exposed to campaign successes and, in general terms, to a volatile electorate. For that reason their results can vary sensibly from the "authentic" electoral results. Table 7.1 presents the results that were obtained for the electoral question: "El 6 de julio próximo habrá elección para elegir diputados. Si el día de hoy fuera la elección, ¿por cuál partido votaría usted?" "On July 6 there will be elections for representatives. If elections were today, for which party would you vote?"

Although this was an early poll, the relative weight of all the electoral categories exhibited results significantly similar to what some weeks later was announced as the official electoral outcome. This is an important validation a posteriori of the poll designed to carry out this research.

The Uncertainty toward the Future Performance of Political Parties

In section I, I explained that due to the electoral of Mexico it was reasonable to suppose that voters tend to be more uncertain about the Mexican

Table 7.1
Voting Intention, Congressional Election (%)

	Survey Percentage	"Effective" Percentage, without No Responses	Official Results (%)
PAN	22	28	27
PRI	34	44	39
PRD	19	24	26
Others	4	4	8
NS	4	—	—
Total	81.2	100.0	100.0
No Response	18.8	—	—

Table 7.2
Certainty Regarding the Future Performance of Political Parties
If They Win the Election* (%)

	About the PRI	About the PAN	About the PRD
Uncertain	43	55	55
Certain	57	45	45

*Percentages were calculated using two different questions. "Uncertain" category was constructed by taking all those who answered "don't know" to Q1 plus all who answered "little or not at all certain" in Q2. This means that "uncertain" appears for all those who don't have an opinion about a party, and for all those who have an opinion (either positive or negative) but are not sure about it.

opposition parties, which do not have a governing record. The information obtained (Table 7.2) corroborates this assumption.

It can be noticed that, as expected, there is uncertainty about all parties, but the PRI is the political option for which fewer cases of uncertainty were registered. For the purposes of this research, results presented in Figure 7.1 are more important.

We can see that uncertainty is present in all levels of education but that it tends to diminish as higher levels are observed. This is consistent with many works[25] which argue that people with low levels of education have a higher probability of not having a solidly formed opinion. In this sense, Figure 7.1 is a validation a posteriori of the measure of uncertainty of this work, as it seems we are really measuring uncertainty.

The PRI is the party that generates less uncertainty at all education levels. This is important because it suggests, as it is assumed in this work, that the difference in the levels of uncertainty is not just a matter of education but of a structural problem with information. This phenomenon could be

Figure 7.1
Certainty about Party Performance, by Levels of Education

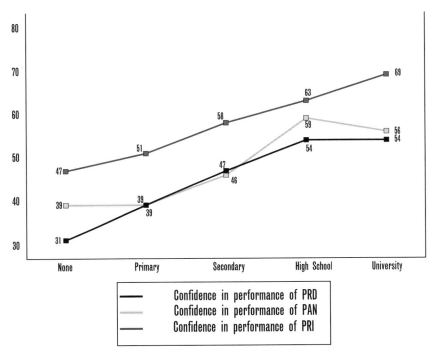

consistently explained with the assumption this work presents: the PRI has more information to offer to different groups of Mexicans, and this counts.

Finally, some considerations must be done about uncertainty and party identification. As shown in Table 7.3, people who identify themselves with a party (two-thirds of the adult population, according to the data) tend to be more certain about this party than the average citizen. As Niemi[26] presented, many works have argued that individuals select the information they receive and only retain the information that serves them to reinforce previous beliefs and values. Yet, as suggested by Table 7.3, party identification by itself is not sufficient to explain electoral uncertainty.

It can be seen that the PRI is the second option that generates less uncertainty for Perredistas as well as for Panistas. Note that the PRI is the party that generates more certainty among those who don't identify with any party. Even controlling by party identification, it seems again that the PRI is the party whose future performance is generally considered more predictable.

Table 7.3
Percentage of Persons Who Are Certain of Their Forecast about Parties' Performance, by Party Identification

"Normally, do you consider yourself as a . . . ?"

	Panista	Priísta	Perredista	Other Parties	Without Party Identification	TOTAL
% of Total	17	32	13	3	35	100
Certain about the PAN	69	40	46	25	39	45
Certain about the PRI	56	59	63	40	51	57
Certain about the PRD	44	39	77	35	40	45

Table 7.4.
Risk Attitudes

"With which one of the following sayings do you identify the more?"
¿Con cuál de los siguientes dichos se identifica usted más?" (%)

	August 1994**	Poll, May 1997
"Más vale malo por conocido que bueno por conocer" Non-risk-taking attitude	40	34
"El que no arriesga no gana" Risk-taking attitude	46	66
Don't know	14	0

**Data are from August 1994 and were obtained by an exit poll conducted by W. Mitofski during the presidential election. The sample was national; 4,832 people responded. This data base can be consulted at the Centro de Investigación y Docencia Economica (CIDE).

Attitudes toward Risk

According to the model used in this work, attitude toward risk defines the intensity and direction of uncertainty in voter's decisions. As explained in Appendix A, uncertainty will only affect a party if individuals are risk averse. Table 7.4 presents an approximation of the risk attitudes of the population, according to question Q3.

Data show that in May 1997 more people had a risk-taking attitude than three years before. This suggests that attitude toward risk is not given but can change according to circumstances. It is important to point out that the question presented in Table 7.4 doesn't necessarily allow one to

Figure 7.2
Expected Performance by Party (%)

"Do you think the (party) can do a good or a bad job of making things go better in this country if it wins the election July 6?"
"Qué tan buen o mal papel cree usted que puede hacer el (. . .) para que las cosas mejoren en el país, sigana las elecciones el 6 de julio?"

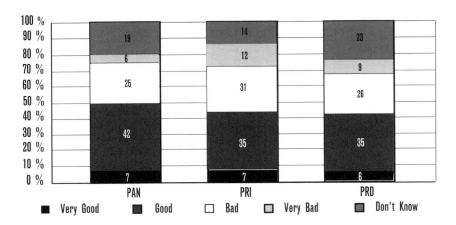

distinguish between voters that are risk averse and voters that are risk takers. It only permits identification of the population group that has a more risk-taking attitude than the other. In reality, both groups presented in Table 7.4 could be either risk averse or risk taking, in which case one group would be less risk averse (taker) than the other.

The Expected Performance of the Parties

Figure 7.2 shows the opinion of Mexicans about the quality of the "job" that could be done by each party if it won the election. Even though it received 12% more votes than its immediate competitor (see Table 7.1), the PRI did not receive more favorable opinions than the opposition. Furthermore, the PRI was the party that received the highest number of unfavorable opinions (43% against 31% for the PAN, and 35% for the PRD).

An inevitable question arises: Why does the party that receives the worst evaluation by voters (with the highest positive difference between bad and good judgments) also receive the highest number of votes? This is not a dilemma if the uncertainty model is considered. The argument follows that the expected value of an output does not alone determine the utility of an agent: variance matters as well. According to the model that

Table 7.5
Forecast of Performance (expected value), and Electoral Preferences (%)

Percentage of Votes for Each Party Depending on the Evaluation It Received

	PAN	PRI	PRD
Very good	75	82	78
Good	41	65	42
Bad	6	18	4
Very bad	4	9	3
Don't know	14	53	12

Table 7.6
Electoral Preferences and Comparative Expected Values (%)

Evaluation about the PAN, PRI, and PRD respectively	Relative weight %	PAN	PRI	PRD
+,+,+	15	25	49	24
+,+,–	10	42	51	4
+,–,+	20	40	6	47
+,–,–	12	79	15	3
–,+,+	4	5	54	34
–,+,–	16	4	90	2
–,–,+	11	3	12	84
–,–,–	4	15	52	12
DN,DN,DN	9	18	61	20
National electoral preferences	100	28	44	24

will be tested in this work, expected value, variance, and attitude toward risk interact to bring about an electoral decision. The relation between all these variables is presented further on.

The Interrelation between the Variables

Cross-tables will be used here as a preliminary step to assess if data behave as the model suggests. The data presented three important characteristics that will be enumerated.

1. *Individuals with the same level of evaluation across parties are more likely to vote PRI.*

Table 7.7
Certainty and the Forecasts about Performance

	Party Evaluated		
	PAN	PRI	PRD
Thinks that the performance of party (see column) will be very good	49	42	41
Is completely sure that performance of party (...) will be good	7	9	8
Is sure enough that performance of party (...) will be good	18	18	14
Is certain about his positive forecast about the future performance of the party	7+18 = 25	9+18 = 27	8+14 = 22
Percentage of persons who have a positive forecast about a party and are sure about it	50	64	53

As it should be expected, there is a strong positive relation between the judgments about future performance and voter intentions. Table 7.5 shows, for instance, that 82% of those who think that PRI would have a very good performance decide to vote for the PRI.

Table 7.5 presents evidence about a phenomenon that is consistent with the hypothesis of this chapter: 18% of those who forecasted a bad performance for the PRI decided to "vote" for this party. Albeit important, expected value is not decisive in electoral decision making. The PRI seems to have a "comparative advantage" that makes people prefer it even when it receives the same evaluation as its opponents. This phenomenon can be better appreciated in Table 7.6.

The first row indicates that, within those who evaluate positively all three parties, one half would vote for the PRI and one quarter for each of the other two parties. Note that the PRI is the option that receives more votes within all the groups where the three parties receive the same evaluation (+ + +; − − −; dn, dn, dn).

2.   *The PRI is the party that generates more positive opinions that are held with certainty.*
Note that even if the PAN is the party that generates more positive opinions (49%), this party is nevertheless not the one that generates more "certain positive opinions." That is, the PAN generates less positive opinions that are held with a strong level of certainty (50%) than the PRI (64%).

Table 7.8
Simultaneous Effect of Three Variables
(attitude toward risk, uncertainty, and expected value) over Vote Intentions

Votes for the PRI depending on expected performance, degree of uncertainty, and attitude toward risk

Forecast and certainty about the forecast		Risk attitude		Average
Expected performance	Certainty about forecast	+El que no arriesga	—Más vale malo	
Very good	Total	85	87	86
	Enough	79	NSC	NSC
	Few	NSC*	NSC	NSC
Good	Total	84	87	85
	Enough	67	78	70
	Few	46	57	50
Bad	Total	10	13	11
	Enough	14	22	17
	Few	21	32	25
Very bad	Total	7	8	7
	Enough	8	NSC	8
	Few	9	NSC	9
Don't know	Don't know (DK)	50	58	53
	Average	38	55	44

*NSC= no sufficient cases (n<40) as for assuring validity.

3. *Individuals who show a lower risk-taking attitude, if they evaluate equal-
    ly all the parties, will tend to vote less for a given party as its evaluation
    (good or bad) becomes more and more uncertain.*

Table 7.8 shows the effect of uncertainty, controlling by vote intentions.
Note that uncertainty affects negatively all voters. This suggests that the
Mexican electorate is mainly risk averse: the *PRI* loses votes as people
are more uncertain about its future performance. Observe for example
that the PRI receives a higher percentage of votes within those that evaluate it as "good" with total certainty (84%), than within those who evaluate
it as "very good," but just are "certain enough" (79%) of their judgment.
It can be now said that the question about risk attitudes (see Table 7.4)
doesn't separate the risk averse on the one hand from risk takers on
the other, but more precisely, it permits to distinguish those voters that
are less risk averse than the others. Voters are mainly risk averse, but to different degrees.

Finally, note that attitudes toward risk are irrelevant for the voting decision if voters claim to be totally certain of their judgments. As suggested by the model, data show that the degree of risk aversion is not important in the electoral decision of those who are certain about their forecast.

This data inspection has allowed us to identify some essential characteristics of the electoral decision-making process. Voters tend to be risk averse because uncertainty about a party affects negatively the probability of voting for it among voters who evaluate the party positively. Second, the PRI is indeed the party that generates less uncertainty, what seems to give it a "comparative advantage," politically speaking.

The next section will present formal tests for the hypothesis of this work; the general econometric model that was used is explained in Appendix B.

IV. TESTING THE MODEL: DESIGN AND RESULTS OF THE ECONOMETRIC MODELS
Results of the Tests

The general model of uncertainty, as presented in section II, was not tested with only one econometric procedure because it contemplates at least (2x2x2x2x2x2x2x3) 384 different possibilities (for instance, a voter thinks PAN is good, with uncertainty, PRI bad with certainty, PRD bad with uncertainty, has a more risk-taking attitude, and votes for the PAN). The number of cases available (2,430), although important, didn't allow a realization of statistic inference with such a large number of possible events.

A first model was established for representing the process in which individuals compare the expected value of different parties. The objective was to quantify the probabilities of voting for the PRI depending on the opinions about different political options.

Logistic model 1: $PRI = 1 / 1 + e^{-(Z)}$

Where $Z = $ Constant + xpan + xpri + xprd + xpanpri + xpriprd + xprdpan.

PRI is the probability of voting PRI.

xpan is the forecast about the future performance of the PAN.

xpri is the forecast about the future performance of the PRI.

xprd is the forecast about the future performance of the PRD.

xpanpri is the simultaneous forecast about PAN and PRI.

xpriprd is the simultaneous forecast about PRI and PAN.

xprdpan is the simultaneous forecast about PRD and PAN.

The possible categories for all the variables used in this model were: 1=a good performance is forecasted; 2=a bad performance is forecasted; 3=don't know. Option (1) doesn't appear in the outcome table because it was chosen as the reference variable .

Table 7.9
Vote for the PRI as a Function of Future Expectations
about Future Performance of Parties

Scaled deviance = 19.889 at cycle 4. d.f. = 15

Estimate	S.E	Parameter
−0.1621	0.1235	1
1.498	0.2917	XPAN(2)PRD(2)
1.424	0.2447	XPAN(3)
1.262	0.4675	XPAN(2)PRD(3)
0.6043	0.2130	XPRD(3)
0.5087	0.2119	XPAN(2)
0.4880	0.2709	XPRI(2)PRD(2)
0.2917	0.1857	XPRD(2)
−0.2784	0.3753	XPRI(3)
−1.150	0.4518	XPAN(3)PRI(3)
−1.322	0.6097	XPAN(2)PRI(3)
−2.383	0.1781	XPRI(2)

scale parameter taken as 1.000

Lecture 1:

P (PRI) / P(No PRI) = exp (β_1 + β_2XPRI(2) + β_3 XPAN(2) + β_4XPRD(2) + β_5 U3).

$\Rightarrow$ P (PRI) / P(No PRI) = exp (−0.162+0.509−2.383+0.292+1.498+0.488) = 1.274.

$\Rightarrow$ P (PRI) = 1.274*(1− P(PRI)).

$\Rightarrow$ P (PRI) = 1.274 − 1.274P(PRI).

$\Rightarrow$ 2.274*P (PRI) = 1.274.

$\Rightarrow$ P (PRI) = 56%.

The model is significant, as it indicates that a person who forecasts a bad performance for all three parties has a probability of 56% of voting for the PRI.

In Table 7.1 the variables were ordered according to its positive effect in the probability of voting PRI. As could been expected, the situation that makes it more possible to vote for the PRI is when a person has a negative forecast for both PAN and PRD at the same time. Notice that it is more probable that a person who forecasts future performance of the PAN as "don't know" to vote for the PRI than when the person forecasts "bad" performance of the PAN.

These results produced the construction of three different models, one for each party, with the form (also see Appendix B):

Table 7.10
Vote for PAN as a Function of Attitude toward Risk,
Forecast about Future Performance of This Party,
and Uncertainty Associated with This Forecast

scaled deviance = 17.438 at cycle 3 d.f. = 16 from 24 observations

Estimate	S.E.	Parameter
0.5822	0.1100	1
−0.2155	0.09859	XR(2)
−0.7243	0.1264	XE(2)
−2.975	0.2087	XE(3)
−3.041	0.4394	XE(4)
−2.355	0.1844	XE(5)
−0.6723	0.3292	XE(1).XV(3)
−0.9875	0.1217	XE(2).XV(3)

scale parameter taken as 1.000

Table 7.11
Vote for PRI as a Function of Attitude toward Risk,
Forecast about Future Performance of This Party,
and Uncertainty Associated with This Forecast

scaled deviance = 10.516 at cycle 4, d.f. = 15 from 29 observations

Estimate	S.E.	Parameter
1.548	0.2408	1
0.5113	0.1175	XR(2)
0.6980	0.4603	XE(2)
−3.962	0.3767	XE(3)
−4.006	0.3483	XE(4)
−1.614	0.2727	XE(5)
−1.777	0.6805	XE(1).XV(3)
−1.485	0.4158	XE(2).XV(2)
−2.420	0.4115	XE(2).XV(3)
−2.234	0.5844	XE(2).XV(4)
0.9519	0.3392	XE(3).XV(2)
1.166	0.3505	XE(3).XV(3)
1.196	0.4756	XE(3).XV(4)
1.920	0.7202	XE(4).XV(3)

scale parameter taken as 1.000

Table 7.12
Vote for PRD as a Function of Attitude toward Risk, Forecast about Future Performance of This Party, and Uncertainty Associated with This Forecast

Scaled deviance = 19.110 at cycle 4, d.f. = 17 from 27 observations

Estimate	S.E.	Parameter
2.154	0.3781	1
−0.2785	0.1441	XR(2)
−1.326	0.4296	XE(2)
−5.180	0.4380	XE(3)
−5.289	0.5605	XE(4)
−3.631	0.4107	XE(5)
−1.426	0.4924	XE(1).XV(2)
−0.5224	0.2450	XE(2).XV(2)
−1.693	0.2449	XE(2).XV(3)
1.622	0.9802	XE(4).XV(4)

scale parameter taken as 1.000

Prob. Vote Party = Attitude toward risk + Forecast about future performance of this party + uncertainty associated with this forecast.

Logistic models 2, 3, and 4: Party = $1 / 1 + e^{-(Z)}$

Where, Z = Constant + xr + xe + xexv.

Party is the probability of voting for a determinate party.
xe is the forecast about the future performance of the party.
xr is the attitude toward risk of each voter.
xexv is the degree of uncertainty associated with the forecast.

The possible categories for all the variables used in these models are:
for   xr, 1= risk-taking attitude , 2= non-risk-taking attitude.
for   xe, 1=very good, 2=good, 3=bad, 4=very bad, 5=don't know.
for   xv, 1=totally sure, 2=enough, 3=little, 4=not sure 5=don't know.

xv is the degree of certainty associated to the evaluation xe about the future performance of a party. In Tables 7.10, 7.11, and 7.12 we only present the statistically significant variables.

The three econometric models offer important information that is consistent with the theoretical uncertainty model and the assumptions that it advances. Note that the PRI is without a doubt the less risky option for the electorate; the coefficient of the variable that represents the attitude toward risk is consistently positive when explicating the electoral preference for the PRI, and negative when explicating the electoral preference for PAN and PRD. This means that those who have a lower risk-taking attitude tend to vote for the PRI more than any other party.

Uncertainty affects all three parties, though it affects the PRI in a minor way. The party that is most affected by uncertainty is the PRD. Unfortunately, no question of symmetry (see note 12) was incorporated in this survey (because no appropriate question passed the focus groups test). Nevertheless, the strong negative impact of uncertainty upon this party suggests that this is the political option considered the most dangerously risky. Even if a formal test of this advancement cannot be done, it may be convenient to comment that these results are consistent with the idea, broadly spread at a national level, that the PRD is a "disorganized and violent party."[27]

Next I present a model in which two different parties are compared simultaneously in an uncertain context.

Logistic Models 5 and 6: $PRI = 1 / 1 + e^{-(Z)}$

Where, $Z = Constant + xo1 + xo2 + xo1xi1 + xo2xi2$.

    PRI is the probability of voting PRI.

    xo1 is the forecast about the future performance of the PRI.

    xo2 is the forecast about the future performance of the (PAN or PRD).

    xi1 is the degree of uncertainty associated with the forecast about PRI.

    xi2 is the degree of uncertainty associated with the forecast about (PAN or PRD).

The possible categories of response where,

    For xo1 y xo2, 1=good performance 2=bad performance.

    For xi1 y xi2, 1=certain, 2=uncertain.

The exclusion of the "risk attitude" variable is not relevant because its effect has already been assessed in other regressions and it was shown that, even if important as a multiplier effect, it does not change the direction of preferences. As I said, it represents two different degrees of convexity for a risk-averse voter.

PRI as dependent variable:

(a) comparative performance PRI/PAN

(b) comparative performance PRI/PRD.

The results of Tables 7.13 and 7.14 model significantly a context of decision making under conditions of uncertainty. Each table permits us to compare and quantify the effect in the vote for the PRI of sixteen different possibilities that result from combining all the possible categories for forecast and uncertainty. Results are presented as probabilities in Table 7.15.

Table 7.13
Vote for the PRI When Controlling for Comparative Performance against the PAN

Scaled deviance = 9.397 at cycle 4, d.f. = 9.

Estimate	S.E.	Parameter
0.4275	0.1837	1
3.004	0.3019	XO2(2)PAN
−2.447	0.2170	XO1(2)PRI
−1.833	0.8054	I11
1.191	0.1915	XO2(1).XI2(2)PAN
−1.782	0.5243	XO2(2).XI2(2)PAN
−1.129	0.2307	XO1(1).XI1(2)PRI

scale parameter taken as 1.000

Table 7.14
Vote for the PRI When Controlling for Comparative Performance against the PRD

Scaled deviance = 13.483 at cycle 4, d.f. = 10

Estimate	S.E.	Parameter
0.4350	0.2284	1
−2.855	0.2726	XO1(2)PRI
3.616	0.2833	XO3(2)PRD
−0.8036	0.2808	XO1(1).XI1(2)PRI
0.8238	0.3096	XO1(2).XI1(2)PRI
1.254	0.2257	XO3(1).XI3(2)PRD

scale parameter taken as 1.000

Note for example that the probability of voting for the PRI when having a good and certain opinion of both the PRI and the PAN is 61%. Furthermore, note that a voter who has a good but uncertain opinion about the PAN and at the same time a bad and certain opinion about the PRI has a probability of 29% of voting for the PRI.

Uncertainty seems indeed to have an important effect in the electoral arena. Reading Table 7.13 differently, suppose voters are certain that the PRI will perform badly and that they also have a certain and bad opinion about the PAN. If the PAN can shift this negative opinion from sure to unsure, then it can cut the PRI share of the vote from 73% to 31%!

The theoretical assumptions made at the beginning of this chapter

Table 7.15
Probability of Voting for the PRI Depending on Forecast and Its Uncertainty (%)

Model PRI/PAN	Prob. Vote PRI	Prob. Vote PRI	Model PRI/PRD
PRI+c*, PAN+c	61%	61%	PRI+c, PRD+c
PRI+c,PAN+I	83%	84%	PRI+c, PRD+i
PRI+c, PAN-c	97%	98%	PRI+c, PRD-c
PRI+c, PAN-I	84%	98%	PRI+c, PRD-i
PRI+i, PAN+c	33%	41%	PRI+i, PRD+c
PRI+i, PAN+I	62%	71%	PRI+i, PRD+i
PRI+i, PAN-c	91%	96%	PRI+i, PRD-c
PRI+i, PAN-I	63%	96%	PRI+i, PRD-i
PRI-c, PAN+c	12%	8%	PRI-c, PRD+c
PRI-c, PAN+I	29%	24%	PRI-c, PRD+i
PRI-c, PAN-c	73%	77%	PRI-c, PRD-c
PRI-c, PAN-I	31%	77%	PRI-c, PRD-i
PRI-i, PAN+c	12%	17%	PRI-i, PRD+c
PRI-i, PAN+I	29%	42%	PRI-i, PRD+i
PRI-i, PAN-c	73%	88%	PRI-i, PRD-c
PRI-i, PAN-I	31%	88%	PRI-i, PRD-I

*symbols "+" and "−" refer to positive or negative evaluations of parties. Letters "c" and "i" refer to the certainty or uncertainty about such evaluations.

have been proved. The behavior expected by the microeconomic model, posed according to these assumptions, adjusts to the data. The main results are presented in the next section.

V. CONCLUSIONS

Uncertainty is a neglected electoral variable, though it is central to Mexican electoral behavior. The role of uncertainty is important because of two fundamental facts, corroborated in this work. First, it was proved that voters think they forecast more accurately the future performance of PRI than the future performance of other parties. Second, in electoral terms, the Mexican population tends to be risk averse. With two identical evaluations, such voters will always prefer the less uncertain option. These two results serve to verify the importance of uncertainty in politics. It was proved further that the microeconomic model of uncertainty offers a good characterization of the electoral decision-making process. As a matter of fact, the uncertainty model helps to solve dilemmas that had never been explored before.

Effectively, the PRI is the party that receives the worst evaluations at a national level, and nevertheless, it represents the option that receives the highest number of votes. This apparent inconsistency has been explained

easily using both a general rational model and empirical data that supported its assumptions and conclusions.

It was proved that risk aversion and the fact that the PRI generates
more certainty combine to confer an important competitive advantage to
this party. Ceteris paribus (*about evaluations*), the PRI will tend to receive
the highest number of votes.

The models used in this work not only allow us to quantify the importance of uncertainty but also they enrich our understanding of the electoral
process. It was proved that the "uncertainty effect" is far from being just a
variable; instead it is a complex process in which (at least) three important
variables (uncertainty, expected value, risk attitude) interact to bring about
a unique outcome.

The role of uncertainty can be amplified or diminished through the
attitudes of the population toward risk. It must be said that an important
change has been detected between the two last Mexican national elections
(1994 and 1997), in favor of a more risk-taking attitudes. Furthermore, it
has been possible to identify not only that the PRI benefits most regarding
uncertainty but also that the PRD pays the highest cost. It was proved not
only that uncertainty matters but also that the uncertainty model is a consistent, rational way to interpret the phenomenon.

Briefly, the PRI benefits from the record of its past performance, a
record that while not fully satisfactory to everybody at least determines the
range of the PRI's possible future performance. This generates certainty, a
good that is generally desired by Mexicans who, being risk adverse, choose,
ceteris paribus, the party for which future performance can be predicted
more certainly: the PRI.

APPENDIX A: THE THEORETICAL FRAMEWORK

Assumptions:

There will be legislative elections, and it is assumed that voters consider them an important moment, with strong consequences for the national economy and politics and therefore for their personal well-being. All acts are terminals in the sense that they precede immediately the consequence. Preferences are complete and transitive (consistence axiom), and individuals act as if they were sure their vote will decide the election outcome. Therefore no strategic vote is contemplated. Voters act in order to maximize their expected utility.

The elements of the individual decision-making process:

1. Set of acts (x): each citizen has to decide from a set of mutually exclusive options, namely political parties "PRI" and "Opposition."

2. Set of states (s): a set of future states or outcomes, mutually exclusive and unpredictable, exists, namely governmental performance.

3. Consequences function, c(acts, states): all possible combinations between political parties and governmental performance. Consequences are expressed as probabilities.

4. Probabilities function, p(state): that expresses the probability of each state or possible outcome. These are subjective estimations made by each voter. We have $0<p<1$ and $\Sigma p=1$.

5. Utility function, v(c): measures the subjective utility that each voter accords to all the different consequences of his or her acts. This function has to assign a cardinal value to consequences. This restriction permits us to compare intensities; it makes it possible to have functions with a well-defined shape (convex or concave).

In this model, citizens decide the best of all possible options using the *expected utility rule*:

$$\text{Rule von Neumann-Morgenstern of expected utility}$$
$$U(x) \equiv p_1 v(c_{x1}) + p_2 v(c_{x2}) + \ldots + p_{sv}(c_{xs}) \quad (1)$$
$$U(x) \equiv \Sigma_{s=1}^{s} p_{sv}(c_{xs})$$

Identity (1) shows that, for each voter, utility U(PRI) of voting for the PRI is the average of all different possible performances of this party (good, average, bad), weighted by the respective subjective probability of these performances to happen.

The main contribution of this model is that, as shown by John von

Figure 7.3
Utility Function over Consequences

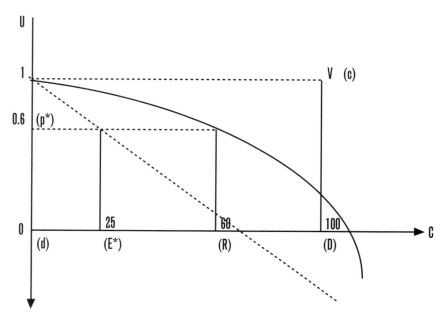

Neumann and Oskar Morgenstern in 1944, it is possible to establish, for each individual, an order of preferences over acts from his order of preferences over consequences. This means that if a voter has to decide between a given performance E (with p=1) and a reference lottery E* (probabilistic lottery with D=p and d=1–p), then there will always be a probability p* such that this voter will be indifferent between E and E*.

Figure 7.3 illustrates the essential characteristics of the model. This voter is indifferent between a governmental performance that gives him 25 units of utility with probability 1, and the option that gives him 0 units of utility with probability 0.4 and 100 units of utility with probability 0.6. In electoral terms, this means that this voter would be indifferent between a political party that certainly will have a mediocre performance, and a party that could be a disaster with some p probability, or an excellent choice with some other (1–p) probability.

In Figure 7.3 we can see why the shape of the utility function is important. The slope will always be positive (because of the assumption that more is always preferred to less), but the second derivative can be either positive or negative. In this case, as the function is concave, function v(c) will always be above any straight line joining two of its points (that is, above any probabilistic lottery). As a consequence, concave utility functions make voters prefer any option where p=1, to all probability lotteries that have the same expected value. Individuals with this kind of utility function are said to be risk averse. Note that if the utility function were convex, we would have the opposite results. People with convex utility functions are said to be risk takers. All implications about the shape of a utility function are summarized in *Jensen's Inequality*, expressed in terms of second derivatives:

> If $v''(c)<0$ then $Ev(c)<v[E(c)]$, concavity $\Rightarrow$ risk aversion.
> If $v''(c)=0$ then $Ev(c)=v[E(c)]$, straight line $\Rightarrow$ risk neutrality.
> If $v''(c)>0$ then $Ev(c)>v[E(c)]$ convexity $\Rightarrow$ risk lover.

This model is very useful to represent decision making under uncertainty:

1. It has a strong normative appeal because its premises are simple and acceptable. As Jacques Drèze put it, "a person that doesn't accept the axiom of simple ordering for conditioned actions, consequences and events cannot expect any help from scientific methods that have been designed to represent decisional problems."[28]

2. It offers descriptive realism and exposes how much making a decision can involve many variables. It is a rationalist approach that can be modeled.

3. The representation of decision making in terms of acts, events, and consequences is flexible, general, and makes formalization of theory easier.

4. The model introduces the powerful theory of probabilities and its analytical instruments. This approach treats uncertainty as a probability problem and not as a "sensation of vacuity and confusion," that impedes any explication of the phenomenon. It gives uncertainty a rational sense that allows its representation.

APPENDIX B: DESIGNING A FORMAL EMPIRICAL TEST

Prob(Vote 1 y no 2) = f (M_{i1}; M_{i2}; V_{i1}; V_{i2}; R_{i1}; R_{i2}) (1)

This identity, presented in section III, presents the electoral preferences as a dichotomous dependent variable expressed in probabilistic terms. The independent variables are the expected values and variances of an opinion about the parties, in this case of the forecasted future performance of parties if in office.

It is a model in which (1) probability enclosed between 0 and 1 is preferred; and (2) relation between the probability (dependent variable) and the vector of independent variables X will be modeled as nonlinear (to avoid the marginal increment of X to be a constant).

The type of model that satisfies these two needs is the accumulated probability Logit, established from a logistic accumulative distribution function. Logit models are constructed according to the next identity:

$$P = 1 / 1 + e^{-(\beta 1 + \beta 2 Xi)} (2)$$

For estimation purposes, identity (2) can be written as:

$Li = \ln (P / 1 - P) = \beta_1 + \beta_2 X_1 + u$, where β_2, the slope, measures changes in L for a unit change in X.

NOTES

1. The possible role of uncertainty in Mexico's electoral arena was first mentioned in academic works simultaneously by Beatriz Magaloni, "Elección racional y voto estratégico: Algunas aplicaciones para el caso mexicano," *Política y Gobierno*, I, no. 2 (1994):309–44. These studies were devoted to another subject of research and presented the problem much more than studying or modeling it. The first attempt to measure the role of uncertainty in Mexican elections was conducted by Jorge Buendía, "Uncertainty, Incumbency and Voting Behavior in Transitions to Democracy" (dissertation proposal, University of Chicago, 1996).

2. The preelectoral poll used in this analysis was financed by the Technical Advisory at the Office of the President of Mexico. Two thousand four hundred thirty national "house interviews" were obtained between May 26–30, 1997. Details about the sample technique and the questionnaire design are given in sections II and III of this chapter.

3. Anthony Downs, *An Economic Theory of Democracy*. (New York: Harper and Row, 1957).

4. Ibid., 40.

5. Douglas A. Hibbs, Jr., *The American Political Economy* (Cambridge: Harvard University Press, 1987).

6. Alberto Alesina, and Howard Rosenthal, *Partisan Politics, Divided Government, and the Economy* (Cambridge: Cambridge University Press, 1994).

7. Luis Javier Garrido, *El Partido de la Revolución Institucionalizada. La formación del nuevo estado en México (1928–1945)* (Mexico City: SEP – Siglo Veintiuno Editores, 1986), 13.

8. In reality, since 1988 opposition parties have started to govern in some important political entities such as Baja California, Chihuahua, and Guanajuato (PAN), as well as in big municipalities such as Mérida and Naucalpan (PAN), and Neza (PRD). Even if these changes effectively provide some new information to the public, it is still regional information. This new type of political information available to the electorate remains relative to the kind of risk-laden public responsibilities involved with macroeconomic and national security policies, all extremely concentrated in Mexico's federal government.

9. For a comprehensive description of all different sources of uncertainty, read Young Back Choi, *Paradigms and Conventions: Uncertainty, Decision Making and Entrepreneurship* (Ann Arbor: University of Michigan Press, 1993).

10. It must be said that Mexico constitutes an extreme example of this particular asymmetric information case. In that sense, it only makes more evident both an old problem and a new research field. In reality, this kind of asymmetric information is common in most democracies, where the incumbent party generally benefits from much more exposure to mass media. For this reason the methodological approach proposed in this work could be useful for advanced democratic countries as well.

11. Morris P. Fiorina, *Retrospective Voting in National American Elections* (New Haven: Yale University Press, 1981).

12. See V. O. Key, Jr., *The Responsible Electorate: Rationality in Presidential Voting 1936–1960* (Cambridge: Harvard University Press, 1966).

13. Guillermo O'Donnell and Philippe Shmitter, *Transitions from Authoritarian Rule: Tentative Conclusions about Uncertain Democracies.* Baltimore, MD: Johns Hopkins University Press, 1986.

14. The national results were the following: PRI 39%; PAN 27%; PRD 26%.

15. Fiorina, *Retrospective.*

16. Magaloni, "Elección."

17. Fiorina, *Retrospective,* 65.

18. Jorge I. Domínguez and James A. McCann, *Democratizing Mexico: Public Opinion and Electoral Choices* (Baltimore: Johns Hopkins University Press), .

19. See, for example, Larry Bartels, "True Voting Under Uncertainty: An Empirical Test," *American Journal of Political Science*, 3 (1986): 709–728.

20. Michael R. Alvarez and Charles M. Franklin, "Uncertainty and Political Perceptions," *Journal of Politics* 56 (1994): 671–78. See also James Enelow and Melvin J. Hinich, "A New Approach to Voter Uncertainty in the Downsian Spatial Model," *American Journal of Political Science,* 25 (1981): 483–93.

21. Besides, there is a body of important literature that concludes that individuals are so poorly informed that issues are not really important. See Angus Campbell, Philip E. Converse, Warren Miller, and Donald Stokes, *The American Voter* (New York: Wiley, 1960).

22. Francisco Abundis, "Issues and Candidates in the 1994 Mexican Election," Columbia University, unpublished manuscript, 1994.

23. Some good practical considerations and advice for designing questionnaires

appear among others in Normal Bradburn and S. Seymour, *Polls and Surveys: Understanding What They Tell Us* (San Francisco: Jossey-Bass, 1998).

24. This question had been used for the first time during the 1994 Mexican presidential election, in an exit poll conducted by Warren Mitofsky.

25. John R. Zaller, *The Nature and Origins of Mass Opinion* (Cambridge: Cambridge University Press, 1993). Note that in this work "forecast of future performance" and "expected value" are synonymous.

26. Richard Niemi and Herbert F. Weisbert, *Controversies in Voting Behavior* (Washington, D.C.: Congressional Quarterly, 1993).

27. In June 1997, 39 percent of survey respondents identified the PRD as a "violent party." See Centro de Estudios de Opinión, "Segunda encuesta preelectoral nacional por muestreo sobre intención de voto" (Mexico: June 1997).

28. Jacques Drèze, *Essays on Economic Decisions Under Uncertainty* (Cambridge: Cambridge University Press, 1987).

8

IS THE PRI FADING?

ECONOMIC PERFORMANCE, ELECTORAL ACCOUNTABILITY, AND VOTING BEHAVIOR IN THE 1994 AND 1997 ELECTIONS

Beatriz Magaloni

During the last two decades, the most divisive issue in Mexican politics has been macroeconomic policy. Inflation, currency depreciation, trade liberalization, and capital flows across the border have crucially defined the pace of politics throughout three presidential terms. The Mexican economy has experienced more than fifteen years of long-term economic stagnation, shortly interrupted by a mild recovery during Carlos Salinas's term. Why then have Mexican voters been willing to reelect the ruling party, Partido Revolucionario Institucional (PRI), despite its mediocre economic record?

Economic voting models of fully competitive democracies cannot easily account for this puzzle. Existing literature has found that incumbent parties seldom survive an economic crisis. This is because voters tend to behave retrospectively: they vote against the incumbent when its economic performance is found wanting.[1] In Mexico, however, retrospective assessments have not played a significant role in voting behavior. In their analysis of the 1988 and 1991 national elections, Jorge Domínguez and James McCann[2] found that voters' economic retrospective and prospective assessments played no role in voting choices. The authors attributed the low saliency of economic factors to the peculiar nature of elections in systems long governed by a single party. The authors argue that Mexicans vote in two steps: first, they ask themselves if they are for or against the "party of the state," with economic evaluations playing almost no role in the individual's stand with respect to such party. Once a voter decides to cast a vote against the ruling party, in the second step policy issues and social cleavages divide the opposition vote among the two major opposition parties, the right-wing Partido Acción Nacional (PAN) and the left-wing Partido de la Revolución Democrática (PRD).

Does low saliency of retrospective evaluations imply that economic factors play no role in voting choices in Mexico? If so, why did the PRI's electoral support start to gradually deteriorate precisely after the onset of the debt crisis of the 1980s? In this chapter I employ a Bayesian retrospective model of electoral choice developed elsewhere,[3] to answer these questions. I evaluate the model with survey data from the 1994 and 1997 national elections. The model is about voting choices in the "first step," employing Domínguez and McCann's characterization of electoral behavior in Mexico. It thus seeks to determine what leads voters to support the ruling party or turn to the opposition camp.

I argue that voters in dominant-party systems face a dilemma: they must evaluate a party with a long history in government against opposition alternatives with no record in government, at least at the national level. The model shows that under some circumstances voters might choose to reelect the ruling party despite finding its economic performance wanting. This is because they will be averse to turning the government to an uncertain opposition alternative that lacks a record in government. These asymmetries of information can explain the low saliency of retrospective assessments in the vote and the reason as to why the process of ruling-party dealignment has been so gradual, despite the depth of the economic recession the economy has experienced during the last fifteen years.

The chapter is organized as follows. I first discuss the main issues surrounding macroeconomic performance during the last five presidential terms. The second part shows the gradual process of ruling-party dealignment since the early 1980s. I then review the Bayesian retrospective model and perform some simulations employing aggregate macroeconomic data to show some of the mechanisms that account for ruling-party dealignment over time. Finally, I provide individual-level evidence of the model by analyzing the 1994 and 1997 national elections. The data come from two nationwide surveys. The 1994 survey was collected by Belden-Russonello one month before the presidential elections (N=1,500). The 1997 data come from a postelectoral survey collected by the right-wing opposition party, the PAN, one week after the midterm elections (N=1,200).

1. A PERIOD OF LONG-TERM STAGNATION

From 1940 until the early 1970s, the PRI presided over a period of stable economic growth. During the years of the so-called "Mexican economic miracle" (the mid-1950s to the early 1970s), the country consistently grew at an annual average rate of 6 percent in an environment of impressive currency and price stability. Mexico experienced rapid industrialization and urbanization within an economic environment protected by high trade barriers. Employment rapidly shifted from agriculture to industry and services. The party also delivered direct benefits to a variety of social groups (e.g., land to peasants; houses and health care to unionized workers; tariff protection and subsidized credits to national entrepreneurs; transport and food subsidies to the rapidly growing urban population).

During the 1970s the Mexican government altered economic policy considerably. Presidents Luis Echeverría (1970–76) and López Portillo (1976–82) replaced the policies of the so-called "stabilizing development" of the 1950s and 1960s, opting to engage in expansionist policies, financed by oil revenues and, above all, external borrowing. During most of the López Portillo *sexenio*, the Mexican economy responded by growing at an average growth rate of 8.4 percent. The last year of the López Portillo *sexenio* was disastrous, however. Contrary to the government's predictions, the international prices of oil were now falling, which created a serious strain on the Mexican economy given that in 1981 72.5 percent of Mexican exports came from petroleum. High international interest rates aggravated the already threatening external conditions. Partly due to the exchange rate risk, capital flight reached ten billion dollars in 1981 and eight billion in 1982.[4] After declaring a debt moratorium, nationalizing the banking system, repeatedly breaking promises not to devalue the currency, and expropriating an estimated four billion dollars in the infamous Mexdollar fraud,[5] President López Portillo (1976–82) handed in a "bankrupt country," as his PRI successor put it.

Since the early 1980s until the present the Mexican economy has experienced long-term stagnation. From 1982 until 1988 the economy had average negative growth rates of –0.15 percent. Mexico has not been able to recover the historic growth rates of the previous decades. Form 1989 to 1994, the economy started to grow again, but at annual average rates of only 3 percent, and after December 1994, the country fell again in deep economic distress.

The decade of the 1980s was characterized by high inflation rates, sharp currency depreciation, decreasing real salaries, and underemployment in the cities (see Table 8.1). During the entire decade, the Mexican economy had average annual inflation rates of two or more digits, reaching an

Table 8.1
Average Economic Indicators: 1982–96*

Year	Inflation Rate	Change in Real Wages		Currency Depreciation	Currency Appreciation Index**
		Industrial	Minimun		
1982	110%				62.59
1983	81%	−23%	−17%	196%	48.32
1984	59%	−7%	−7%	24%	64.24
1985	64%	−3%	−1%	71%	63.11
1986	106%	−6%	−8%	124%	54.57
1987	159%	−2%	−6%	138%	55.85
1988	52%	0%	−13%	80%	75.93
1989	20%	−9%	−6%	8%	83.88
1990	30%	3%	−9%	14%	93.72
1991	19%	6%	−4%	7%	108.34
1992	12%	9%	−5%	3%	121.18
1993	8%	7%	−2%	4%	127.93
1994	7%	4%	0%	6%	129.55
1995	52%	−13%	−12%	90%	95.18
1996	28%	−13%	−11%	34%	104.19

* Annual Averages constructed with monthly data.
** The index is constructed by dividing the nominal exchange rate expressed in pesos per dollar by the consumer price index. If the currency is appreciating in real terms, it means that the value of the Mexican peso, relative to the dollar, is "improving" because the rate of inflation is larger than the rate at which the peso changes.
Source: Author's calculations with Banco de Mexico data.

unprecedented annual rate of 180 percent in 1988. The de la Madrid government (1982–88) attempted to lower inflation by implementing an IMF-sponsored stabilization package that included restructuring public finances, abruptly devaluing the currency by more than 100 percent, and raising public sector prices. Despite the fiscal adjustment, the government could not control inflation.

High inflation levels shrink the incomes of voters, even more so of the poorer ones. As can be appreciated in Table 8.1, during the years of chronic macroeconomic instability (1982–88), the minimal and industrial wages of Mexicans lost their real value by almost 60 percent. Only when inflation appeared to be under control, did average real industrial wages start to increase, with minimal wages lagging behind. After the 1994 peso crisis, inflation made a comeback and with it real wages declined again.

Although the de la Madrid government initiated the economic adjustment, it was not until the Solidarity Pact, signed six months before the 1988 presidential elections, that macroeconomic stabilization was achieved. When Carlos Salinas (1988–94) took office, the annual inflation rate had dropped to around 20 percent. The Salinas government further moved toward macroeconomic stabilization, renegotiating the external debt and balancing the budget (using, among other strategies, the privatization of state-owned enterprises), and deepened trade liberalization by negotiating NAFTA with the United States and Canada.

The Mexican economy did not grow at particularly high rates during the Salinas years. Nonetheless, all the macroeconomic indicators started to improve. Inflation was dramatically reduced and industrial real wages consistently increased, recovering to about where they were in the early 1980s, until the end of 1994, when the second crisis hit the country. In addition, during the whole Salinas presidential term, the exchange rate appreciated. The government used the fixing of the exchange rate as a nominal anchor in the economy, a focal point to coordinate expectations and promote investment credibility. After three *sexenios* of chronic currency devaluation and capital flight, the Salinas government chose to fix the exchange rate to signal a commitment, that is, that investment and savings would no longer be expropriated through abrupt and unexpected devaluation. Table 8.1 shows a real exchange rate index. The index is constructed by dividing the nominal exchange rate expressed in pesos per dollar by the consumer price index. If the currency is appreciating in real terms, it means that the value of the Mexican peso, relative to the dollar, is "improving" because the rate of inflation is larger than the rate at which the peso changes.

A side effect of the government's exchange rate policy was that Mexicans could cheaply consume imported goods. Due to the liberalization of trade and the buoyant internal demand, consumer imports flooded urban markets in Mexico. The increase in the internal demand was partly driven by an extravagant expansion of consumer credit. During the Salinas years, most middle-class Mexicans borrowed to purchase cars, homes, trips, and all sorts of final consumer products, mostly imported. The deficit in the current account thus jumped from nearly fourteen billion in 1991 to more than twenty-eight billion in 1994. Imports could somehow be financed by the massive amounts of portfolio investment entering the country throughout the Salinas *sexenio*. The balance-of-payments disequilibrium became problematic, however, when capital flows stopped and even reversed, as occurred during the election year of 1994.

After the debacle of December 1994, when the peso collapsed, Mexico experienced the most serious economic downturn since the Great Depression. In 1995 GDP dropped by almost 7 percent; industrial wages declined in real terms by more than 30 percent in just two years,[6] the currency was devalued, overall, by around 250 percent and unemployment reached unprecedented levels (as high as 7 percent in some months of 1996). The economic crisis took the population (and many foreign and national investors) by surprise. The public had apparently trusted that the economic reforms would soon lead the country onto a new pathway of growth.[7] The electorate reelected the long-lasting PRI, apparently trusting that its presidential candidate, Ernesto Zedillo, would continue with the economic program of the previous administration and soon bring "welfare to the Mexican family," as he promised during the campaign.

The recession soon destroyed what today is regarded as a false optimism. Instead of a new pathway of growth, Salinas's term now appears as a bubble in the midst of recurrent economic crisis in a period of more than fifteen years of long-term stagnation. In addition to the recession, corruption scandals[8] and the surge of crime have contributed to the public cynicism about government and politicians. Today, President Salinas himself is one of the most despised politicians, most likely because Mexicans blame him for the economic recession.

2. THE ELECTORAL PANORAMA

The economic bust of 1994–96 had a profound impact on Mexico's electoral politics. In 1995 several gubernatorial elections took place: the PAN was reelected in Guanajuato and Baja California, won Jalisco, and came very close to the PRI in Yucatán.[9] These changes are not as dramatic as the ones produced in the municipal and local deputy elections that took place in 1995 and 1996. In the 1995 local elections, the PRI's vote dropped from close to 70% to an overall 52%, and in the 1996 elections the PRI had major losses in states were it traditionally had had important hegemonic or semi-hegemonic holds such as México, Guerrero, and Morelos. During the 1995 and 1996 local elections, the PRI lost to the PAN most of the important cities in dispute, including the state capital cities of Jalisco, Baja California, Yucatán, Michoacán, Oaxaca, Chiapas, Puebla, Aguascalientes, Coahuila, Sinaloa, and Morelos.

Figure 8.1 shows the aggregate levels of PRI electoral support in all gubernatorial, local deputy, and municipal elections from 1980 until 1996. Ruling-party dealignment is an ongoing process at the local level. The data in Figure 8.1 should be read taking into account that there is a strong electoral cycle-pattern involved: the PRI has consistently performed worse in the gubernatorial elections taking place during the first year of the presidential term.[10] The PRI performed better in the third, fourth, and fifth years and a little bit worse during the year of the presidential elections.

These cycles are clearly driven by local patterns of party competition— that is, they depend on the "type" of state involved in the election. Thus, the relevant comparison is really across same presidential term year and same

Figure 8.1
PRI Vote Share in Local Elections: 1980–96

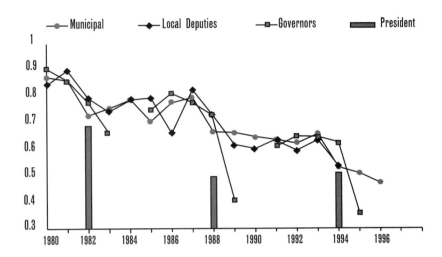

type of election: one should compare, for instance, gubernatorial elections only with gubernatorial elections taking place during the *same* year of the presidential term or look at the same states over time. Analyzing the data in this manner, it is clear that in all the gubernatorial, deputy, and municipal elections there has been a *systematic* PRI aggregate vote loss from 1980 until 1996. The most dramatic changes, however, took place in the gubernatorial elections of 1983 and 1986 and in the local deputy and municipal elections of 1994–96; all of these elections took place during times of high economic distress. In addition, in the local elections taking place in 1997, the ruling party lost to the left-wing opposition party, the PRD, the newly created gubernatorial office in Mexico City and to the PAN the gubernatorial races of Querétaro and Nuevo León. As of the beginning of 1998, the PAN controls six governorships and, as Cuauhtémoc Cárdenas was sworn into office in December of 1997, the PRD governs the largest city in Mexico.

The 1997 midterm elections also produced unprecedented results: the PRI obtained only 38% of the national vote and it lost the absolute majority in the Chamber of Deputies.[11] Figure 8.2 shows the PRI's vote share in presidential and congressional elections from 1964 to 1997.[12] It can be seen that although the PRI has been losing electoral support from one election to the other, two sharp changes can be distinguished: the first in the 1988 presidential elections and the second in the 1997 midterm elections. That is, between the 1982 and 1988 presidential elections, the ruling party lost close to 20% in electoral support and in the 1997 midterm elections, it lost

Figure 8.2
PRI Vote Share in Presidential and Congressional Elections: 1964–94

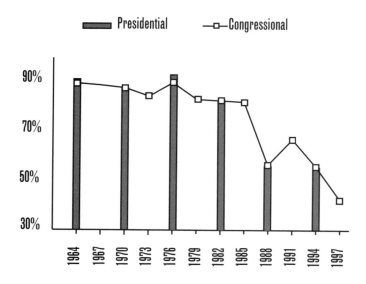

22% of the national vote relative to the previous midterm elections. Again, both of these elections took place after periods of severe recessions. It should be noted that in almost all midterm elections with the exception of 1991 there was a decline in the PRI's electoral support relative to the previous presidential election. This is consonant with the finding that in presidential elections there is usually a "midterm decline"—a decline that has been explained, at least in U.S. elections, by presidential approval and the performance of the economy.[13] The 1991 elections were the only midterm elections in which the PRI experienced an electoral *gain* relative to the previous presidential election and such electoral swing was unusually high (close to a 10% gain). Investors and consumers overreacted with optimism during the Salinas years; the electorate did likewise.

3. BAYESIAN LEARNING AND ELECTION TO ELECTION DYNAMICS

How has the economic record affected voting choices in the Mexican national elections? Do voters attribute responsibility for economic performance to the government? If so, why did the majority of voters wait until the 1997 midterm elections to vote against the PRI? In this section I employ a Bayesian retrospective model developed elsewhere to explain why the process of electoral change in Mexico has been so gradual. The model argues that voters cast a vote for the party that is expected to yield the highest returns when in office, as measured by economic performance, and systematically derives the manner in which voters construct their expectations on how the alternatives are expected to shape future economic performance.

Constructing expectations about the future might be a complicated process. Quite often, as Anthony Downs made explicit, voters will employ information shortcuts to assess the competing parties and their proposed economic policies and will pick whichever they believe will yield the highest returns.[14] In Downs's framework, they concentrate on what is easiest and fastest to assess: *actual* performance of the incumbent party during the last term. In the Morris Fiorina and Chris Achen framework,[15] voters observe not only the current record of the incumbent but also what each of the alternatives has *done* while in office, together with their platforms, during the years of political awareness of the individual, creating a summary retrospective measure of each of them that serves to judge for the future.[16] Most recently, MacKuen, Erikson, and Stimson argued that the voter's economic forecasts are not only simple extrapolations of past performance but also result from the leading economic indicators, as filtered through the news media.[17]

In Mexico the voters' information problem is magnified. The problem faced by voters does not simply lie in that the challengers are more uncertain, for this is true even in fully competitive systems. The problem is, on the one hand, that retrospective information is highly asymmetric given the long years of single-party rule, and on the other, that opposition parties hold no record in government whatsoever. The Bayesian model systematically shows how both of these information problems affect the voters expected utility calculations and ultimately their voting choices.

The model posits that voters use three pieces of information to form their assessments on the PRI's expected economic performance: (1) long-term retrospective information given by the cumulative economic record of the ruling party observed by the voter since he started to be aware of politics (for the sake of simplicity, one can assume that voters start to monitor the PRI after they become eighteen years old); (2) short-term economic information given by the voter's evaluation either of the current state of the economy or the incumbent's performance during the last period; and (3) the party's campaign announcements or what the PRI promises to deliver if reelected.

The model posits that voters form their expectations about the future economic performance of the PRI by updating, according to the Bayesian principles, their prior beliefs with the new data observed. The cumulative economic record of the ruling party observed by the individual constitutes the voter's "prior beliefs" and the new data are current economic performance and campaign promises. The key insight of Bayes's theorem, applied to voting behavior, is that voters do not form their judgments about a political party in a historical vacuum. Voters monitor over time the performance while in office of a party, storing such information in their memories and gradually modifying these prior judgments with more recent information. But the amount by which the voter alters her a priori perceptions on the ruling party in light of the recent events depends on the precision of the long-term information. The more erratic the long-term economic record of the ruling party becomes, the more voters will focus on the most recent piece of information to infer what the party might do if reelected.

The following propositions emerge from the model: a dominant party, if successful in producing stable economic growth during several years, can profit from its past performance and still enjoy considerable levels of support despite a recent economic crisis. If, on the contrary, the dominant party has produced an erratic economic performance during several years, an economic downturn before the elections might actually mean losing power. In this case, historic performance is too "noisy" to make safe forecasts, leading voters to concentrate more on the most recent pieces of information and thus increasing the relevance of short-term retrospective assessments on the vote.

But voters do not only form prospective assessments on one party; they perform *comparative* judgments upon which they base their choices. In forming their expectations about how an opposition party might perform if elected, voters face a serious information shortage: there is no retrospective information to evaluate the opposition parties because these parties have no record in government, at least at the national level. A lack of record in government implies that there is no information on the way in which opposition parties might handle crucial aspects of governance. All the information voters possess about these parties are their campaign promises, "mere words" which they might not necessarily trust.

To infer the opposition's expected performance, the model states that voters also behave according to the Bayesian principles: they update their prior beliefs with the party's campaign promises. However, since opposition parties have no record in government, the voter's prior beliefs are "diffuse" and generally noninformative. The nature of Bayesian learning leads voters to discount what the opposition offers due to a priori uncertainty about these parties. An implication of the model is that opposition parties need to reduce the voter's uncertainty to win elections. Their available strategies for doing so largely depend on the institutional setting. Opposition parties can, for example, attempt to reduce the voter's uncertainty by winning increasingly more elections at the local level.[18] Although *local* performance cannot be directly projected to future *national* performance, voters might still use local records as imperfect "proxies" to construct their priors on the opposition expected performance.[19] An opposition party that increasingly controls more and more electoral offices at the local level can indeed be regarded as less uncertain than one that does not. It is common to find some opposition parties following a "local" strategy when competing against a dominant party (in India, Mexico, or Taiwan for example). Presumably, in following such strategy, opposition parties are calculating that by becoming a *party in government* at the local level, they contribute to reducing the voter's uncertainty, which in the long run might help them win at the national level as well.

The Bayesian retrospective model provides an explicit and systematic accounting of the way in which individuals might learn from experience, combining newly encountered information with their past experiences and understanding of the political world. For such reason, the model is quite appropriate for understanding changes in voting behavior across time depending on the cumulative performance record of the ruling party. Some implications of the model, reflecting on election to election dynamics, follow:

1.   *Given its economic performance record, the PRI could enjoy high (almost universal) levels of electoral support before the debt crisis.*

2.   *The debt crisis triggered a process of ruling party dealignment.*

The mechanism is the following: given eight years of economic crisis, the voter's prior beliefs on the PRI's expected economic performance necessarily decreased. Prior beliefs can be interpreted as a long-term summary measure of the voter's past political experience with the ruling party, similar to Morris Fiorina's interpretation of party identification.[20] In Fiorina's definition, the summary measure includes evaluations of the parties' performance while in office, their platforms and postures, and their fulfillment over time.

Figure 8.3 shows long-term retrospective evaluations on the economic performance of the PRI as represented by the average growth rates observed during a voter's lifetime from the age of political awareness (eighteen years old). I employ growth rates to simulate the model because a long time-series dating back to the 1920s on inflation, unemployment, and real wages is not readily available. Figure 8.3 shows the voter's prior beliefs on the PRI's expected economic performance at three historical moments: before the debt crisis of 1982; around 1988, once the debt crisis had hit the country; and after the recent peso crisis. It can be seen that before the debt crisis, all voters had experienced an average of annual growth rates of 6 percent or more. Voters that became aware of politics during the years of the oil boom (those born between 1958 and 1963) even experienced an average of growth rates of 8 percent. The debt crisis had two effects on the voters' prior beliefs. First, it dramatically reduced the prior beliefs of *all*

Figure 8.3
Prior Assessments on PRI's Economic Record, by Age Cohort, at Three Historical Moments

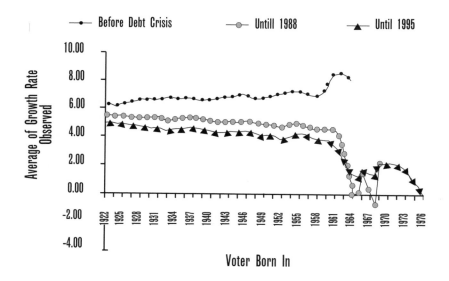

Note: Prior assessments come from the average of growth rates observed by an individual since she or he became eighteen years old.

voters, particularly those born between 1950 and 1963 (the *priors* of those born in 1963, for instance, dropped by 7 points). Second, the debt crisis generated extremely *low* prior beliefs among the younger generation, those who became aware of politics once the recession had started. These voters did not experience the "good old" years of stable and high economic growth. When they started to be aware of politics (roughly around the 1980s), the economy was on the verge of a bust, which lasted for almost eight years. The years of mild economic recovery during the Salinas term slightly increased the prior beliefs of those born after 1970 (voters who started to be aware of politics precisely after he took office). The second economic crisis experienced after December 1994 further hurt the party's overall record, as summarized by the voter's prior beliefs. In this second occasion, the prior beliefs of those born before the 1960s (the older generation) dropped more than the prior beliefs of the younger.

The empirical implications of these arguments are twofold: party sympathy toward the ruling party must decrease precisely after the debt crisis; and the younger generation of voters must show lower levels of attachment toward the PRI. According to Darryl Dieter, ruling-party sympathy decreased from 56 percent in 1982, to 33 percent in 1988 to just under 20 percent in 1994. He also provides evidence that the younger generation of voters tends to show lower levels of sympathy toward the ruling party.[21]

3. *The corollary is that to remain in power, the PRI has become increasingly more dependent on short-term economic performance.*
    The model tells that the larger the variance of the historic record of the ruling party, the more voters will tend to concentrate on the most recent pieces of information to form their forecasts. Before the debt crisis, the average variance on the economic performance of the PRI observed by the Mexican electorate was 2.2. This number comes from calculating the average variance of annual growth rates observed by individuals depending on the year they were born. After the debt crisis, the average variance of growth rates increased to 3.9 and after the December 1994 peso crisis to 4.3. This implies, on the one hand, that voters will increasingly focus on short-term economic performance to make their inferences about the ruling party's expected economic performance, and on the other, that the PRI of today could not win an election, as it did in 1982, if it takes place during a year of negative annual growth rates. This implication of the model can be restated as a more general hypothesis in the following terms.

4. *Mexican voters will tend to be more tolerant to poor economic performance because they will be averse to turning the government to an uncertain opposition alternative. For alternation of political power to take place, the cumulative economic record of the incumbent must fall below a threshold so as to compensate for the uncertainty of the alternatives.*
    Figure 8.4 simulates the model by generating voters' expectations of the future economic performance of different types of parties and the current situation of a hypothetical economy. There are two types of incumbents. One type holds a good performance record that roughly approximates to that of the Mexican PRI from 1940 to 1980. The other type holds a mediocre economic record that roughly corresponds to the record of the PRI until the present. Figure 8.4 also considers two types of challengers, A and B, each competing on different party systems, a dominant-party system and a competitive-party system, respectively. Thus, challenger A has never been in office, while challenger B has. Since challenger B has previously been in office, its expected performance can be calculated applying almost the same equation as that used for the incumbent. That is, for challenger B, there is prior information, which is given by the economic performance produced when in office. The simulation assumes that while such challenger was in office, the economy had average growth rates of 5 percent. Voters update this prior information with challenger B's campaign

Figure 8.4
Simulation of the Bayesian Model: Expected Party Economic Performance for Two
Types of Incumbents and Two Types of Challengers

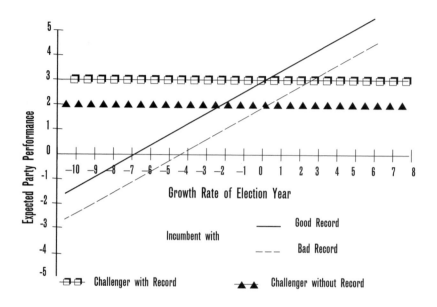

Note: Expected party performance is defined as the average of growth rates the party is predicted to produce during the following term if elected.

promises. For challenger A, voters possess no such a priori information and this leads them to discount this party due to uncertainty. The simulation assumes that voters discount this party's campaign promises by the same amount as they discount the other parties' promises. Thus, the only difference between challenger A and the other parties is that it holds no record in government. In the simulation, all four political parties promise to deliver during the campaigns a similarly "good" economic performance, measured in terms of growth rates.

It can be seen that the better the incumbent's current economic performance, the larger its chances of winning; conversely, the stronger the economic recession, the more likely the incumbent will lose. However, the threshold needed for the incumbent to lose the election is smaller when it faces a challenger who holds previous experience in government. The only difference between challenger A and challenger B is that the former has never been in office, while the latter is supposed to have a good record in government (an average of annual growth rates of 5 percent). In this particular simulation, challenger B would still be strictly better than A even if its long-term record fell to an average of annual growth rate of 2 percent—that is, even if B were a rather incompetent political party relative to the incumbent, it would still be better than the unknown challenger A. The difference between the points at which challenger A's and B's expected performance intersect with that of the incumbent might be called the "tolerance threshold" of dominant-party systems—the amount of government laxity voters are willing to tolerate before voting the incumbent party out. Thus, the threat to replace a bad incumbent is less credible in the dominant-party system and incumbent politicians can take advantage of this.

It should be noted that the chances to replace the dominant party are much lower if it possesses a good long-term economic record. Figure 8.4 shows that a dominant party with a good performance record, which roughly approximates that of the PRI until 1980, could be reelected against an uncertain opposition party even if the economy where not growing during the election year. Nonetheless, as is illustrated in Figure 8.4, if the dominant party possesses a record that roughly approximates to that of the PRI until the present, increasingly voters will be more willing to vote for the uncertain opposition alternative given a poor current economic performance.

4. INDIVIDUAL-LEVEL EVIDENCE OF THE MODEL

In this section I seek to evaluate the Bayesian model of learning with individual-level data for the 1994 and 1997 national elections. As discussed above, the model states that voters employ three pieces of information to form their expectations about how the PRI, compared to the opposition, will shape future economic performance: the long-term economic record of the ruling party, their evaluations of the current state of the economy, and what the parties promise to do if elected. Thus, the dependent variable of the model is the voters' comparative economic prospective judgments. I evaluate the following hypotheses derived from the model:

1. Voters who have better long-term experiences under the rule of the PRI (i.e., higher prior beliefs) are expected to have higher chances of holding comparative prospective judgments in favor of this party.

2. Voters who have better judgments about the current economic performance of the government are expected to have higher chances of holding comparative prospective judgments in favor of this party.

To evaluate these hypotheses, I therefore estimate the impact of long-term retrospective information and of short-term *direct* and *mediated* retrospective information on the voter's comparative prospective assess-

Table 8.2
Expectation of the PRI's Economic Performance (%)

Comparative Prospective Assessments	(1) Distribution of Responses 1994	(2) Voted PRI 1994	(3) Distribution of Responses 1997	(4) Voted PRI 1997
PRI Better than Opposition	57.0	87.0	32.3	89.6
Neutral	10.1	52.9	2.9	0
Opposition Better than PRI	32.3	13.3	64.7	8.5

Note: Columns 2 and 4 do not add up to 100 because they are percentages of responses in columns 1 and 3 respectively.

ments. Fiorina distinguished between "simple" and "mediated" retrospective assessments.[22] The voter's *simple* retrospective evaluations are assessments of the direct effects of political outcomes on the personal or the national economy (e.g., how she perceives things have changed during the last term of office). In this sense, *simple* retrospective assessments are really assessments of *results* observed during the last term of office. *Mediated* retrospective evaluations do not ask about results, but seek to measure the voter's evaluation on the incumbent, mediated through his assessments on *people*. Mediated retrospective assessments normally come from the voter's evaluations of the incumbent president's job. I will not combine these two measures into a single retrospective short-term assessment because I want to assess which holds a stronger relationship with the voter's prospective assessments.

Data

The model's dependent variable is the voter's comparative prospective economic assessments or how she evaluated the PRI would shape the future of the national economy relative to either of the opposition alternatives. In the 1994 and 1997 surveys each respondent was asked to state which party was seen as more capable in handling different economic problems. In the 1994 survey, respondents were asked to state which party was thought as more capable in improving their personal finances, shaping the future of the national economy, and fighting against poverty. In the 1997 survey, respondents were asked to evaluate the party most capable in generating jobs, increasing wages, and fighting against poverty. An overall measure was constructed by counting the number of times the voter saw the PRI or either opposition parties as more capable of improving each of these items. The marks each alternative received of these three assessments were calculated, creating two summary prospective marks, one for the PRI and the other for the opposition, the PAN and PRD combined.[23] To create the comparative economic prospective assessment, the summary prospective mark given to the opposition was subtracted from that given to the PRI. If it is positive, respondents expect the PRI to perform better than the opposition; if it is negative, they expect the PRI to be worse than the opposition; and if the prospective measure equals zero, the respondent was indifferent between the PRI and the opposition.

Table 8.2 shows the voter's comparative prospective assessments and their relationship with the vote. Voter's prospective economic assessments appear to be strongly related to the vote. Those believing that the PRI's economic performance was expected to be better than the oppositions' overwhelmingly supported such party, and those who believed the opposite was the case voted either for the PAN or the PRD. Table 8.2 also reports how the electorate was distributed on this combined prospective measure. In the 1994 elections, the majority of voters expected the PRI to be more capable than the opposition parties in handling future economic performance. The economic crisis that followed appears to have altered dramatically those expectations since in the 1997 survey the overwhelming majority of the electorate no longer evaluated the ruling party as more capable in shaping future economic performance.[24]

The independent variables of the model are the voter's prior beliefs and her mediated and direct retrospective assessments. Prior beliefs come from the average of growth rates the voter has observed since she started to be aware politically. The numbers, which come from those reported in Figure 8.3 on page 214, are imputed to each respondent in the survey depending on her age. This measure of actual performance is, of course, a proxy of prior beliefs or of how the voter might have experienced and evaluated economic performance during her lifetime. As argued above, voters care about a large set of economic variables and do not care only about growth rates. And they might attach different weights to these various components of performance. I use only growth rates because they constitute the one economic indicator for which a longer systematic and reliable time-series, which dates back to the 1920s, can be found, and because the other macroeconomic variables that might be equally relevant (e.g., inflation, unemployment, real wages, currency depreciation) have tended to vary downward or upward with cycles of growth and recession.

Direct retrospective assessments are a summary measure of the voter's evaluations of economic performance during the last three years. In the 1994 and the 1997 surveys, respondents were asked to assess whether the national economy and their personal finances had improved, stayed the same, or deteriorated during the last three years. This creates a 4-point scale ranging from electors who are strongly against the incumbent to

Figure 8.5

Percentage Voting for the PRI by Summary Measure of Retrospective Evaluations, 1994 and 1997 National Elections

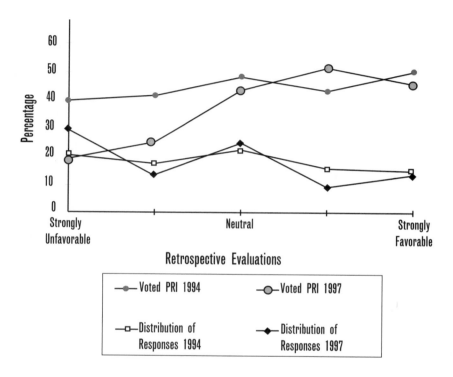

Note: Retrospective evaluations are defined by two items: whether respondents evaluated that her personal finances improved, stayed the same, or deteriorated during the last three years, and whether respondents evaluated that the national economy improved, stayed the same, or deteriorated during the last three years. With these answers I create a summary retrospective evaluation that ranges from 0 (strongly unfavorable) to 4 (strongly favorable).

those strongly in favor of it. For instance, those who thought their personal finances had deteriorated and the national economy was in worse condition received a score of 0, strongly against the incumbent.[25]

Figure 8.5 reports how respondents were distributed on this summary retrospective evaluation and the percentage that voted for the PRI in both elections. Two important implications become apparent. First, in both elections, the support for the PRI increases as the summary retrospective evaluation becomes more favorable to the incumbent. However, in the 1994 presidential elections, the PRI received very high levels of support from those holding unfavorable retrospective assessments. That is, among those who evaluated that each of the economic problems had deteriorated, more than 40% reported intending to vote for the PRI. In the 1997 elections, only 20% of those holding extremely unfavorable direct retrospective assessments reported voting for the ruling party. Thus, it appears that the electorate's disposition to punish the PRI for short-term economic performance increased in those elections. This might result from two quite different factors. On the one hand, midterm elections generally tend to be much more plebiscitarian than presidential elections; on the other, it might indicate that the PRI vote has, indeed, become more dependent on short-term economic conditions, as the Bayesian model makes explicit.

Mediated retrospective assessments come from the voter's evaluation of Salinas and Zedillo. In the 1994 survey, respondents were not directly asked to evaluate Carlos Salinas's performance in office. They were asked to state their opinion of him, which can be taken as a proxy of their evaluation of his *job* as president. The measure ranges from 0 (a very bad opinion) to 4 (an excellent opinion).[26] In the 1997 survey, respondents were directly asked to evaluate how Zedillo had managed the national economy, inflation, and unemployment. With these answers I create a 6-point scale summary measure of the voter's evaluations of Zedillo's economic performance. For instance, those who evaluated that Zedillo had done a good job handling the national economy, inflation, and unemployment receive a score of 6, strongly approving of Zedillo's economic performance.[27]

Table 8.3 presents how the electorate was distributed on these measures of presidential approval and its relationship with the vote. Those who held favorable evaluations of the president's performance were significantly more likely to vote for the PRI than those who held unfavorable evaluations. An important difference in terms of presidential evaluations can be seen among these two elections. While the majority of respondents had slightly favorable evaluations of Salinas, the overwhelming majority disapproved of Zedillo's economic performance.

The next section presents a systematic evaluation of these arguments by estimating how voters constructed their expectations of the parties' future economic performance in both elections.

Estimating Voters' Comparative Prospective Assessments

For estimating the voter's comparative prospective assessments I employ a maximum likelihood logit procedure.[28] Respondents who expect the PRI to perform better than the opposition are scored as the high category and those who expect the opposition to be better in handling future economic performance as the low category. The small percentage who did not see the PRI or the opposition as more capable is excluded from the analysis. Results are shown in Table 8.4.

Table 8.3
Voting Intention by Approval of Salinas and
Summary Measure of Approval of Zedillo's Handling of the
Economy, Unemployment, and Inflation (%)

	Distribution of Responses	Voted for the Incumbent	Voted for the Opposition	
			PAN	PRD
Approval of Salinas				
Strongly Approves	14.8	65.7	13.6	2.3
Approves	48.1	54.2	18.9	5.7
Neutral	28.4	39.0	25.3	11.9
Disapproves	5.0	20.6	30.1	29.9
Strongly Disapproves	3.6	6.2	21.5	17.1
Summary Measure of Zedillo's Approval				
Strongly Approves	9.1	74.1	11.8	9.1
Moderately Approves	4.3	62.5	22.5	4.3
Slightly Approves	9.5	60.7	13.5	9.5
Neutral	18.9	46.7	33.3	18.9
Slightly Against	13.7	33.6	28.1	13.7
Moderately Against	19.7	16.3	32.6	18.7
Strongly Against	24.9	17.2	38.6	24.9

Note: In the 1994 survey, presidential approval comes from a question that asked the respondent's opinion of Carlos Salinas. The measure ranges from 0 (very bad) to 4 (excellent). In the 1997 survey, presidential approval comes from three questions: how respondents assessed Zedillo's handling of inflation, unemployment, and the national economy. With these answers I create a summary measure of Zedillo's performance that ranges from 6 (good in all three items) to 0 (bad in all three of them). Percentages are weighted for the 1994 data. Those who did not report for which party they voted in the 1997 elections are excluded. Those who reported voting for other minor parties are not shown.

These results lend considerable credence to the manner in which the Bayesian retrospective model derives the voter's calculations on the parties' expected economic performance. In each case, the coefficients are significant and of the expected sign. As expected, prior beliefs have a positive impact on the voter's comparative prospective assessments: the higher the priors, the more favorable to the incumbent comparative prospective assessments become. This means that the older generation of voters, who have experienced a better long-term economic record on the part of the PRI, have higher expectations of how the ruling party, as opposed to the opposition alternatives, will shape future economic performance. Both direct and mediated retrospective assessments also perform as expected:

Table 8.4

The Voter's Comparative Prospective Economic Assessments,
PRI vis-à-vis the "Opposition," 1994 and 1997 National Elections

Independent Variables	CPA (PRI-Opposition) 1994		CPA (PRI-Opposition) 1997	
	Coefficient	Std. Error	Coefficient	Std. Error
Constant Term	−2.24***	.3145	−2.83***	.2441
Voter's Prior Beliefs (long-term information)	.1494***	.0614	.1202**	.0639
Voter's Short-term Retrospective Assessments	.2086***	.0536	.2202***	.0728
Voter's Evaluation of Incumbent President	.7767***	.0794	.5784***	.0569**

** p < .05   N=1091   N=661
*** p < .01   −211 1252.60   −211 645.634
              Goodness of fit 1099.202   Goodness of fit 656.583
              71.04% Predicted correctly   75.84% Predicted correctly

the more favorable the voter's direct and mediated retrospective assessments, the more favorable to the incumbent comparative prospective assessments become.[29] These results mean that voters employ their memories about the long-term economic record of the PRI, together with their evaluations of the current state of the economy and presidential performance, to form their evaluations of how this party will shape the future of the national economy.

In logit analysis one cannot discuss the effects of a particular variable in isolation. In order to give some indication of the range of effects presented in Table 8.4, I examine some hypothetical cases for the 1994 and 1997 models. Consider three individuals: (1) a voter holding strongly negative economic retrospective assessments (uniformly unfavorable opinions on the state of the national economy and the voter's personal finances, thus receiving a score of 0 in the summary retrospective measure); (2) a voter holding neutral assessments on these issues (a score of 2 in the summary retrospective measure); and (3) one holding uniformly favorable economic retrospective assessments (a score of 4 in such measure). Now suppose that these three individuals differ in their prior beliefs on the incumbent's expected economic performance. Some are young voters who became aware of politics precisely during the debt crisis (for the 1994 elections) or who became eighteen years old precisely at the end of the Salinas's period (for the 1997

Table 8.5

Effect of Prior Beliefs and Retrospective Evaluations on Expectations of Party Performance: Some Expected Probabilities of Evaluating the PRI as More Capable than the Opposition Parties

Age Cohort	Voter's Prior Beliefs	Voter's Retrospective Evaluations		
	(average of growth rates observed)	Strongly Unfavorable	Neutral	Strongly Favorable
1994 Elections				
18 to 29	2%	.5232	.6248	.7165
50 +	5.2%	.6355	.7258	.8007
1997 Elections				
18 to 25	.16%	.1742	.2468	.3374
50 +	5.2%	.2789	.3753	.4827

Note: These probabilities were derived from the estimated logit coefficients presented in Table 8.4. Prior beliefs come from adding to each respondent in the survey a value that comes from the average of growth rates experienced according to his or her age. Direct retrospective evaluations are defined by two items: whether respondents evaluated that her personal finances improved, stayed the same, or deteriorated during the last three years and whether respondents evaluated that the national economy improved, stayed the same, or deteriorated during the last three years. Mediated retrospective assessments are set to their mean value.

elections). These voters, that is, did not experience the so-called "Mexican economic miracle." All that these voters have seen is the economy in recession, with a mild recovery during the Salinas presidential term. Others are older voters who have seen better times under the rule of the PRI. These voters directly experienced the long years of high growth rates and, of course, have also witnessed the economic recession. The predicted probabilities of evaluating the PRI as more capable than the opposition in shaping future economic performance are shown in Table 8.5. The voter's evaluation of Salinas and Zedillo are set to their mean values.

In both elections, retrospective assessments play an important role in moving the individual's comparative prospective assessments in favor or against the incumbent. The first and second rows of Table 8.5 are the predicted probabilities of expecting the PRI to be more capable than the opposition in shaping future economic performance that come from the 1994 model. The third and fourth rows report the predicted probabilities coming from the 1997 model. Thus, for instance, in 1994 a voter between eighteen and twenty-nine years old, who holds low prior beliefs and strongly unfavorable direct retrospective assessments, had a 0.52 probability of expecting the PRI to be more capable than the opposition of handling future economic performance. This predicted probability increases to 0.71 for those holding low prior beliefs but strongly favorable retrospective assessments. In the 1997 model, the impact of direct retrospective assessments on the voter's comparative prospective judgments is very similar. Consider those holding the lowest prior beliefs. The predicted probability of holding prospective judgments favorable to the PRI by those who had extremely unfavorable retrospective judgments is 0.17. The probability increases to 0.33 by those who had strongly favorable retrospective assessments. Thus, in both models, the magnitude of the impact of direct retrospective assessments on prospective calculations was very similar, increasing the chances of expecting the PRI to be more capable than the opposition by close to 20% when changing the voters direct retrospective assessments from strongly unfavorable to strongly favorable.

It should be noted, however, that in the 1994 elections, the relationship between retrospective and prospective assessments is far from perfect. In particular, one would expect that the predicted probability of holding higher economic expectations on the PRI by those holding neutral and strongly unfavorable retrospective assessments to be closer to 0.50 and 0 respectively; but this is not the case. Voters behaved quite differently in the 1997 elections. It can be seen that a voter holding strongly unfavorable and neutral direct retrospective evaluations had a very low chance of expecting the PRI to perform better than the opposition in the future.

In both elections, prior beliefs also play a role in shaping the voter's expectations. As predicted by the model, the older generation of Mexican voters possesses better reasons than the young generation to expect this party to perform better in the future. The impact of prior beliefs on the voter's prospective assessments is similar in both elections. In both models, the predicted probability of holding prospective assessments favorable to the PRI increases by 10% or more if prior beliefs increase from its lowest to its highest value. Older voters have not only seen in the past longer years of economic growth but also they are clearly willing to employ their memories to form their future forecasts.

There are important differences between both elections in terms of the impact of prior beliefs. First consider only those voters holding extremely unfavorable retrospective assessments. In the 1994 elections only the youngest generation of voters (i.e., those holding the lowest prior beliefs) were predicted to have a close to 0.50 chance of expecting the opposition to be more capable of shaping future economic performance than the PRI. These voters, who were between eighteen and twenty-five years old, behaved more in accord with the simple retrospective rule that tells them to reject something bad when they see it. The older generations, for their

Table 8.6

Effect of Presidential Approval and Direct Retrospective Evaluations on Expectations of Party Economic Performance: Some Expected Probabilities of Evaluating the PRI as More Capable than the Opposition Parties

| | Voter's Retrospective Evaluations | | |
Voter's Opinion on Salinas	Strongly Unfavorable	Neutral	Strongly
Strongly Favorable (4)	.79	.85	.90
Neutral (2)	.45	.55	.85
Strongly Unfavorable (0)	.14	.21	.28
Voter's Opinion of Zedillo			
Strongly Favorable (6)	.70	.79	.85
Neutral (3)	.29	.39	.51
Strongly Unfavorable (0)	.07	.10	.15

Note: These probabilities were derived from the estimated logit coefficients presented in Table 8.4. Retrospective evaluations are defined by two items: whether respondents evaluated that her personal finances improved, stayed the same, or deteriorated during the last three years and whether respondents evaluated that the national economy improved, stayed the same, or deteriorated during the last three years. Presidential approval in the 1994 survey comes from a question that asked respondents their opinion of Carlos Salinas. In the 1997 survey, approval of Zedillo comes from a summary measure of answers to three items: respondents' evaluations of his handling of inflation, unemployment, and the national economy. Prior beliefs were set to their mean value.

part, still expected the PRI to be more capable of shaping future economic performance even when they judged the current economic record as inadequate. These voters, that is, were willing to allow the incumbent a chance to repair things in the future because they adjusted their expectations gradually in the face of new information.

In the 1997 elections prior beliefs still had a statistically significant impact on the voter's expectations. Note that the magnitude of the coefficients reported in Table 8.4 is very similar in both elections. However, in 1997 those holding unfavorable and neutral direct retrospective evaluations had a higher predicted probability of expecting the opposition to perform better than the PRI in the future, regardless of age. Only the oldest generation of voters who, in addition, had favorable retrospective evaluations, had close to a 50% chance of expecting the PRI to perform better than the opposition. The majority of the electorate, that is, was clearly ready for a change in the 1997 midterm elections because the average evaluations of President Zedillo's economic performance, and of the PRI's long- and short-term economic record, were clearly unfavorable due to the recent economic recession.

Mediated short-term retrospective evaluations play a strong role in shaping the voter's expectations. Consider, for example, three types of voters (holding strongly unfavorable, neutral, and strongly favorable direct retrospective assessments) that vary depending on their evaluations of Salinas and Zedillo. These voters are assumed to hold average prior beliefs. The predicted probabilities of expecting the PRI to be more capable than the opposition of shaping future economic performance are shown in Table 8.6. As the voter's presidential evaluation increases and as retrospective assessments on the incumbent become more favorable, voters are more likely to hold comparative prospective assessments in favor of the PRI. In both elections, the evaluation on the president strongly affected the voter's comparative prospective assessments. Thus, when forming their expectations on the incumbent's future performance, voters not only evaluate results, as measured by their direct retrospective assessments but also consider the performance of the president, as presumably some of his policy initiatives, as filtered by the mass media.

4. ESTIMATING VOTING CHOICES

The final task to complete the argument is to show that voters indeed employ their comparative prospective assessments to make their voting choices. The hypothesis is that the voter will pick the alternative that is expected to be more capable of handling future economic performance. Since the Bayesian retrospective model seeks to account the determinants of ruling-party support and when voters will be turned off the PRI to the "opposition," I employ a maximum likelihood logit procedure where a vote for the PRI serves as the high category and a vote for the opposition, the PAN and PRD combined, as the low category.[30]

I define the voter's utility as a function of comparative prospective economic assessments and a set of sociodemographic characteristics. Comparative prospective assessments have been shown to be a function of prior beliefs and direct and mediated retrospective assessments. These variables, however, might not only have an indirect impact on voting choices (that is, through the voter's comparative expectations of the future economic performance of the parties) but also may have a *direct* impact on the vote. I

Table 8.7
Logit Analysis on Vote for the 1994 PRI Vote: Alternative Models

Independent Variables	MODEL I	MODEL II
Constant Term	−2.376***	−4.42***
	(.5578)	(.8848)
Regions		
South Gulf	−.2226	−.0121
	(.2674)	(.4300)
South	−.6577***	−.5408
	(.2520)	(.4095)
Mexico City	−.6320**	−.7290*
	(.2851)	(.4256)
Western Highlands	−.0527	.1492
	(.30117)	(.4510)
Northeast	−.0008	.2181
	(.2828)	(.4516)
Northwest	−.1247	.1953
	(.3108)	(.4989)
Demographic		
Gender	.4509***	.2184
	(.1585)	(.2473)
Education	−.3589***	−.2731**
	(.0815)	(.1278)
Peasant	.4964**	.9644***
	(.2403)	(.3832)
Manual Laborer	−.0840	.2600
	(.2245)	(.3715)
Public Employee	−.0843	−.4685
	(.3643)	(.5551)
Student/Retired	−.2788	−.0975
	(.2444)	(.3837)
Choice Theoretic		
Direct Retrospective	.1847***	.0298
	(.0505)	(.0805)
Mediated Retrosp.	.8296***	.4497***
(Opinion of Salinas)	(.0939)	(.1500)
Prior Beliefs	.1929**	.2778**
	(.0765)	(.1227)
Comparative Prospective		.8785***
		(.0550)

*p<.10	N= 942	N= 915
**p<.05	Pseudo R^2 .1877	Pseudo R^2 .5987
***p<.01	−2 LL −498.056	−2 LL −238.67
	% Correct 74.42	% Correct 91.26

thus estimate two voting models. The first includes prior beliefs and direct and mediated retrospective judgments and excludes comparative prospective judgments. The second model adds up the voter's comparative prospective assessments. If prior belief and direct and mediated retrospective assessments are still statistically significant in the second model, it would mean that they also have a direct impact on voting choices. If they are statistically significant only in the first model, their impact on voting choices must be said to be indirect, that is, through the voter's comparative prospective economic assessments.

The 1994 Vote

Table 8.7 reports the results of two models for the 1994 elections. Model 1, which includes sociodemographic variables, the voter's prior beliefs, and retrospective assessments, and Model 2 which adds up prospective economic assessments.[31]

The first model shows that in the 1994 elections, the PRI received support from less-educated voters, from women, and from peasants. The regional pattern of PRI electoral support during the 1994 elections shows an interesting development: the PRI not only performed worse in Mexico City, as has traditionally been the case, but also in the South and the South Gulf of Mexico.[32] Only the variables "peasant" and "education" remain statistically significant in the fully specified vote equation shown in Model 2. This suggests that the regional variables and gender affected voting choices only indirectly, that is, by affecting voters' retrospective and prospective assessments. Model 1 indicates that a purely retrospective model appears somewhat successful in explaining support for the PRI in the 1994 elections. Direct retrospective assessments show a positive and statistical significant relationship with the vote, meaning that the more the voter evaluated that the economy had improved during the last three years, the higher the probability of supporting the PRI. The impact of this variable is, however, rather weak. Holding the other variables at their mean values, the predicted probability of voting PRI by those who hold strongly unfavorable retrospective assessments, that is, evaluating that the national economy and their personal finances had *both* deteriorated, had a 0.48 chance of supporting the PRI. This result shows that in the 1994 elections Mexican voters could not be portrayed as "gods of vengeance and reward," as V. O. Key put it.[33] The simple retrospective rule, that is, does not predict voting choices well because a high proportion of the electorate voted to reelect the PRI despite holding strongly unfavorable direct retrospective assessments. It should be noted, moreover, that the statistical significance of this variable collapses once prospective economic assessments are introduced in Model 2. Thus, the 1994 elections cannot be interpreted as a referendum on the economy.

Model 2 strongly supports the hypothesis that electoral choice in the

1994 elections can be explained, above all, by the voter's expectations of how the PRI and the existing opposition alternatives will shape future economic performance. In their analysis of the 1988 and 1991 elections, Domínguez and McCann obtained analogous results.[34] The voter's mediated retrospective assessments show a powerful positive impact in explaining a vote for PRI, which suggests the key importance of presidential support in explaining PRI vote, a relationship also found in Domínguez and McCann and in Buendía.[35] A strong positive relationship between the voter's prior beliefs and his voting choices was also found, suggesting that in the 1994 elections the PRI received disproportionate levels of support from older voters.

The 1997 Vote

In Table 8.8 I report the results of two models that estimate the voting choices of Mexicans in the 1997 elections. The PRI received less support from lower-educated voters, as it did in the 1994 elections, and also from students, the self-employed, and manual laborers. Women and peasants were no longer more likely to vote for the ruling party. The PRI performed worse in Mexico City and also in the Western Highlands. However, none of the sociodemographic and regional variables with the exception of "self-employed" remained statistically significant once prospective calculations were introduced in Model 2. Prior beliefs no longer affected voting choice directly in the 1997 elections, suggesting that the older generations had started to dealign to either of the opposition alternatives. Models 1 and 2 indicate that the most robust predictors of voting behavior in the 1997 elections were: direct retrospective assessments; evaluations on the economic performance of President Zedillo; and the voter's comparative expectations about the future economic performance of the different alternatives. For such reason, the 1997 elections can be interpreted as a negative referendum on the economy and on the performance of the president. These negative evaluations, moreover, contributed to the voter's highly unfavorable prospective economic assessments on the ruling party, which as in the 1994 elections, show a powerful impact on the vote.

Measuring the Effects of the Independent Variables

Table 8.9 reports the predicted probabilities of voting PRI in both elections over a range of comparative prospective assessments, mediated retrospective evaluations, and direct retrospective judgments. The rest of the variables are set to their mean values.

In both elections, the voter's comparative prospective assessments show a similar effect on the vote. Those who evaluated that the opposition was more capable than the PRI in shaping future economic performance (ranging from a value of 0 to a value of 2 in the comparative prospective measure), are predicted to have a greater chance of supporting the opposi-

Table 8.8
Logit Analysis on Vote for the 1997 PRI Vote: Alternative Models

Independent Variables	MODEL I	MODEL II
Constant Term	−.8330**	−2.9685***
	(.3699)	(.7745)
Regions		
South Gulf	.4070	−.0374
	(.2962)	(.5685)
South	.1109	.2519
	(.2790)	(.5260)
Mexico City	−.6521*	.1798
	(.3499)	(.6296)
Western Highlands	−.6223**	−.3713
	(.2703)	(.5108)
North East −	.0634	−.3864
	(.2661)	(.5101)
North West	.0673	.0349
	(.3006)	(.5747)
Demographic		
Gender	.0969	.1979
	(.1852)	(.3420)
Education	−.1864***	−.0854
	(.0653)	(.1306)
Peasant	−.2420	−.3853
	(.3381)	(.6623)
Manual Laborer	−.8494***	−.6471
	(.2704)	(.4988)
Self-Employed	−.5746***	−.9364**
	(.2395)	(.4684)
Student	−.6421**	−.1423
	(.3141)	(.5367)
Professional	−.7440	−1.0569
	(.4900)	(.8032)
Choice Theoretic		
Prior Beliefs	−.0053	.0273
	(.0603)	(.1178)
Direct Retrospective	.2737**	.2698**
	(.0634)	(.1196)
Mediated Retrospective	.4310***	.2677***
	(.0477)	(.0885)
Comparative Prospective		.8286***
		(.0646)

*p<.10	N= 853	N= 642
**p<.05	Pseudo R² .2016	Pseudo R² .5678
***p<.01	−2 LL 907.431	−2 LL 315.324
	% Correct 73.04	% Correct 91.74

Table 8.9
Predicted Probability of Voting PRI in 1994 and 1997, by Comparative Prospective Evaluations and Direct and Mediated Retrospective Judgments

	1994	1997
Comparative Prospective Assessments		
Opposition Expected (0)	.07	.07
Economic Performance (1)	.16	.15
Better than PRI's (2)	.31	.28
Indifferent (3)	.52	.48
PRI's Expected (4)	.72	.67
Economic Performance (5)	.86	.82
Better than Opposition's (6)	.93	.91
Presidential Approval		
Excellent	.80	.52
Neutral	.62	.33
Very Bad	.37	.18
(Difference 1–3)	.43	.34
Retrospective Assessments		
Strongly Favorable	.70	.42
Neutral	.68	.30
Strongly Unfavorable	.66	.20
(Difference 1–3)	.04	.22

Note: These probabilities were derived from the estimated logit coefficients presented in Tables 8.7 and 8.8. A voter's comparative prospective judgment is a summary measure that comes from three questions that asked respondents to assess which party was most capable in improving three economic problems. The measure ranges from 0 (when the respondent thought either the PAN or the PRD was more capable in improving each of the three economic items) to 6 (when the respondent thought the PRI was). All the sociodemographic and regional variables are set to their mean values.

tion parties. Conversely, those who evaluated that the PRI, relative to the opposition, was more capable (ranging from a value of 4 to 6 in the measure) are predicted to have a greater chance of voting PRI. Those who were indifferent between the PRI and the opposition (a value of 3 in the comparative prospective measure) had an equal chance (.502) of supporting the PRI or turning to the opposition.

Thus, there is ample evidence that the more the individual expects the PRI to be more competent in handling future economic performance, the more likely he will vote for the PRI. Conversely, the more he expects the opposition to be more capable that the ruling party in shaping future economic performance, the higher the probability of voting for the opposition, all other things held constant. Moreover, the average voter was risk-neutral since those who calculated that the PRI and the opposition were equally capable in shaping future economic performance are predicted to have almost an equal chance of voting PRI and voting for the opposition.

FINAL REMARKS

In this chapter I have argued that voters in dominant-party systems face a dilemma: they must evaluate a party with a long history in government against opposition alternatives with no record in government, at least at the national level. These asymmetries of information can explain why the process of ruling-party dealignment has been so gradual despite the depth of the economic recession the Mexican economy experienced during the last fifteen years. When comparing a party with a long record in government against the uncertain alternatives, voters might choose to reelect the long-standing incumbent, even if they hold negative short-term retrospective assessments, for two reasons. First, voters might employ their long-term memories on the economic performance of the PRI, leading them to adjust their expectations gradually in the face of new information. Second, voters might be averse to turning the government over to an uncertain alternative. For alternation of political power in office to take place, the cumulative economic record of the PRI must fall below a threshold, that is, it must be sufficiently poor and "noisy" such that voters are willing to turn the government over to an uncertain opposition alternative.

I provided individual-level evidence of these arguments, showing that both in the 1994 and 1997 elections, voters employed their memories, together with the current state of the economy and presidential performance, to form their prospective judgments of the future economic performance of the PRI relative to the opposition parties. I showed, moreover, that in both elections comparative prospective judgments had a powerful impact on voting behavior. The difference in the election results of both elections can largely be accounted for by the voter's comparative prospective judgments. While in the 1994 elections the majority of voters predicted the PRI to be more competent in shaping the future of the national economy, in 1997 the majority expected either of the opposition parties to be more capable than the PRI. The economic recession of 1994–96 and poor evaluations on the performance of Zedillo on his handling of the national economy, inflation, and unemployment were shown to account for the change in comparative expectations among the majority of the Mexican electorate.

Thus, voters' comparative prospective judgments in both elections can be accounted for by the same mechanisms identified by the Bayesian retrospective model. There were, however, important differences in the voting choices of Mexicans in the 1994 and 1997 elections. The crucial differences were, on the one hand, that in 1994 long-term evaluations of the performance of the PRI had a direct impact on voting choices while in 1997 these impacted voting choices indirectly, that is, only affecting the formation of expectations about the future economic performance of the parties. This suggests that in 1997 even the older generation of voters had started to dealign from the PRI. The second crucial difference in voting choices in both elections was that in 1997 voters did employ their short-term economic evaluations on the PRI's economic performance. Thus, it appears that Mexican voters are increasingly more willing to hold the ruling party accountable for short-term economic conditions.

NOTES

1. See, among others, Morris P. Fiorina, *Retrospective Voting in American National Elections* (New Haven: Yale University Press, 1981); Gerald H. Kramer, "Short-Term Fluctuations in U.S. Voting Behavior, 1986–1964," *American Political Science Review* 65 (1971): 131–43; Douglas A. Hibbs, Jr., *The American Political Economy* (Cambridge: Harvard University Press, 1987); Roderick D. Kiewiet, *Macroeconomics and Micropolitics* (Chicago: University of Chicago Press, 1983); William R. Keech, *Economic Politics* (Cambridge: Cambridge University Press, 1995); Karen Remmer, "The Political Economy of Elections in Latin America, 1980–1991," *American Political Science Review* 87 (1993): 393–407.

2. Jorge I. Domínguez and James A. McCann, "Shaping Mexico's Electoral Arena: Construction of Partisan Cleavages in the 1988 and 1991 National Elections," *American Political Science Review* 89, no. 1 (March 1995): 34–48.

3. Beatriz Magaloni, "A Bayesian Retrospective Model of Electoral Choice in Dominant Party Systems" (paper presented at the American Political Science Association Meeting, Washington D.C., 1997).

4. The government had first chosen to maintain the peso through external borrowing. Nonetheless, given the amount of capital flight, this policy soon became unsustainable and the peso was repeatedly devalued (in only one year, from January to December 1982, it lost about 450 percent of its value relative to the dollar).

5. In August 1982, the government chose to freeze dollar deposits, followed by a forced conversion at below-market rates.

6. Real wage decline is measured from December 1994 to December 1996.

7. For such reason, Zedillo ran his campaign under the slogans "continuity to consolidate the changes" and "welfare to the Mexican family."

8. For instance, Raúl Salinas, the brother of the former president, is being subject to trial for a long list of crimes, ranging from the murder of the PRI's secretary general, José Francisco Ruiz Massieu, to tax evasion and misuse of public funds. Other much more minor PRI politicians are also under investigation for corruption.

9. The most recent gubernatorial election of Michoacán was won by the PRI by a narrow margin.

10. There are no gubernatorial elections in the second year of the presidential term.

11. Several gubernatorial elections took place concurrently with the 1997 midterm elections. The PAN won in Querétaro and Nuevo León.

12. These are official results and their reliability can be questioned. I follow other analyses in taking these data as a good measure (the only available) indicating the pace of political change in Mexico. See, for example, Juan Molinar Horcasitas, *El tiempo de la legitimidad: Elecciones, autoritarismo, y democracia en México* (Mexico City: Cal y Arena, 1991).

13. Samuel Kernell, "Presidential Popularity and Negative Voting: An Alternative Explanation of the Midterm Congressional Decline of the President's Party," *American Political Science Review* 71 (1977): 44–66; also see Edward R. Tufte, "Determinants of the Outcomes of Midterm Congressional Elections," *American Political Science Review* 69 (1975): 812–26.

14. Anthony Downs, *An Economic Theory of Democracy* (New York: Harper and Row, 1957).

15. Fiorina, *Retrospective Voting*. Chris Achen, "Social Psychology, Demographic Variable and Linear Regression: Breaking the Iron Triangle in Voting Research," *Political Behavior* 14 (1992): 195–211.

16. This summary retrospective measure, as in Fiorina's analysis, is captured in the individual's party identification. Achen further developed this framework, constructing a rigorously developed rational choice model of party identification in which citizens receive a party identification from their parents and then constantly update it, consistent with Bayesian principles, with their own political experiences, direct benefits received from the parties, and current campaign data. Party identification so constructed serves to forecast the future stream of benefits from each of the alternatives. Fiorina, *Retrospective Voting*; Achen, "Prospective Voting."

17. Michael B. MacKuen, Robert S. Erikson, and James A. Stimson, "Peasants and Bankers: The American Electorate and the U.S. Economy," *American Political Science Review* 86 (1992): 597–611.

18. The costs of entering local electoral markets are naturally lower. On the one hand, opposition parties can focus their often-scarce organizational resources on smaller geographical regions; on the other, from the voter's point of view, the risks involved in experimenting with a new political alternative appear to be lower in smaller electoral offices.

19. Beatriz Magaloni, "Elección racional y voto estratégico: Algunas aplicaciones por el caso mexicano," *Política y Gobierno* I, no. 2 (1994): 309–44.

20. Fiorina, *Retrospective Voting*.

21. Darryl Dieter, "The Decomposition of the Party System? Electoral Change in Mexico" (paper presented at the 1995 Latin American Studies Association, September 28–30 (Washington, DC).

22. Fiorina, *Retrospective Voting*.

23. For instance, if the respondent saw the PRI as the party most capable of improving the situation of the national economy and his personal finances but the PAN or the PRD as more capable of addressing the issue of poverty, according to this respondent the PRI receives a mark of 2 and the opposition a mark of 1. Naturally, when the respondent reported not to know which party was more capable or reported that no party was more capable, each alternative receives a mark of 0.

24. It should be noted that there is a sharp discontinuity in respondents' comparative prospective assessments reported in columns 3 and 4 of Table 8.2. That is, in the 1997 survey, there are close to zero "neutral" assessments. This appears to be the product of a strong polarization in the electorate during those elections.

25. The summary measure was constructed as follows: if the respondent said things

had improved, it was scored as 2; if he said things were the same or did not know, the answer received a score of 1; and if he said things had worsened a score of 0 was given. I take this type of scoring from Paul R. Abramson, John H. Aldrich, and David W. Rhode, *Change and Continuity in the 1992 Elections* (Washington, D.C.: CQ Press, 1994).

26. Unfortunately, the survey did not ask respondents to evaluate Salinas's handling of different economic problems such as inflation, unemployment, and the like, so I cannot further investigate with this data how much Salinas's evaluation was driven by the way he handled the economy. There is some evidence, however, that Salinas's approval ratings were related to economic performance. See, for example, Jorge Buendía, "Economic Reform, Public Opinion, and Presidential Approval in Mexico, 1988–1993," *Comparative Political Studies* 29 (1996): 566–91.

27. The summary measure was constructed as follows: if the respondent said Zedillo had done an excellent or a good job, it was scored as 2; if she said the president had done a regular job, the answer received a score of 1; and if she said he had done a bad or very bad job a score of 0 was given.

28. The voter's comparative prospective assessments are a function of prior beliefs and mediated and direct retrospective assessments. Thus, the equation I estimate is the following:

$$CPA_i(\text{PRI-Opposition}) = \text{ß}_1 1 + \text{ß}_2 \text{Prior}_i + \text{ß}_3 \text{Retrospective}_i + \text{ß}_4 \text{Pres.Approval} + \varepsilon_i.$$

29. A broader implication of these results is that the voter's comparative prospective judgments on the parties' expected economic performance are not simple rationalizations that reveal their partisan biases. I have provided a systematic account of where the voters' expectations come from, which is wholly consistent with theoretical expectations.

30. For a multinomial probit analysis of PAN and PRD in the 1994 and 1997 elections, see Beatriz Magaloni, *The Dynamics of Dominant Party Decline: The Emergence of Multipartism in Mexico* (Ph.D. dissertation, Duke University, 1997).

31. The models employ a summary comparative prospective measure. Recall that each respondent was asked to state which party was regarded as most capable in improving three economic problems. If the respondent answered the PRI was, the answer received a score of 2. If he answered "do not know" or that neither the PRI or the opposition was seen as most capable, it received a score of 1. If he answered that the PAN or the PRD were more capable, a score of 0 was given. Thus, the summary prospective measure ranges from 6 to 0, where 6 means that the PRI was seen as the most capable in improving each of the three economic problems, 0 means that the opposition was, and 3 that the respondent saw the PRI and the opposition as equally capable.

32. The excluded regional category is "Center" in both elections.

33. V. O. Key, Jr., *The Responsible Electorate: Rationality in Presidential Voting 1936–1960* (Cambridge: Harvard University Press, 1966).

34. Domínguez and McCann, "Shaping Mexico's Electoral Arena."

35. Domínguez and McCann, "Shaping Mexico's Electoral Arena"; and Jorge Buendía, "Economics, Presidential Approval and Party Choice in Mexico: The 1994 Elections" (paper presented at the September 28–30, 1995 Latin American Studies Association meeting in Washington, DC).

INDEX